Working the Sea

Misadventures, Ghost Stories, and Life Lessons from a Maine Lobsterfisherman

Wendell Seavey

North Atlantic Books
Berkeley, California

Published by
North Atlantic Books
P.O. Box 12327
Berkeley, California 94712

Cover photo: Mike Radcliffe and Wendell Seavey, the first day out
in *Great Balls of Fire,* by Ann Seavey
Cover and book design by Paula Morrison
Printed in the United States of America
Distributed to the book trade by Publishers Group West

Working the Sea: Misadventures, Ghost Stories, and Life Lessons from a Maine Lobsterfisherman is sponsored by the Society for the Study of Native Arts and Sciences, a nonprofit educational corporation whose goals are to develop an educational and crosscultural perspective linking various scientific, social, and artistic fields; to nurture a holistic view of arts, sciences, humanities, and healing; and to publish and distribute literature on the relationship of mind, body, and nature.

North Atlantic Books' publications are available through most bookstores. For further information, call 800-337-2665 or visit our website at www.northatlanticbooks.com. Substantial discounts on bulk quantities are available to corporations, professional associations, and other organizations. For details and discount information, contact our special sales department.

Library of Congress Cataloging-in-Publication Data
Seavey, Wendell, 1938–
    Working the sea : misadventures, ghost stories, and life lessons from a Maine lobsterfisherman / by Wendell Seavey.
        p. cm.
    Summary: "A first-person account of life in the fishing communities of coastal Maine"—Provided by the publisher.
    ISBN 1-55643-522-3 (pbk.)
    1. Seavey, Wendell, 1938– 2. Lobster fishers—Maine—Biography. 3. Lobster fisheries—Maine. I. Title.
    SH20.S4S39 2005
    639'.54'092—dc22
                            2005004303

1 2 3 4 5 6 7 8 9 UNITED 10 09 08 07 06 05

*This book is for Ann, who has always encouraged me
and my storytelling.
She says that books help a lot of people more than you know,
so this is my book.*

Acknowledgments

As in all projects that take this much time, I had some wonderful people to encourage me, and I would like to thank them.

First of all, I would like to thank Richard Grossinger for encouraging me to tell my stories for this book. Thank you, Richard, for the endless hours we put in together forming these memories into a "readable" book. I am grateful, Richard, for your patience with making a "storyteller" into an "author"—that is a big jump! And, most of all, for thirty-five years of friendship.

Next I owe great thanks to my wife Ann, who has tried for years to get me to tell my tales. I thank you for your support, prodding, and suggestions.

I would like to thank Elizabeth Paulin of Celebration, Florida, for strongly advising me to get on with this book. Also my long-dead father Frank Seavey, Sr., who in his way showed me his pocket watch, indicating it was time for me to get going. That *is* what got me going. Thanks, Dad.

Many thanks to Lee Kuck for taping a majority of the stories while I told them to her, and the bigger job of deciphering my strange "Downeast Grammar" into written word. You surely had your work cut out for you. I enjoyed telling you my tale.

My gratitude always to the many fine "old people" who many of these stories are about, whose lives intertwined with mine, and in some ways made me the man I am today. I hope you will be pleased with my memories of all of you.

—Wendell S. Seavey

Contents

Editor's Note

Though most of this account was transcribed directly from Wendell Seavey's speech, the text is *not* presented in Downeast diction. It was our choice to set the material, for the most part, in standard English, with the usual grammar, spelling, and punctuation. This honors the content and narrative rhythms over the regional dialect.

Everyone speaks in one dialect or another, a reality which is traditionally disguised by the formality of "book-writing." To put Wendell's account in dialect would have been to call undue attention to the unconscious linguistic patterns of his subculture at the expense of the story. However charming the idiosyncrasies of the Eastern Maine accent, they are not the purpose or the heart of this book; Wendell's story is. We have tried to keep that readable and clear. However, we have also tried to preserve the flavor of his language, which has meant including the occasional misspelling, jargon, or odd idiom.

An audio version of this book might be made available by popular demand. Please write us if interested.

Working the Sea

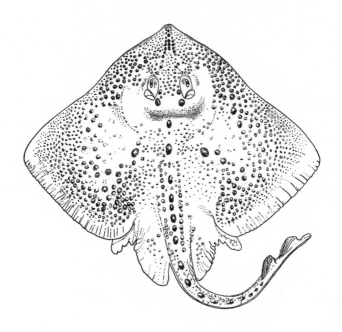

I Come Onto This Earth

Can I take you back to the beginning? I want to start right back on the evening that I was born, and that was August 3rd, 1938. It was late in the afternoon when Dr. Tapley came over and my mother was preparing my Dad's supper. Dr. Tapley is a figure I will weave in and out of this story. He said, "Letha, what in hell are you doing up? You should be in bed. You and I have got work to do tonight. You are going to have your baby."

And she says, "Well, I've got to get Frank's supper on the table."

Frank is my Dad.

"To hell with Frank's supper, you get up and go to bed. After you have delivered your baby," he says, "if Frank hasn't had his supper, then I'll cook his supper for him!" My dad could handle that all by himself just fine.

Dr. Tapley sent my youngest sister, Olive, across the road to use the telephone. We didn't have a telephone then, but Lottie's little general store across the street did. He said to Olive, "You go over and get Lottie to call Blanche Gott (who was a midwife) and tell her to come over to Frank and Letha's. Tell her I am going to need help tonight." Olive, who was about fourteen, did not know my mother was pregnant, and they quickly sent her down to stay with her aunt Dot—my Dad's sister down over the hill. Then my older sister Phyllis, who was eighteen at the time, went over to the next-door neighbor's to stay. She knew full well that my mother was pregnant, and when she told Olive, Olive denied it. She said, "Phyllis, you lie! You lie, Phyllis!"

Phyllis remembered the hour and the minute I was born. She said it was ten minutes past ten in the evening: "I knew you were born because that is when mother stopped screaming." I was a very, very difficult birth. I was breech and, when I come out of my mother, I had a caul over my head (a sheath or membrane) and Dr. Tapley had to run his finger up my back and break that sheath before I could breathe.

Well, back in English folklore it is said that they used to save the caul of any boy baby born with it. Should the boy, when he gets of age, decide to go to sea, he takes his caul with him and all he has to do is present it to the captain of the ship. Such a boy could get on any ship he so desired. They would take him in, so I am told, because they believed as long as he was on board with his caul, the ship would never sink. More than that, he would bring good luck; he was like a charm. A boy born with a caul would never meet his death by drowning, and he would possess psychic abilities.

When I was born and the caul taken off of me, Dr. Tapley looked at the midwife and said, "Blanche, you and I get all the difficult ones."

That was the night I came into this world.

The First Thing I Remember

Now usually my mind can go way back — or anyway, it used to be able to — and remember different things. The first memory I have upon coming to this Earth was during the month I was born. I was just an infant. I couldn't move on my own. I can remember opening my eyes and I was right under an overhead lamp that hung down from the ceiling. It had three light bulbs on it. I was in a bassinet in my mother's living room.

I can remember that my brother, my youngest brother

Wilbur, was right at the foot of the bassinet; my mother was on my right; and my next-door neighbor Ida Dix was on my left. I can see how they were dressed, so I knew it was summer. They were singing to me what I always thought was a nursery song, but it wasn't; it was a hymn called "Jewels." I can remember the melody of them singing that to me. I knew then that I was one of them, but much smaller. What they were doing was letting me know that I was welcome to this world. That is my first memory of being here.

I can remember all that just as plain as day.

They have a picture—the first picture that I know of that was taken of me. It was my sister Phyllis holding me outside the house. Now, my two sons, who are much larger than I am, say, "That's a fine picture, but the only problem is he never grew!"

Some Seavey Genealogy

My father Frank was born in October of 1895, and my mother and father married in the year 1916. The first trace of the Seavey clan was a Richard Zeve who was born in the 1470s in Devon, England. In about 1500 he had a son named Thomas Zevie (notice the difference in the spelling), born in Devon, England. In 1600 there was a William Sevey born on the 25th of October, also in Devon, England. William was the first one, as far as I know, to move to the U.S., and he died in 1688 in Portsmouth, New Hampshire. When the Seaveys migrated here, they landed in Portsmouth, and in about 1688 a Captain Stephen Seavey was born there. By that time the name was spelled the same way we spell it today. These folks settled in New Hampshire and owned an island called Seavey's. Today the Navy has a stockade on it.

The first Seavey we can run across coming to Maine was a second Captain Stephen Seavey (not an ocean captain, but a captain in the Army), who was born on the 12th of June, 1747, in Portsmouth; he died in 1826 in Cushing, Maine. This Stephen Seavey served with Colonel Benjamin Foster's regiment from Massachusetts for a brief time, and it is claimed by his family in Portsmouth that he also served with General Washington's army at Valley Forge. Later, he moved into Maine and bought Georges Island—fifty acres for two hundred dollars.

My grandfather, Edwin Seavey, was born in 1872 in Friendship, Maine, and was the first one to move downeast to Mount Desert Island. He arrived here about 1890, and the Seaveys have been here ever since. Relatively speaking, this makes us newcomers to Mount Desert, and we haven't decided whether we are going to stay or not!

When my grandfather Edwin was working in Hall's Quarry on Mount Desert, his job was to drill the holes into the granite, place the dynamite, and blow the rocks out of the quarry.

Back then, they didn't have the machinery we have, and a man couldn't drill a hole by himself; one man would hold the drill while the other would strike it. The man holding the drill would then rotate it a quarter of a turn, and the striker would strike it again. As long as the man holding the drill did just exactly what the striker told him, he would never hit him with that maul. I suppose that when the holder of the drill and the striker were at work, it was a good idea that the holder of the drill did not piss the striker off. He might get bonked.

My grandmother's maiden name was Alice Norwood and she was from West Tremont on Mount Desert Island. Alice and my grandfather on my father's side were married in 1892. They had twelve children that they raised to adulthood and two that did not make it.

The Carters of Louds Island

My mother was Letha Carter and she was born on Louds Island in Muscungus Bay on July 11th of 1896. Her father's name was Constantine, not your common name. This island—about a mile and a half to two miles long and probably about half a mile wide—was used by the early Europeans as a fishing station. Only it was not known as Louds Island; in those days it was Somerset Island, named after Lagomore Somerset, its only year-round resident. Rumor has it that his remains are buried on the island, but no one knows where the grave is. The island did not carry the name of Somerset for all that many years. It was more commonly known as Muscongus Island after the bay it sets in; it probably carried that name for a hundred years or more.

Constantine was born in 1855; he'd been married before, so my mother had half-brothers and sisters. He loved to argue, and he loved to talk. Especially if there was a conservative minister around, he loved to debate the Bible. He was a piece of work unto himself. He is buried in Rockland.

Up to the middle of the 1600s Muscongus had year-round residents on it, but in the late 1600s, there were four Indian wars, and by the second in 1689, it was not considered safe, needless to say, to live there year round. When there was a large group of people it was secure, but staying out there by yourself with only two or three could easily get you killed. From 1703 to 1713 the French and the Indians got along pretty good with each other. They were both the wretched ones as far as the English were concerned. The result of this difference of opinion was known as Queen Ann's War, and it ended, I am told, with the Treaty of Utrecht. That's when the English got Acadia from the French—not any sooner—and Newfoundland and Hudson Bay were part of the package. But during the war years Muscongus was a frontier island; no one dared get caught with their trousers down there.

Along about 1749 to 1752 Louds acquired its second year-round resident. William Loud was a junior ranking officer in the British Navy. From his journal, I gather, he must have been a fairly well-educated man. He was intelligent, and he wrote well. He did not haze or harass the men under him. He treated them with respect and, long as an order from above was sensible and reasonable, he was fine with it—and his men respected him for this.

He did have one drawback—a short fuse—and, when lit, it set off an explosive temper. One day a superior officer issued an order, and Loud thought it was a pile of horse dung. He did not like it one bit, so he blew his ever-loving stack at the superior officer. He told him that he had no intentions of carrying the order out. It brought his career right to a fine stop; he was relieved of his rank, stripped of his commission, and thrown in the ship's brig. In fact, they were going to transport him back to Portsmouth, England, to stand trial for treason.

Like I said, he had his good points, and his men liked him. They did not want to see their commander go to England to stand trial, so at night, when he knew that their ship was sailing through Muscongus Bay, one of the guards in charge, staged an escape. Loud broke out of the brig and eased himself down over the side in the night. He was told where there was land; hopefully he could make it. He was a strong swimmer, so that wasn't a problem. The rest of the crew probably thought that he jumped overboard and drowned.

People on the nearby mainland helped Loud survive. They

got him supplies, farming tools, a gun for hunting, fishing equipment, a dory, and some clothes. In other words, I guess they took him to Wal-Mart and outfitted him up. They even gave him a dog named Roger. That mutt was as strong-willed and full of character a dog as William Loud was a man. They were well suited to each other; this was true companionship.

Loud and Roger went to Muscongus and built themselves a home. They meant to do some subsistence farming, fishing, and hunting. Once they built a good shelter they would go back to the mainland periodically, get restocked, and then return to the island. Well, over a two-year period William fell in love with one of the women of the mainland, as could have been expected, and her family liked him too. After all, he was a likable man. They were not at all against their daughter going over and living on Muscongus, so that is what happened. And that is how Louds Island got its second and third residents and, eventually, a new name.

Right from the start Roger hated William's new wife. He couldn't stand her, wanted nothing to do with her. In dogs, it's not so much hate as jealousy. She persisted in improving the relationship, and over a period of time Roger accepted her, enough so that when their first baby was born the dog was very protective of both the wife and daughter. No one got to them before Roger had a chance to check them out.

That is how life went on with the Loud family for twenty-odd years during which they had three or four children and the island changed from Muscongus to Louds, a name it has kept for two hundred years.

Once William Loud was established, more families came and, until the 1960s, the island always had a year-round population. Since then, it is just seasonal.

Back to my mother. In 1779 Ephraim Carter was her first

ancestor to come to Louds Island. While he bought 100 acres of land, four other people bought from 100 to 150 acres at about that same time. Soon there was a whole community.

As I said before, my mother's father was Constantine, a descendant of Ephraim. He was born on January 10th, 1855, and died on August the 11th, 1923. My mother always said he was buried at Acorn, one of Rockland's two large cemeteries. But I found out later, when I searched for his grave, that was incorrect. The secretary of the Acorn Cemetery had no record of him being buried there.

It's a long story about how I found out where my grandfather really was. It includes calling funeral homes, researching old *Rockland Gazettes* in the library, finding his obituary, and getting his authentic death certificate. I found from the City of Rockland that *they* had paid for his remains to be buried. That meant he was at Farmer's Field, not Acorn. Though the poor house next door has been torn down, the cemetery is still standing.

At Rockland's paupers' cemetery I performed a ceremony myself for my grandfather to make it feel like family closure. I also brought home a copy of the old newspaper and showed it to my sister Olive. It fell on the floor and my dog Lily took a bite out of it. Wouldn't you know that the one thing she ate was my grandfather's obituary. I guess that was the universe telling me, it's over; let go of it.

Constantine's first child, Sherbon Carter, was born on August 3rd, 1878. Flora Carter was born on September 27th, 1881. Sadly, her mother died in childbirth with her and, as far as I know, she was given up for adoption. He married again—Susan Butler was her maiden name—and she was my mother's mother. Susan raised Sherbon and many of her own children, including my mother.

My mother went to an elementary school that was built on Louds Island in the year of 1865 when she was a young girl. Later, they ran that school up to the eighth grade; it stayed in operation until 1962.

Constantine moved his family to Big Gott's Island or Black Island, probably in the early 1900s when my mother was a little girl. I know he worked the quarries of Black Island but very little else about the Carter side of my family. There is a picture of our grandfather and Linny, my mother's sister, together on Black Island. When my mother moved off of Gott's at the age of thirteen, she became a maid at a home in McKinley, rooming with the family and sharing a bed with an older maid. Because of superstition, the woman of the house soon changed her mind against this arrangement, believing that the old woman would sap my mother's strength. She saw that my mother got her own bed and also promised that, if she worked for her as a maid, she would see that she got a high-school education, a promise she failed to deliver on. My mother never did go to high school, though it was something she had wanted very much and regretted missing for her whole life.

My mother only had one eye, but she never told anyone, and so no one knew how it happened. The only way I even knew about this was that I overheard my father telling a person that when Mom was a little girl, a person broke a bottle, and a piece of glass went flying into her eye, cutting it so badly that they had to remove it. It wasn't until she was eighteen that she had saved enough to buy a glass eye in Portland.

Dr. Tapley's Story

The doctor who oversaw my birth, Thomas S. Tapley, was born a few years before my grandfather, in 1868. Though the son of a sea captain, he was a progressive and modern man. Because the medical school at Bowdoin did not do dissecting, he quit there and, after a year's break to care of his ailing father, returned to the University of Vermont where they taught dissecting. He graduated in 1899 and moved to McKinley on Mount Desert Island four years later. He was known as a horse-and-buggy doctor because that was how he traveled. Dr. Tapley could do surgery, he could do anesthesiology, he could do dentistry, and he could do veterinarian work. I don't know if he could walk on water. My grandfather and grandmother started using him as their physician when he got here in 1903, and he delivered a number of both my parents' and grandparents' children.

Dr. Tapley lost his wife in a hospital, a loss he felt tremendously the rest of his days. After her death, he sent people to the hospital only reluctantly. He said that they were nothing but death houses. He did everything in his power to get a person healed before they might have to go to a hospital. However, he made a mistake with my sister Barbara. She died of pneumonia at two and a half. She might have died anyway. My mother apparently tried to shake her back to life when it was too late.

Later on, my brother got pneumonia, and Dr. Tapley did not want to send him to a hospital either. My mother said to my father, "You have lost a daughter, do you want to lose a son? Send this boy to the hospital," which he did. At the hospital, doctors were able to drain his lung and save his life. My mother always held Dr. Tapley responsible for Barbara's death, but to a certain extent she also forgave him—for God knows how long that man worked or how many people he delivered, how many lives he saved. My family continued to rely on Dr. Tapley. He delivered me and, as you heard, I was a hell of a hard childbirth.

Dr. Tapley was a tall, gaunt-looking man, and I thought he looked just like the pictures on the schoolhouse wall of Abraham Lincoln, without the beard. My sister used to say, "As soon as the man walks through the door, you feel better." He always made sick kids laugh.

Once I cut the end of my index finger off with a straight razor and I was bleeding like a stuck pig. He asked Olive if she had saved the part of the finger I lopped off and, when my sister gave it to him, he asked for a jar of molasses. He took the molasses, put it in there on my finger, and stuck the cut-off part of it right back where it was, and said, "Make sure it stays there for a few days, and he'll be all right."

It stayed there till this very day, and if you want to come to Southwest Harbor, Maine, I'll show it to you.

Lottie's Store

A neighbor named Charlotte, nickname of Lottie, ran a general store in town. The men and the women would gather there, morning, noon, and night, talking. From sports to politics to fishing to God knows what—anything people talk about they'd talk about in Lottie's store. Debates could get pretty heated, but most of the time it was just fun. Lottie sold meat and candy, cookies and bread, much like a little convenience store that we'd have today. It was no supermarket.

Tremont was dry for years and years and, when the dry law was lifted in the town, some of the fellas used to tease Lottie, "When is that new law coming up here?"

"*That* is *not* coming to this store!"

They would have to go elsewhere to get alcohol.

Lottie was a practical, old-fashioned woman. Sometimes, if she had to urinate, she'd just use a little tin container, go to the bathroom in it, and then throw it out the door onto the bushes and lilacs. Lottie had the best-looking lilacs in town.

She was also a midwife and the town librarian and, if she happened to read some book and didn't like it, she'd ban it by throwing it away! My mother would tend store for her while she tended library. It used to irritate my father sometimes, to have mother over at Lottie's store. I came home one day and said, "Dad, where is mother?"

"Oh, she is over there at that goddamn peanut stand of Lottie's!"

Back in those days, if there was a woman in town—say her husband had a drinking problem, the type of man who would go on a binge and take all the money so until he went fishing again she would be tight up—well, people would go into the store and leave money anonymously. Later the wife would come into the store and say to Lottie, "I have got to ask you if I can charge some groceries?"

"Oh no, my dear, that's been taken care of; you have fifty dollars in credit here."

That is how people would do it—leave some funds wherever that woman might go shopping.

World War One Years

World War One began in August of 1914 and ended in November of 1918. Boys from Tremont served in that war. Four million military people died and six million civilians, a total of ten million, but my father Frank did not have to go; they thought he might have had rheumatic fever when he was young, and he was always short of breath. There were, however, local men who went to the front lines. Carl Larson was in the artillery; he saw combat in Germany. Sherl Galley was in the infantry; he also saw combat in Germany. He told me that one of the things the Germans used to do was to put the spotlights up on the clouds. These acted like a mirror and would reflect the light down on the ground. Sherl said, "When you ever see those lights go up, the first thing you do is bail right into the mud, just lie flat as can be. Hopefully, they won't see you."

Also, during those years there was a very bad flu, the Spanish Influenza they called it, which is odd because it started in the Orient. On a global scale it wiped out twenty million. With the war casualties, it adds up to thirty million people dead in those four years, almost like a generation being wiped out. The world was transformed without even knowing it.

Some of the men that went into the Army never saw combat. They became very ill from influenza; many died. Some, like Clarence Harding and Ralph Benson, were just sick the whole time they were in service.

The story I am going to tell you now came straight from Ralph Benson himself. He said, "Wendell, when I got discharged from the Army in World War One, I was so sick I came home to die; that is how sick I was. I didn't feel I had any chance at all of living. The first thing I done when I got here was go down to the wharf, the one that Lester Radcliffe has owned for about two hundred years, to greet the fishermen and say goodbye. Then I went to my bed to die. But the old horse-and-buggy man, Dr. Tapley, came over and examined me. He said, 'Ralph, I think I know what your trouble is. It is your teeth. They're poisoning you. Why don't you let me extract them? If my diagnosis is right, I bet you will regain your health.'"

That was probably around 1918. So, instead of dying in 1918 Ralph passed on in about 1975.

Dr. Tapley used to say, "I take no credit for saving anyone's life." But I bet Ralph was grateful to him for some fifty-seven years.

Ralph came across as a fastidious, methodical, quietly efficient kind of man. Whatever he owned he took care of it like it was sacred. When I was young he gave me a paper cap-gun that he shot when he was a boy. It had a long barrel, a short handle, and on it was printed "Old Ironsides." It was a single-shot gun. You put one cap in it, and bang, that was it! When he showed it to me, it was just as good as the day it was made.

Years ago men shaved with straight razors, but back in 1895 a man by the name of King Camp Gillette invented the safety razor. At the time, no one knew if the device was going to catch on or not.

Ralph was probably about ten years old when this happened and, when it came to the point that he was going to need to begin shaving, you know what he did? He bought one of the first razor dispensers that Gillette ever made, and he shaved with that dispenser for the rest of his life. Talk about taking care of your things!

Ice Age

Starting during the first of the World War One years, up to 1920, the winters were extraordinarily bitter. They were not normal winters. Even Blue Hill Bay froze over. Somewhere in those years our mother's two brothers, Raymond and Fred, with a sled in tow, dared walk from Underwood's factory wharf in McKinley across the saltwater to Black Island, about three miles out to sea. When they got their business done there, they turned around and tried to walk back. Raymond, being the larger man, fell through the ice about fifty feet from the packing wharf. Luckily, a man hove him a line and pulled him into the dock. But Fred was a gnome of a man about the size of Snuffy Smith, and he made it in under his own power.

On March 16th, 1920, my sister Phyllis was born. Our mother and father, Frank and Barbara, were living in an apartment, the upstairs one, in a house where the Bass Harbor town pier is today. As usual, they called up Dr. Tapley to come over and assist my mother with the birth. But the snow that day was so deep that he couldn't get his horses through, so instead of Dr. Tapley, a midwife by the name of Hattie Farley delivered Phyllis.

They tell me about the same year that Phyllis was born (eighteen years before me), my grandmother was pregnant with her last child. The baby was going to be a daughter, but Alice was so exhausted from all her pregnancies that she could not deliver it. Dr. Tapley had to make a very big decision that day. He knew he couldn't save both of them. It had to be one or the other, either the mother or the child. Ordinarily, the doctor will save the child, figuring the mother has had some chance at life and the child hasn't, but in this case Dr. Tapley, so it is said, reasoned, "She has got so many young children depending on her, I am going to save the mother." That was the sort of decision this horse-and-buggy doctor had to make. My goodness, he almost had to play God.

Depression Years

My mother was forty-two years old and my dad was going on forty-three when I was born. I came as a surprise—I was so much younger than my brothers and sisters, about a generation apart from all of them. Yet my father and mother raised me just about the same way they did my brothers and sisters, even though they grew up during the Depression and I did not. My oldest brother was twenty-one years older than I; my sister Barbara who died at two-and-a-half would have been twenty years older; my sister Phyllis was eighteen years older; my brother Wilbur was sixteen years my senior; and my youngest sister, Olive, was thirteen years eleven months ahead of me.

My mother was very conservative. She learned right from the word go that to survive, you had to be thrifty. Once, during my mother's childhood, Grandmother gave her two biscuits to share with a friend and my mother broke one up and shared it with the friend. "But your mother gave you two biscuits," the friend protested, and mother said, "Yes, but you have to save for tomorrow because tomorrow there might be nothing to eat." That was before the Depression; it was being dirt-poor in the 1890s. Even at the time I was growing up, we didn't have an automobile. If we got invited to go somewhere, like Bangor or Rockland, we knew we would be on an all-day trip because we'd be going with a neighbor or friend. We car-pooled before it was fashionable. We always packed a lunch and camped alongside the road, dining like a family of gypsies. Restaurants were wasteful, sinful, in my mother's eyes.

World War Two was going on when I was little, and that made a difference. My father was making much better money during the war years because there was a greater demand for fish and the price was higher than when my parents were raising my brothers and sisters. I probably had more things than my brothers and sisters did: bicycles, sleds, skates, and all that jazz.

My sister Olive told me this story once about the years in the Depression before I was born. One day at the little school there was a race run between one of the boys and one of the girls. The boy won that race hands down, but the girl was not about ready to accept defeat. She told the boy, "The only reason you won this race is because you boys can wear pants and us girls have to wear dresses. If you had to wear a dress like I do, I'd beat you fair and square." So, after lunch that day, the boy came back to school dressed in one of his mother's dresses just to prove the girl wrong.

That very afternoon the superintendent of schools happened to show up at the little schoolhouse. During recess, while the kids were out frolicking, he came up to the teacher and said, "Mr. Johnson, I realize these are hard times and there are some very poor people in this town, but—really—is that boy's family so poor that he has to wear his mother's dresses to school?"

We weren't that poor, but we didn't have a bathroom; we didn't have a telephone. Those things were not common anyway at that time. We had a black iron woodstove that we cooked on in the kitchen, and in the living room we had a wood- and coal-burning stove that gave out more of a steady heat. The bedrooms had registers in the floors; we could open them to get heat upstairs. Still, we used to sleep downstairs during the winter months because it was just warmer.

In 1932 a man went out fishing one day and died. He and his wife had a lot of children. Now apparently he wasn't the best-dispositioned man in town, and my mother's sentiment, when she heard of his death, was sharp: "Good riddance. His poor wife will never have to put up with another abusing day from that man." All my father would ever say was that he died in his boat.

Sometime later the mother began seeing another man. She was receiving State aid to raise her children and, back in those days, rules were strict. The State deemed (in its infinite wisdom) that this mother should have her children taken away from her.

The day the human-services people from the State of Maine were coming to take the children away, not a fishing boat went out of Bass Harbor. All of them were on their moorings, and every fisherman was standing on the mother's lawn, waiting. When the State representatives arrived, the men of the town let them know that, in their opinion, the mother was a decent woman and a good mother. It was the town's opinion that she should have her children and she should also retain her aid. When the State people saw the local support for this hopeless mother, they decided that maybe they had overreacted a little bit. Finally the chief representative decided that the mother could keep her children as well as her aid, but she would have to compromise a little bit. The State would send the aid money to Alice Smith, who was an ordained minister in the town. Every month the widow would have to go ask Alice for the money.

The fishermen made certain that Alice gave her every dollar she'd got coming to her.

I like that story very much. In my opinion, the fishermen of Tremont stood taller that day than the skyscrapers of Manhattan. Tremont was showing what it is made of, even in lean years.

Gramp

Grandfather Edwin, who was a quarryman, would go fishing from time to time, but not steadily. He'd go for a while, then return to quarry work. He was not primarily known for either his quarrying or his fishing, but for an unusual capacity.

Gramp showed if he was getting angry by changing his color, just like a chameleon. He would turn as black as a piece of coal. That was his first giveaway. My dad said, when he was living to home, if they were doing something and noticed Gramp turning black, it was time to stop whatever they were doing. If they acted right then, they'd be all right. But if they kept going, they would be in deep shit.

When I was in the Army, my youngest uncle, Irving, went hand-lining with my father. Out fishing together, the two brothers would talk things over. That is how this story came down to me. One day Irving decided to tell my father about an event that happened when he and his wife Violet first got married. Every so often, Irving would drink too much and, when he did, he'd get silly. He and Violet lived just up across the field from my grandfather's house. One night he got teed up. Bad choice! Violet had it with him. She went down to get my grandfather. It was not so much like calling the police as reaching into the comics for someone like Popeye or Li'l Abner.

Irving sees his wife and Gramp coming up through the field. When they bust in the house, Gramp says, "You are making a damn fool of yourself! Go to bed and sleep it off."

But Irving says, "Dad, we have gone long by the time when you need to put me to bed anymore. I'll go to bed when I damn well please, okay?"

Gramp went just as black as the kitchen stove. Irving realized his mistake, but it was too late. Popeye reached out, grabbed Irving with both hands, picked him up, took him over to the bedroom, and just slammed him into the mattress. "It was like hitting a trampoline," Irving said. "I bounced off the bed onto the floor. I looked up at Gramp and he was still glaring at me, and I knew if I done it again, he'd break my goddamn neck. So I jumped up but stayed on the bed, and Dad said, 'You stay there! Violet, if he gets out of that bed or gives you any trouble, you come and get me. If I have to put him to bed again tonight, next time he won't be able to separate himself from the sheets at all!'"

And that is the story of how Uncle Irving got put to bed as a full-grown man.

Rowing to the Movies

Whenever Father wanted to go to visit his parents, I could tell. He'd get out his shaving equipment. He wouldn't shave with a safety razor; the blade wasn't so good and you could only get one shave out of one blade. He used a straight razor and leather strap like a barber would. He had to get 'em out and sharpen 'em up: "I'm going up to see my mother and the old man." He would wash himself, shine his shoes, put on a three-piece suit and a necktie with a stickpin. Last came a felt hat. Whenever he did that in the daytime, you'd know where he was going.

My father was old-fashioned. He didn't drive. He never held a driver's license in his life. His father, Edwin, who was born in 1872, had a car and was more modern than my father.

Grandfather Edwin and Grandmother Alice lived up in Duck Cove, two miles from where I grew up in Bernard. He always walked; he took a shortcut up through the woods to the main road. He must have looked like a piece of work, coming out of the woods, but it was his way of showing respect, to dress like that. He'd never wear his work clothes to see his parents.

We used to have a movie theater in town, the Neptune, above Reed's, the general store across the harbor in McKinley. They sold boots, clothes, radios, electrical appliances, and the like. When I was a small boy, my father would take me to the movies now and then. He'd always call it "the pictures." Instead of the two-mile trip by land up around the harbor, we'd walk down to the shore and row across in a punt. I remember seeing *Fighter Squadron, The Wake of the Red Witch,* and *The Doolins of Oklahoma,* and lord knows what else—the memory's not that good. During the War, they would show the American flag, and everybody in the theater would clap. I saw the first Joe Louis–Joe Walcott fight in 1947 in McKinley. Everyone thought Walcott won, but they gave it to Louis.

At night after the movie was over, we'd row back. The boat had no light, but I thought nothing of it because we did it so often. We knew exactly where we were at every moment and marked how we were going by each boat we passed on the moorings. They were as much fixed points as a hill or church. Much of them were white hull, and they'd loom up real easy, even without a moon.

School Days

I went to the same two-room schoolhouse that my father attended. My brothers and sisters went there as well. The children were broken down into kindergarten through third grade —that was called the little room. The big room was from fourth grade to seventh grade. There was one teacher for each room. As the teacher was instructing one grade, the other three grades would be doing their studying or whatever, and then she'd locate to the next grade. We learned reading, writing, arithmetic, and what have you. In the big room it was the same way again: one teacher for fourth, fifth, sixth, and seventh grade. I was in the last class that went completely through that school before they closed it down.

At recess time we weren't just on the playground; we would be in the woods and trees out in the back of the school. It was much less structured and more free-spirited than schools are today. We could climb trees or play guns, cowboy and Indian games. In the wintertime there were two ponds we could skate on, two hills we could slide on.

Everyone walked to school. Kids that had to go a long ways brought their lunches, but I lived within about a five-minute walk of the schoolhouse, so I went home for my lunch. Mother would fix hamburger, potatoes, fish—fish! We ate a lot of seafood: hake, haddock, cod, pollock, mackerel, flounders, shad, scallops, lobsters, cusk. My father hated meat. He said it was not fit to eat, that you didn't know what the cattle or hens were fed—seafood was pure. Pure then, yes! He'd be very saddened by what we've done to the ocean.

The only way he'd eat meat was if my mother burnt it to a crisp.

The First Time My Guardian Angel Appears

The first time I can ever remember that my guardian angel kicked in was in the wintertime when I was in about third grade. It's a wonder that my life didn't end right there. Me and one of my classmates, Gerald Walls, were at recess playing up on the hill. We saw this small black car coming; I guess they called them coupes back in those days. It had a front seat, and that was it. There was a man driving, and there were two women in this car beside him.

I thought I had time enough to get across the road, and I started to run. The man was looking straight ahead, but I could see he wasn't focused. He was laughing and talking with the women. I knew he couldn't see me. He was coming fast, and I didn't have time to make it. His car was going to go right over me if I kept running, so I reversed my course and ran back.

I was too late turning, though. The front part of the car went by me, as I turned in a clockwise motion, but the rear fender on the right side hit me on the shoulder. It gave me a hell of a bump! There was black ice on the road, and it sent the car swerving from one side to the other. I can remember looking at the car and the faces of the two women and the man looking back to see how bad I was hit. The car never stopped. It kept on going down into Bernard. I never knew who the man or the two women were. They were strangers. I wasn't hurt.

I got back to the school ground all right. Other than getting a good bump on the shoulder—I don't recall any lasting pain—I was no worse the wear. My friend Gerry said, "Wendell, that was a close one!"

I didn't report it. I never told anyone. You are probably the first one I ever told of that story.

A Boy during Wartime

Except for coupes with strangers in them distracted by women, Bernard was a very safe place to grow up in. Those were war years, but I was too innocent to have any idea of the hell going on in the world. To a kid, there was always the fascination with war. We recycled cans and things like that; they said it was going to make stuff for the soldiers. I liked imagining a sardine or tomato-soup can turned into a rifle or bullet. At school we used to get little military stamps on our papers: the flag, or a tank, or a battleship, or a plane when we happened to earn an "A" on our paper. If it was *that* good, it deserved a plane.

There were a lot of aeroplanes flying around here in World War Two. And blimps. Blimps are something that always fascinated me. I thought they were almost mystical—fantastic creations in the sky. I used to chase them when they would be going over. Usually they outpaced me, but once in a while they'd just hover over the land and I'd be able to get right under them and look up at them. I suppose what they were doing was looking for submarines in the ocean, but I never saw any. However, I know that there were blimps shot down over the Maine coast during the war, and I imagine it was German submarines that did it.

Granville Reed

September, 1948, I entered the fifth grade. I was sick on the first day of school, and my mother had to take me to the doctor's in Ellsworth. So I started on the second day, and that's when I got to meet Mr. Reed.

He was born in 1924, same year as my youngest sister Olive, and he fought in World War Two. When he got out of the Army, he went to study to be a lawyer but, after completing his degree, instead he came to Bernard to take a position as an elementary school teacher.

Mr. Reed was small in physical size and he had a gentle soul. From the word "go" I liked him very much. He carried a long stick that was pointed like a musical director's baton, and if any student got out of line, he would give that person a quick strike with it.

He would not beat a kid but, if he had to get your undivided attention, he wouldn't think twice to give you a rap. If you misbehaved enough, he'd make you copy pages out of the dictionary. Once he rapped me right on top of the head—bap! But he did it to get my attention, maybe the way a Zen master would with his staff.

I did have to stay after school on occasion and copy the dictionary. I wasn't there every night, but periodically. I can't even remember anymore what I done wrong, but it must have been something.

Usually a number of us would be copying while he'd be down

in the cellar chopping wood to keep the stoves going the next day. You see, he was the janitor as well as the principal of the school. Of course, the minute he was gone to the cellar, us kids would have a wonderful time laughing and joking.

He was a good teacher. He worked your foolishness out of you. The previous fifth-grade teacher had a really mean streak in him. He would take a stick and wail the hell right out of a kid—boy or girl. That would just set people back.

Granville Reed was not with us for long. He only taught from September of 1948 till May of 1949. Then the Korean War broke out, and he decided to reenlist.

I was home sick with the measles when he resigned, and they got a substitute teacher who took over our class until the school year ended. Before he went into the Army, Mr. Reed came back to say goodbye to the class. And good-bye it was. In Korea he was a second lieutenant, probably a platoon leader. He was killed within a year and two months from the time he left Bernard.

Thirty years after his death I had a dream about him, a very powerful one. In this dream I was walking from my home up by the Bernard elementary school and, as I passed near, I saw some activity going on in the school where nothing had happened for decades. I went in, and there was Mr. Reed and a woman, another teacher. The woman was going to take kindergarten through third grade, and he was getting the fourth through the seventh. I said, "Mr. Reed, what are you doing here?"

"We are renovating this old building, and we are going to teach intense environmental education. You have to get them on the elementary level. Once they have gone to high school you have lost them. We believe that the environment is a very important issue in our times."

I said, "Mr. Reed, you came here in 1948 and became an elementary school teacher, but you resigned your position and you reenlisted. You got shot and killed in Korea. This can't be!"

"You are right, but I am going to tell you something: I was never meant to be a soldier; I was never meant to be a lawyer; I was meant to be a teacher. I made a fatal mistake when I reenlisted, and it cost me my life. But I have been very lucky. I got a second chance. This time I am going to do it right."

"But Mr. Reed," I said, "You have to realize things are not today like they were years ago. Tremont no longer has little elementary schools. We consolidated in 1951. Everything is together."

When the dead appear in dreams, they generally know what they are talking about. Mr. Reed was no exception. He said, "We realize that, but we feel time is short and we will be able to attract those of the new generation who want serious environmental education. That is what we are going to do. We are going to teach now what we couldn't teach then. I am going to teach what I should have taught instead of going to Korea. I didn't understand, but I do now." He even had his baton ready!

Twenty-five years after the dream I went with my wife to the cemetery where I knew my old teacher was buried, and we walked each row, looking for a gravestone marked Granville Reed. After a while I realized we were getting nowhere. I tried something different. I stopped where I was; I looked right up in the sky and said, "Mr. Reed, if you want me to find your remains, you guide me to them." I focused my attention between my eyebrows. All of a sudden there was a magnetic pull, and I followed it in a southeast direction, and then it turned and pulled me to the south until it stopped; I looked down and what did I see on the gravestone? "Granville E. Reed, second lieutenant 24th infantry, 25th infantry division, WWII Korea PH, born May 10 1924, died July 30 1950."

I said, "Thank you, Mr. Reed."

My Brothers Go to War

People back home never referred to the servicemen as "men"; they all called them "our boys." "Our boys are coming home," or, when they were fighting a big invasion, "Our boys are going to have a hard time." It was always "our boys." Each house in Bernard hung a flag that had a star for each person from that family that was in the war. I had two brothers, so my personal household had a flag with two stars on it in the window.

I can't remember when my oldest brother Frank went into the Army. At the time he was drafted he was married, with a daughter. He went fishing with my dad before he left for the war. As for my other brother Wilbur, who was born in 1922, I can remember the exact day he went into the Army. Webb had to leave early one morning. It was in the winter—the sun rose late and it was dark. I got up very early, before the sun rose, and I asked my mother, "Where is Webb?"

"He has gone to war, " she said.

During basic training both of my brothers came home for short leaves in the summer around the same time. One got back on the day the other one had to leave, so they met each other once more before one went to Europe and the other to the Pacific.

When they came back for good I didn't recognize Frank; I had forgotten him totally. My dad just said, "You'll get used to him again." My brother Webb, it was like he never left; I recognized him instantaneously when he came home.

I used to wait for the bus—we had a service from Ellsworth to the Island all through those years; we were expecting him anytime. Each night the bus would stop, I'd be there, and he wouldn't get off. I was terribly disappointed. Finally—I can picture it in my mind's eye—the night came that he got off the bus, a man in a uniform. My Dad said, "That's your brother," but I knew him immediately.

Of course, not all of "our boys" came home. When I was in the third grade, word reached our schoolhouse that Clarence Galley had been shot. He had been in Germany and was killed by machine-gun fire. His brother was a year older than I was in class, and I can remember his being excused from school. He left the schoolhouse crying. At lunchtime we went to his home and he was standing out on the doorstep by a rain barrel, still crying, and his mother and father were in the kitchen.

My Father the Fisherman

My father was a fisherman all his life—the last of the early American fishermen. He was a man of character, honest, the kind of man you can trust. The greatest thing of my life back in childhood was going to the shore with him and watching those men work on the dock. I would be very quiet and listen to them tell their tales. They didn't leave a written history; they told it by word of mouth in stories. I realized real young that there was an art to telling stories, and those men had it. They were the ones I admired, the fishermen. I realized if I kept my ears and eyes open, I could sit there like a fly on the wall and learn. My father was one of the storytellers, too.

Dad got broken into offshore fishing about February of 1912 and, if I remember right, that was the year the *Titanic* went down, the year my dad started working the sea. At sixteen years old he joined a schooner of men fishing off George's Bank. Here's how it happened: Clarence Turner used to skipper a number of different vessels, using Portland as his home port. One day down at the wharf, he said to Dad, "Your father tell you that I wanted you to go fishing with me?"

And my father said, "No, he didn't."

"Well, do you want to go pack your bag? We are leaving tonight."

That was it—no papers to fill out, no bureaucracy, no good-bye party.

On Dad's first trip out, which was in February, he got fear-some seasick. The cook on board was Henry Dow, a man from Bernard, and he came up to my father and asked him, "What's the trouble, Frank? Let me finish baiting your trawls for you. You go lay down in your bunk." My father said it seemed like he no more got to sleep when the skipper called him out to set the trawls that had been baited. After a nap he was feeling better, maybe not perfect, but fishermen didn't have a choice; they were already on the boat, so they had to get used to the sea.

It was just a short trip that first time; then they ran back into Portland the next day and sold the catch, codfish and had-dock. My dad said that, after going out on trips that lasted from one to three weeks, the longest up to six weeks, it wasn't long before he realized he had gotten over seasickness. I guess you'd call it the "cure by sea" or, as my Dad would say, simply "going till you get used to it."

When my father first started tub trawling with Clarence, they fished the banks, about a hundred, a hundred-a-fifty miles offshore. They mainly traveled by sail, but they did have an aux-iliary motor. They trawled for hake, haddock, pollock, and cod; those fish are all cousins to one another, roundfish rather than what you'd call flatfish.

Cod was an important part of colonial America, more important than people may realize. If it wasn't for fishermen, the pilgrims would have starved. The Indians may have given them a Thanksgiving party, but my ancestors were out getting the cod and feeding 'em. It's codfishermen not pilgrims who founded this nation. They were here first and they learned to survive and make a home base here. Everything else that followed came out of this.

Trawling involved setting long hooked lines in the water; these sank to the bottom of the sea where the fish would bite the hooks, and that would be their undoing. Four tubs of trawls per dory, eight lines apiece, each fifty fathoms long, would run a good mile and a half across the ocean, which gives you an idea of the scale we are talking about. The men'd go out at four-thirty in the morning in dories from the main vessel, set out their trawls, be back by six as the sun was making its way up, have breakfast, and then after breakfast go right out and haul them back by ten-thirty. Then they'd bring the dory up alongside the vessel, unload the fish, dress them down, wash and ice them in the hole, and bait all their trawls back up again for the next day. Some afternoons they would not be finished work until 11 o'clock at night. Clarence used to say, "That's the trouble with these short days, you can't get nothing done."

When my dad fished in a powerboat out of Bass Harbor, it was totally different than vessel fishing, which was a group enterprise; he had to do everything by himself. He used to throw out a bamboo pole and keg with an anchor line on it of about one hundred fathoms. From this he would set out eight tubs of trawl that had hooks three feet apart—there was more room for the tubs in the powerboat than the dory. They would spread out a distance of three to three and a half miles, about the same as the crow flies from Southwest Harbor to Bernard. Every two trawls Dad would throw out a middle keg with an anchor line wrapped around it so that it would unwind. That gave him about five different reference points he could haul from to get these trawls back.

Every summer Dad would go trawling like this or, on occasion, swordfishing with harpoons, sometimes with Clarence Turner, sometimes with other men. Then he'd come back home and fish coastwise—hand-lining for cod and pollock, trawling for hake mostly, a little for haddock; dragging for scallops. And then he'd leave again for the banks: George's, Brown's, Lahave, Cashes, the Kettle Bottom, the Rips, German Banks, the great offshore grounds. Vessels he fished on were the *Locking Var,* the *Willard,* the *Marion Turner,* and the *Barbara.*

Close Call out on the Banks

The worst days to fish offshore were Monday and Tuesday because passenger ships and freighters from Boston and New York would make the banks. Especially in fog and snow, it was hectic. They'd blow their horns, and the fishing boats would have to try locate them and keep track of their positions. If one of these big ships hit a fishing vessel, she was a goner. Dad told me the passenger ships were the easiest to deal with because they went so fast their sounds could be dead-reckoned. You could first hear them blow off in the distance. The next time they blew they were alongside, and the next time they blew they had gone by you. It was clear-cut like an express train on a track. But those tramp steamers were slow; they would blow all night long and you couldn't tell where they were.

At night the fishermen would set sails and light torches along the side of their vessels to illuminate the sails so the big ships would spot them quickly. The fishing vessels also had sirens they could crank. If there was any question about lights approaching in the fog or darkness and the guy on watch was in doubt, he was supposed to wake the skipper. Clarence told my Dad, "You know, I have been brought out of my bunk more times for the morning star than anything else."

But one could never be too cautious. The closest call my father ever had was when a vessel he was on saw a ship bearing down on them. The watchman woke Clarence. Clarence did not want to get up; he said, "She'll probably go two miles to the south'ard of us."

The watchman went to check, then came down below again, and very firmly told the skipper, "If she keeps on her present course, she will not go two miles south'ard of us; she will ram us." Then he called all hands on deck. The freighter could not see the fishing schooner and was still coming straight for it. It was too late to make an effective move. The watchman hollered to my father, "Let's launch a dory and see if we can get clear of the vessel before she hits us." At that moment the freighter blew her horn, which meant that she had spotted his vessel and was doing her utmost to avoid it. When she went by his stern, she smashed a dory that was in a davit hanging out over the edge—cleaned it right off without actually hitting the schooner.

The Sleepy-Headed Crewman

On one trip a particularly sleepy-headed fisherman was working with my father. They always had trouble waking this guy up. This time, it was on towards winter and my dad had just come off watch. He had on thick woolen mittens, and it had started to snow. His drowsy friend, who was supposed to relieve him of his watch, had been reading on his bunk and had a candle lit. Just as my dad came down below, the man dozed off and pitched over, driving his head right into that candle, igniting his hair. My dad grabbed him with snowy mittens and brushed the fire out.

When they got done trawling for that season and were going to get ready to come home, this sleepy-headed friend of my father's said, "Frank, I can get you a job on a halibut fishing boat, no problem." Dad wanted to take it, but Henry Dow, the cook, talked my father out of it. He said, "You have been gone for quite a long period of time, and I think your mother and father would like to see you now. I am going to discourage you from going out on this boat. I think it is time you went home. I just got a strong feeling about it." Henry Dow was able to talk my dad out of it.

Dad's friend went out on that boat, and there was a snow-storm while they were at sea. A freighter bore down on them out on George's Bank. The watchman called all hands on deck, but my father's companion did not appear. Collision was imminent, so another man voluntarily went down below deck to rout him out of his bunk. While the two men were below, the freighter hit the vessel, split her in half, and both men were lost. Of the entire crew, half were killed that day, including the skipper's son. I think my dad realized that he owed his life to Henry Dow, the cook who encouraged him to come home.

In the annals of offshore fishing of that era, this was a commonplace traffic accident. The loss of life aboard vessels was tremendous back in those days. As near as I can gauge, during the Civil War years, around three hundred and sixty-five men from Gloucester, Massachusetts, were lost in combat, while during those very same years, nine hundred and forty-five were lost to fishing. Even in my father's time, in the early part of the last century up to the first World War, he had seen as many as nine vessels at a time with flags at half-mast in Portland harbor, indicating that they had lost men.

Submarine Attack

One summer my father was with Clarence swordfishing on George's Bank. With a trip of fish already in the hold, Clarence said, "We'll lay over tonight and, if it is good tomorrow, we'll fish one more day—that is, if the weather holds. Then we are going to Portland, for sure." The next morning, a fog bank arose about twenty minutes' running time from where they were anchored, and Clarence decided it wasn't conducive to good fishing. "To hell with it," he said, "we are not going to fish today." They got the anchor up and prepared to go.

The boat had just got into the fog bank when they heard a gun go off. It was near a boat that had anchored right alongside of them all night, a brand-new vessel on her maiden voyage. Clarence knew instantly from the sound that it was a German submarine that had opened fire. His boat was safe in the fog so they kept going, away from the danger. When they got into Portland, they heard the news. There *had*, in fact, been a German submarine that came up and shot the hell out of the American fishing fleet. The vessel that had been alongside of them was the first one to get sunk, but the captain lived to report on it. He met Clarence later and told the whole story: "When that submarine surfaced, she came up right where you pulled your anchor. The German skipper shouted to all the ships in the neighborhood, 'I will give you ten minutes to get food and water, launch your dories, and get clear of the fleet. I'll hold fire for just ten minutes. I know some of you will try and make that fog bank, but remember, if I run across you again, there is no second chance.'" The captain of that brand-new vessel knew they stood no chance of reaching the fog, and so they abandoned ship in dories.

"'I have really been waiting for the merchant ships coming out of Boston and New York and going overseas,'" the German skipper explained while the men were leaving their fishing vessels. "'That is what I really wanted.'" He went on to say that Tuesday was a glorious night to find ships coming out of Boston and New York crossing the banks, but on this day they were so dispersed that he hadn't seen even one of them. "'I've got no showing, I am out of fuel, and I've got to go back to Germany but, before I do, I've got to make a showing.'" So he shot up the fishing fleet, or a lot of it, and that's all my father ever knew of this story, except that all the members of the fleet either made it to shore or were picked up by the Navy.

Charlie York, another man out with the fleet that day on the *Locking Var,* gave his version to a professor. When the German sub issued her ultimatum, the crew of the *Locking Var* cut their anchor. Her skipper headed for a sandy shoal called the Cultivator where he knew the sub would not follow. They were going to take advantage of both the shallow water and the fog bank and try to escape. Like Clarence's ship, the *Locking Var* made it into Portland under its own sail in one piece.

About three years ago I saw a magazine article about the history of the German sub. The American Navy caught her and sunk her out in the Atlantic. They never did reach Germany.

Trawling with Dad

When I was young, about seven or eight years old, my father let me go fishing with him quite a bit in the summer. I was too young to do any serious work, of course. He would set out when it was still dark, so the only nights he would trust to take me were those of the full moon or a big moon. He didn't have radar or Loran; it was compass, course, and time. If I was with him, he wanted to be able to see good. He and I would go to the harbor at one-thirty in the morning and, only if it was clear would he take me with him.

I remember being fascinated by the phosphorescence, the water-fire the boat would go through in the darkness. And I was always amazed how my dad could cut through the night and know just where he was going. The reflection of the moon in the black waves, always changing, breaking apart and never quite coming back together, was my definition of beauty as a child. Or the moon going in and out of dark cloud banks such that the sky was another sea. I believe it was Thoreau who asked, "How many encounters has the moon had with the clouds?"

Dad had twelve trawls then, so he could have one gang of six ashore being baited while he was fishing the other six. The first trip that I went on with him, when he was hauling back the first trawls, he got bit off by the sharks four different times and lost much of his gear. We were about twenty miles offshore, and I can remember him dragging a grappling hook behind the boat, trying to sweep the gear back up. It didn't work. It didn't catch the trawls. So, we had to call it quits, and a lot of that gear was left out in the ocean. He said the next day he was going to go and take the other six trawls from back on shore and run the same course and time. He would try to set those trawls right on top of what he done the day before. Of course, I wanted to go with him. He said, "No, no, this is going to be a hard, difficult day. I can't take you."

What really impressed me was that this man ran out twenty miles into the ocean with his pocket watch and his compass only, right back out to the exact same spot we had been in the day before. At the time he had no tachometer on the boat. He simply listened to the engine to hear how hard she was turning, and he set right square on top of those lost trawls!

When he come in that night, he not only had the fish he caught that day, he had the fish he caught the day before. That boat was so full of fish it was just barely floating in the water. He had all the standing room filled, and the cabin, too. He was just plumb loaded with fish.

The Rhythm of Nature

Life was slower-paced in those days. The entertainment that we had wasn't television; it was radio and books. You'd listen to all these programs: *The Shadow, Roy Rogers, The Lone Ranger, True Detective.* The thing was that you had to use your imagination because the stories were like somebody reading to you. You couldn't see the visual image, so you had to do that part in your head. I think we had more patience back then. We didn't get bored quite so easily.

We invented a lot of our own games. We learned to entertain ourselves with baseballs and bicycles—whatever we had—and we seemed to enjoy it.

It was entertainment enough to go out in a boat all day and watch the sun come up out of the ocean, slowly go across the sky, and finally see the day shut down on itself in reds and oranges. You'd get the rhythmic pace of nature. We'd observe the ocean and its denizens—whales, porpoises, schooling fish, swordfish jumping out of the water, gulls trailing the ship, vocalizing about something or other, maybe the entrails from the cleaned fish. The colors were brighter than Technicolor; the dangers were more real than cowboys and Indians; the creatures were stranger than Superman comics. I mean horned sculpins, skates, stingrays, starfish, and even the fish innards were more unusual looking than anything in a science-fiction show. And they were real things! You never knew what was coming next, not like in an action movie or video game, but because the sea was alive and moody in its own way; it was mysterious and could bring the most unexpected things up from underneath itself. That's when the vastness of the world really hit you. It wasn't something from inside your own mind or electric display. It was true excitement and had a beauty all of its own.

Kids these days get bored when they go out in a boat: "This is monotonous! That's not exciting! Nothing's happening! When's something gonna happen, Wendell?" But I suppose—God, they have been so overstimulated! When you've got *Star Trek,* computer games, and instant this and instant that, you never have to wait for nothing! We realized back then that you have to wait for things to happen at their own pace, at their own rate, like the sun, like schools of fish. Maybe life had more romance back in those days than it does for kids nowadays. They see too much too fast. Our way back then was more of an actual working rhythm of things. I know modern kids have got everything—so they say—but sometimes I wonder if they miss the adventure that we had as boys. I don't know, but I think along those lines.

My Dad the Movie Star

When I was about eight years old, my father said to me, "You know, I was in a movie once. I was fishing with Clarence Turner and we were on the *Willard.* It was in the fall of the year, back in the days of silent movies. I was twenty-seven. We put into New Harbor, Maine, and planned to be there long enough to repair our net and overhaul our gear, which would take us a few days. When we got in, there was a film company from Hollywood there, filming a movie called *The Seventh Day*."

The director wanted to work the fishing vessel into his movie, which was a love story, so he hired Clarence and the *Willard* and all Clarence's men. " 'When I need to take shot of it,' the director said, 'I want you to take her out and put her under sail.' " Sometimes they'd get the fishermen to participate along with the actors and actresses. My father was in one brief scene, hoisting fish out on the wharf.

The director was actually a successful man with a number of notable films, a big-name filmmaker in his day, but he was temperamental. My dad said he'd give those actors and actresses merry hell if they didn't do things just the way he wanted. They had to shoot every scene over and over to get 'em so he'd accept them. There was a scene that had one of the crew members in it, but the crewman didn't get it right, and the director flew into him, gave him hell as if the fisherman were one of his actors. This man was an independent fisherman, an early American tub-trawler. His kind were characters; they were their own bosses, free men. It went like this, as I remember my father acting it out for me: The fisherman said to the director, "Look, you goddamn son of a bitch, I don't have to put up with your horseshit like these people. If you are going to treat us like that, you can take your goddamn christly camera and go right on to hell with it. Is that clear?"

The director was used to dishing it out but not to taking it. There was a pause. "I deserved that," the director said, "I apologize to you. I promise you that will never happen again." The fisherman and the producer shook hands.

After a few days they had the nets all repaired and were set to go back fishing, so Clarence told the director, "We are ready to go to sea now."

"God! You can't leave me now!" the director protested, "I have got more scenes to shoot of your vessel."

"Look, we are not movie actors; we are fishermen. We make our livelihood from the sea."

"What would it take to get you people to stay? Money?"

"For one thing," Clarence replied.

"Money is no problem. What do you want?"

Clarence requested a certain amount for the use of the vessel and fifty dollars for each man, which was a lot of money in 1921. For that fee, they stayed what little time was needed to finish shooting the movie.

About ten years or so ago, I went into the barbershop over to Southwest. There were a bunch of customers in front of me, so I sat down with the *Bangor Daily News*. On the front page I saw a headline: "Silent Movie Relocated." Apparently, Czechoslovakians liked our silent movies. Recently, archivists there located a number of them. They had to re-translate the subtitles back into English.

There was an image from a movie with a fishing vessel, a real fishing vessel not a yacht, with her dories stacked right up inside of her, and I thought, "Wouldn't that be something if that movie was *The Seventh Day?*" I turned to the page where the story continued. And it was!

A couple of weeks later they showed the movie down the coast and I went to see it. Two elderly women were sitting in front of me.

"What brings you people here?" I asked them.

"We were both fifteen years old when this movie was filmed," they told me. They had been childhood friends and remained such through life.

"It was my father that owned that wharf the film was shot on," one said. "When they were filming, we went down to the dock to watch them do it. The director tried to shoo us off. 'Look, girls, we are working here. I don't want you around. Get yourselves right up off the dock!' I said, 'You know you are on my father's wharf and, if I report this to him, you might have to find yourself another wharf to shoot your movie on!' He let us stay."

The plot centered on a rich unmarried couple who go from New York to Maine on a fabulous yacht, but the woman had no real love for the man. Then, near the end of their trip, in off the banks comes a fishing vessel,the *Willard,* and on the after part of the boat is an actor portraying a fisherman. She looks at him, sparks fly, and that is how it goes. In the end the two suitors meet and get into a pissing contest on the wharf. The fisherman pushes the rich guy into the water. The two women I met at the screening said that scene had to be shot and re-shot so many times the poor actor almost drowned!

Lobstering for a Dollar a Day

The first year I started working for money with my father was back in 1948. I was ten. He usually went coastal tub trawling from May until into September, but that year they quit buying fish early and he set traps out in July instead of fishing and took me lobstering with him. He let me bait the bags and he paid me a dollar a day.

To work his traps, he would want to be on the fishing grounds by the time he could see, which was about a half hour before sunrise.

We'd get up about three-thirty or quarter of four, which was not as early as when I went out trawling with him on full-moon nights.

I can remember when we'd start out—it would still be relatively dark; it might be predawn. As we would go down over Bass Harbor Bar, you'd see the sky lighten up over the east. I always loved when the sun would come up—how it would paint the sky! Then, before you knew it, it was daytime. The gulls fascinated me with their tameness, the way they would feed on the water while they talked to no one in particular, how they would clean up everything in the bait pocket.

If you listened real close to the engine, it had a melody. I can remember being able to pick that up. With the belts and everything snapping and cracking, it played a song unto itself. To listen to the whole thing was not only to hear it work but to be sung a map of our journey. My father could use that map, as I told you, to place us on fishing grounds with precision.

My father's engine was salt-water-cooled. In the winter he'd keep the water that engine had heated and let the hose run it on the deck of the boat. He'd plug the scuppers so the water wouldn't run out. A gull would light in that pool and, first thing, look at its feet out of curiosity, then settle back down there to warm them. Liking what it felt, it might stay there the whole day.

The boat itself was small—about 31 feet long, 9 feet wide—and she didn't have no bunk down in the cabin like most boats today. When I got seasick I used to lie down and sleep by the companionway, right on the floorboards alongside the engine. And when I'd get over it, I'd come back up and go to work again.

I wasn't pressured to work all that hard. Filling the bait bag with herring wasn't heavy work, but it was a contribution, and it got me started in lobsterfishing.

I went for lobster all that summer with my dad, till school started.

Rites of Passage

On the coast of Maine we were expected to work as soon as we were old enough. If we didn't we would be called lazy, and that was no compliment. When I was eleven, I started baiting trawls on the dock. Each line had hooks with a herring on each hook. We had to learn how to attach the herring properly and how to pack the trawls in the tub so the men could set them out smoothly at night. The lines had to feed into the tubs neatly, so the hooked trawls would come out evenly with a minimum of entanglement. It was quite a procedure for me. With seven hundred and fifty hooks every three feet apart per trawl, the fishermen were glad to have us kids to do it, as long as we did it right. The more trawls we could get baited, the more fishing they could get in. When I first started, we were paid a dollar a trawl.

Once we were working on the wharf, we were not boys anymore. We felt useful and knew our place. We did not have to wait to get out of high school or study for a college degree before we knew what we were going to do with our lives.

As teenagers, we started working on the fish wharf also; we were strong and responsible enough to handle knives. The fishermen would hire us, along with the men who worked on the wharf, to dress the fish down—cut the heads off them, rip open their bellies, take out all the innards, wash 'em, put 'em on ice, and load the catch into trucks. Nowadays there would be laws against kids doing that kind of work, handling knives and such, but back then, there was no thought of that, no insurance companies regulating things neither. One simply learned how to use a knife, and accidents were a part of learning, an important part of life. We didn't have Big Brother to tell us which job was too dangerous for young boys. And if you did get hurt, well, that was a part of growing up.

The younger workingmen would play and roughhouse with us. They'd give us young bucks a chance to test our antlers on them. Sometimes there might be two or three kids tackling one man. I called it The Rites of Passage, these wrassling matches. A man would say, "Well, I think somebody wants to go for a swim," and two men would get on either side of a kid and send him right off the dock into the harbor. All of this was done with good nature. No one was ever hurt by it. When we got older, we did it to the younger kids. There was no such thing as suing. It was an innocent time.

The Ocean

To me as a boy the ocean was awe-inspiring. It was a bountiful thing. I couldn't imagine where it began or where it ended. I was impressed how men would talk about it and refer to it, each in his own language, almost as if they were talking about God. Clarence Harding always said "the water"—just "the water." That was enough. "Some men work on the land; some men work on the water"—that's how he referred to it. Herbert Thurston referred to it as "the sea"—it was all one thing for him too, but a "sea" rather than "the water." A man worked the sea; that was real men's work, almost divine laboring. It was "the ocean" when my father referred to it—"we're gonna run off in the ocean tonight and set our trawls." It was like he was talking about a place, but it was all water and moving, nothing you could stand on without a boat. How men identified something so limitless, the words they used—"the sea," "the water," "the ocean"—meant something to them; it indicated wonder and respect.

As impressive as God's ocean was, man's boats were remarkable foils for its water. I remember being struck initially by how much a boat can take and not capsize. My father told me, "A boat will scare you to death before she'll drown you." Knowing that, I never was afraid in a boat. I figured it was an object designed for the water, tested and improved over generations. Fishermen, probably as long ago as the Stone Ages, drowned to make better boats for their children. The men came up as sturdy as their boats.

Hand-Lining and Trawling

I didn't begin formally trawling and hand-lining with my father till I was eighteen. In my childhood, I was just a guest, an onlooker. Then I did it for real my first five years out of high school, from 1956 to 1961. When we went out together, he and I would fish eight tubs of trawl. You may remember: a tub of trawl is made up of eight lines; there are fifty fathoms to each line and a hook about every three feet, approximately seven hundred and fifty hooks to a trawl. We would fish eight trawls spread out for about three and a half miles.

Usually at hand-lining it was Dad fishing a line and me fishing another; he on the starboard side, me on the port. There would be about fourteen hooks between the two of us. Even then it was a very old-fashioned method of hook-and-line fishing, yet nonetheless successful for it. If we were out for codfish those days before the sea was fished out, we could catch between 2,500 and 5,000 pounds of fish a day, ordinarily. When we got into pollock we could haul from 3,000 to 6,000 pounds a day. When we went for hake we would catch from 3,000 to 9,000 pounds of fish a day. The biggest catch I ever made was on the twenty-fourth of May in 1965. Three of us together, my father, me, and a man named George Sawyer, hauled in a single day 12,747 pounds of pollock—the biggest catch I ever saw anyone make while hand-lining!

That was back in the fifties and sixties, and we kept catching those amounts till the early seventies. After that, things changed, as we sadly know. The honorable trade of the fisherman became the grim reaper of species extinction.

Saving My Father's Life

I also went lobsterfishing with my father during those same years. In the winter of 1957 one day, Dad and I were fishing our traps in pairs, and I was back of the steering shelter, pegging lobsters and baiting bags. My father was running out a pair of traps, and the boat was underway at a fast working pace. When I heard his feet thumping the platform, I knew immediately he was in trouble. What I saw was that he got a turn of the rope around both his wrists like he was handcuffed. Knowing there was nothing he could do to save himself, I ran forward and hit the clutch handle of the engine into neutral. Then I ran back to the stern of the boat. My father was two-thirds out over the stern when I slammed my body right down on his and grabbed on the end of the boat and pinned him there so that he wouldn't go overboard. When the boat lost momentum, I was able to reach forward, get ahold of the rope, haul in some slack, get the turns of rope off his wrists and him back aboard the boat. First question I asked him: "Are you all right, Dad?"

He says, "This is what I tried to tell you. You've got to pay attention to what you're doing, or you can get yourself in a goddamn mess awful quick."

I says, "Dad, was that message for me or for you?"

Never again did he ever mention this incident to me, but in the summer of '59 I overheard him relate the story to another fisherman, and he said, "If Wendell hadn't been there that day, I wouldn't be here now."

Two Old Fishermen: Stories about Them

Each generation would introduce the younger generation to working the sea. The generation that introduced my father to the ocean was born during the Civil War era. When I was young, six, seven, and eight years old, these men were in their eighties and dying. My father's generation—the World War One fishermen—were in their prime of working. They were men in their fifties, and I would listen to their stories. My brothers' generation were all in the Second World War and, when they came back, some of them returned to fishing, but others went ashore to work. Life in coastal Maine was starting to change a little. Their stories did not have the same ring.

When I was a boy, I knew two elderly fishermen, both born in the year of 1878. One was John Clossen, and the other was George Trask. Back then, I thought they had been here forever—there never could have been a time when they were young. Of course, that's a young person's viewpoint. George Trask told my dad, "The first time I met John Clossen I was thirteen years old. I had sailed over with my father in his Friendship Sloop from Gott's Island. This young fellow came up to me on the wharf. He had a piece of chalk in his hand, and he drew a circle on the wharf and then looked at me very challengingly and said, 'I bet I can put you in that circle.'

"I retorted, 'You'll have to shove me,' and then what did he do? He went up and wrote the letter 'U' in the circle."

They were friends ever since.

John was a very craggy man. He looked like he was carved right out of granite. My father said that he never met a man in his life that he felt enjoyed his work as much as John Clossen. John relished every phase of being a fisherman: building and repairing the equipment as much as fishing the equipment. Dad said if you ever wanted anyone to go to work the sea with, John Clossen was ready.

George Trask liked to tell stories of when he himself was young and how strong he was. Such stories! You'd think he was Samson—always this and that about his body and shoulder muscles. When I was a young buck, George told me, "You know, sonny, some of these men who call themselves prize fighters today, well, when I was twenty-five I wouldn't have minded stepping into the ring with 'em."

Later I sounded it out on my father—I always used him as a sounding board—and I told him what George had said. My father replied, "Yeah, and after George'd gone a couple of rounds he probably wouldn't have minded stepping out of the ring either!"

George had this old Model A Ford that he drove very slowly—never over twenty-five miles an hour. He would lecture us now and then about how speed caused accidents. Speed was thirty. Old men like him never adapted to the modern way.

In the summer when I was nine years old, my mother, father, and I as well as some of George's grandchildren, who were all much younger than me, went to Bar Harbor to go blueberrying. My mother and George sat in the front, and my father and the kids and I were all jammed up in the back. Every time we came to a hill, he'd have to shift down. The gas pedal and the clutch were never in sync with each other. It was lurch and lunge all the way there.

As we were approaching Bar Harbor, my father was getting

more and more impatient. The kids had started banging on the pots and buckets they had brought to put the blueberries in. Now, my father was a man who had a low tolerance for noise. He would have made a good librarian. We were never allowed to holler in the house or he would explode. Pretty soon he was swearing under his breath, "Jesus, Jesus, Jesus."

Of course, my mother could hear him, and it was tickling her to death. She sat up front giggling, knowing that he was going nuts back there with all those kids but that he wouldn't be able to do much about it. After we finally came into Bar Harbor, did our blueberrying, and lurched and lunged back home, my father said, "By God, that is the last blueberrying trip I am ever going to go on. The people watching us drive by must have thought that Ringling Brothers Circus had landed."

George's wife was named Emily. They had been married for eons and had two children, Millicent and Orville, who were all grown up when I was a boy. When I got to be a teenager, George couldn't fish by himself anymore, so he would go with Orville. Then, when he got too old to go out in the boat at all, he would work ashore building traps and painting buoys to help Orville.

Emily used to work in the Underwood Sardine Factory. She did that well into old age. A bus used to come right down the main drag in Bernard and pick her up, along with the other factory workers. It would bring them home at lunch. I saw her getting off that bus in her eighties, trotting like a soldier, double-timing just to get back to the bus stop for a second shift.

Down at the wharf they had a big area they called the Pool Room where men worked on their equipment and built their traps out of pre-cut pieces of oak. The parts of the trap would be two sills, three crossings to connect the sills, three pre-bored bows that went down into the tops of the sills, three door cleats, and the laths. The heads were knitted out of marline, and they had to be laced into the traps. We made them that way until the early '80s when we changed to wire.

They also overhauled and fixed trawls, scallop drags, and old traps, and painted their colors on buoys. They had a card table in there, and the men would socialize around it. One time, when he was in his eighties, George came down to the wharf and said, "Well, Emily told me today that she wants me to go out and get a steady job like any other man." If he was too old to work in a boat, as far as she was concerned, there was no earthly reason he couldn't hold down a steady job on shore. She didn't count helping his son at the wharf; she figured he should be out working for pay. But that was the old economy, the way we grew up.

All the men just burst into laughter.

Louie Cries at Tremont Town Meeting

A lot of those old-timers were very politically minded, at least local politics. Town Meeting was important to them, and they'd get up and hoot and holler and express their opinions, whether anyone wanted them or not. Louie Norwood was one of those kinds of hollerers. My mother told me that every time he got up and talked publicly in Town Meeting, he'd cry. It didn't matter that the subject was only taxes or the roughness of the roads or school policy. It made him cry. The whole town used to turn out just to see and hear Louie bawl. He couldn't help it. He'd get up and talk and talk and start crying.

Once, before I was born, his wife got him to promise that he would not get up and talk in Town Meeting ever again. He agreed. That year, the whole town turned out, and the morning went on fine, working through the agenda. The whole time Louie sat right there in his chair, silent as a church mouse, keeping his promise. They adjourned to go to lunch. I might mention here that every Town Meeting my father and mother made a big clam chowder, and then after that it was back to finish up the agenda in the afternoon. Well, this particular year, the townspeople were saying around their clam chowder how disappointed they were that Louie was holding fast. But in the afternoon he couldn't stand it anymore, and he stood up and he told them this and that and the other about the town dump or some such subject and then soon burst right into tears. The people weren't disappointed after all.

Tom Kelley and Henry Sawyer

Among the other old-timers in town when I was growing up was Tom Kelley, who must have been born somewhere around 1870. He was a Merchant Marine with an unlimited captain's license; he could go by sail or steam. I asked him once how long he worked the sea. "Forty years," he told me, "twenty years under sail and twenty years under steam."

Tom used to handle tramp steamers, the ones with no steady port who would take their cargoes anywhere in the world. He had been to many places where it was not safe to go ashore or, if you did, you wanted a sidearm on you. He had seen much of the world from a rough perspective. In the evening of his life he got into town politics and was first selectman for many years.

Henry Sawyer was another man I knew. He was three or four years older than my father and was good friends with Tom Kelley. When Tom would return from one of his trips, he'd always look Henry up and talk with him. Henry was a stay-at-home man, an old-time lobsterfisherman. Now and again he would get a letter from Tom when Tom was at sea, and he would share it around town and then tell Tom some of the observations and wisecracks about him when Tom was home, which would amuse him.

One time, after Tom went back to sea, he described a huge storm out on the Atlantic. Well, one of the locals named George, not to be outdone, told Henry that he had seen far fouler weather hauling traps out at the Outer Ledge than Tom Kelley had ever seen. Sometime after that, Henry got a letter from Tom stating, "Well, Henry, we hit a storm going over cross last trip that I'll bet was almost as bad as that storm George was hauling traps in down at the Outer Ledge."

George Murphy

George Murphy was tall, maybe six foot two, and had tremendously big bones in his body. He had long legs, long arms, and his hands were the largest I have ever seen on a human. They looked like coal shovels. His wrists were as thick as his arms. When he stood, his hands fell with his forearms facing forward and his palms back, the opposite of most people. He never seemed to have had an ounce of fat on his whole physique. Back then they had what they call over-knee boots, which, when hauled up, came up past the knee almost five or six inches on a normal man. With George they only came up to his knee and that was it.

After his wife Wavy died, I used to take him out. We'd go to basketball games and restaurants. He'd tell me stories. It was almost like he was my dad. He laughed a lot; he also loved to drink and dance. George wasn't a bully but, if trouble came his way, he would not turn the other cheek. Whoever took on this Neanderthal didn't make out too well.

He used to call me "Uncle." Once he told me, "You know, Uncle, I am not an innocent man. When us young fellas would go fishing out of Portland, we liked to celebrate. You see this scar?" It went down two inches long on the right side of his forehead. "Me and the boys got in a scuffle in Portland and this cop hit me with a nightstick and put a gouge in my head. At the time I didn't think there was any call for it. We had stopped fighting and we were not fighting with the police anyway, but they sent the paddy wagon over. That son of a bitch struck me with that nightclub anyway. We ended up in Portland Jail."

Unbeknown to his men, Clarence Turner, the captain of the boat George was working on, had a deal with the Portland police. If any of his men ended up in the slammer, he'd simply take them out of there when he was ready to go fishing again. "Clarence came over and bailed us out, but I was angry. I swore to look that cop up when we got back to town. When we did get back to Portland, I went to the police department and asked where he was. They said, 'Just forget it, George. While you were gone he had a heart attack and died.' I guess he didn't want to face the consequences of his act. Well, I have a scar in remembrance of him."

George had a little coupe back in the 1930s and he used to like to go out to the dances. Well, one night coming home, he saw a car stranded on the side of the road, so he stopped to see if he could help. There were three men: one as big as George, one medium-size, and one little guy. Right out of nowhere the big fellow stepped forward and struck George. "He knocked me down off the side of the road. I tried to get to my car and get the crank that we used to start it with—three on one, they had the advantage so I needed a club. But before I could get to it, the small man came at me. I caught him right in the face with one swing, and that was the end of him. Then the big man was back at me, and he struck me across the side of my face. He was uphill of me, and I came up with all I could muster and caught him under his jaw. The medium-sized man ran. The ambulance came and they took the big man to the hospital, where he had to stay for three weeks. Eventually the police knocked on my door. I expected to be arrested, but they thanked me. 'We have been after those three for some time. They have been faking an accident, stopping cars, beating people up and robbing them, and finally they tried to stop the wrong guy. You helped us stop *them.*"

One time he and friends went out to a dance after drinking. It was a cold winter's night. They stopped at an old country store, and they joined some men there talking. George had a pretty good skinful in that night and was having more. He was chewing tobacco, too, one of his favorite things. The stove handle at the country store was red hot that night and, as another man tells it, as they stood around talking George would reach over with his bare thumb and finger and open the stove door each time he needed to spit tobacco. It never bothered him then, but the next day he wondered how he got burns on his hand.

Another time he had been drinking and he didn't want Wavy to know, so he had the fellows help him up his doorstep. They pointed him to the door and he said, "I'll be fine now." He went in and they ran around the house to look in the kitchen window. George walked towards the kitchen table where Wavy was waiting, pulled back a chair to sit down but, when he sat, he didn't come within three feet of that chair. It was just all arms and legs crashing to the floor. The men outside could hear his wife say, "Oh Pa, you are home drunk."

The Two Thurston Brothers

There were two brothers, Herbert and Morris. Morris was the older one; he was born in 1874. Herbert was born in

1886, twelve years' difference in their ages. They were as opposite as you can imagine. Morris had no sense of humor; his laugh was very forced. He made a lot of money for a man of those times—he bought the wharf in Bernard—he was well off simply from what he had done through his own ingenuity. Morris was spotlessly clean, like he came out of a Chinese laundry, even though he wore mostly working clothes. He was very fast-moving, pushing himself, and always getting hurt, banging himself up like you wouldn't believe. Once he was trying to get his boat ready for the season. Within a week, he sliced his thumb with a saw, hit himself in the forehead with the claws of a hammer, and dropped a plank on his foot and broke his toe. All in the process of trying to get the boat in the water to go fishing, which you'd think was the more dangerous part! That too. He'd fallen overboard more times than even I have, which must set some kind of a Guinness Book of World Records.

It was just unbelievable how clumsy the man was. Around the time in the early spring when the ocean is still very cold, Morris had gone fishing with Les Rich. They sold their catch on this scow they had out in Bass Harbor after the fish wharf burned in '53. Coming back aboard the boat, it seemed that Morris just couldn't wait, and he jumped from the scow onto the stern of the boat and just kept right on going, boots, oil jacket, oil pants—right into the harbor. He lost his glasses and ruined his hearing aid. His fishing buddy had to pull him out.

Morris himself told me once that back in the 1800s, when he was young, he was up on the mast of a sailing boat when she began to roll. Well, Morris went right overboard, and his father, with whom he was fishing, had to go back and pick him up. He was a living example of things you'd think only happened in Disney cartoons. One time, working in a boatyard with the boat out of the water, he jumped out of the boat onto a staging plank, and the plank came right up and smacked him in the face! He looked like a bulldog for a week.

Morris was a teetotaler, and the fishermen would kid him about it. One day they asked, "Morris, if taking a drink would save your life, would you do it?"

"By ghost," he said (he would never swear), "I think I'd rather die first."

While Morris was strict in his principles and his beliefs, his brother Herbert was completely different. Herbert's clothes would sometimes shine—it would be that long before he'd change them. He chewed tobacco, smoked a pipe, smoked cigars too, and he was one of the slowest men you can imagine, just like a Japanese tea pourer doing the ceremony. Speed was not of the essence for him.

As if to make up for his brother's abstinence, Herbert drank plenty and, when he would go on a bender, it would last for two weeks at a time. When it was over, he'd disappear back home and sober up, clean himself up, put on clean clothes; then a few days later he'd come back like nothing ever happened and go on about his work.

Herbert just lived from hand to mouth. Well, one day he had a large trip of fish—this was back in 1956—and he got in late that night. He was selling his fish in Vinalhaven, which in those days was about a three-hour run from Bass Harbor. It was so late when he got into Bass Harbor, he left the fish in the boat and was going to take them in the morning. I was about eighteen at the time, and I asked him if I could join him.

Herbert said, "Sure, if you want to." On the way to Vinalhaven, the wind blew a gale to the nor'west. As Herbert steered the craft, he told me stories, which is how I know so much about him: "As far as my drinking goes," he began "my mother said that when she was carrying me, she craved liquor; she craved it, but she wouldn't drink. Maybe if she had had a good hooker, I wouldn't be the way I am today! When I have a drink, it makes a new man out of me. And then the new man has to have a drink, and that is what gets me into trouble."

When Herbert would go off on one of his toots, he loved to sing. Oh, he'd sing and sing and sing. There was a lady in town who also liked to get drunk and sing, and when they'd get together you'd see 'em hand in hand, walking down the road singing, just as happy as can be. When the party was over, she'd return to her home, and Herbert would return to his.

Herbert told me all this himself straight from the horse's mouth: "When I was about sixteen, I ran away from home. I couldn't stand it any longer. I went up into the northern part of Maine, way up in the County, as we call it. I got a job in a logging camp." I could never picture Herbert as a logger, but, as he told it, they had been out in the woods for a couple of weeks chopping wood. "This was my first time at it," he said of that job, "and after payday, we came out of the forest and went to town. I got me a room in this rooming house; then I went out on the town and got drunk that night."

Now this was back in the 1800s; things were a bit different than what they are today concerning toilet facilities and everything. "When I woke up in the morning," Herbert said, "I had to have a bowel movement. I looked everywhere for a chamber pot and could not find one in the room, so out of desperation I opened the bureau drawer and I shit in the bureau drawer. After that I had to get out of town fast. I knew they'd kill me if they caught me. I never did log after that—I went fishing."

From then on, Herbert fished from Maine to New Jersey. He used to sell his fish on Fulton Street in New York City and at Boston markets. Back in those days, with the hard characters and what have you, Herbert carried a loaded revolver. He didn't bear arms any longer, not in my day.

Once Herbert was fishing on this vessel out of Portland and there were Newfoundlanders on it. They were an aggressive lot, and the skipper was an arrogant man. Out there on the banks, in some foggy weather, Herbert asked, "Skipper, do you think you know where you are?"

The skipper said, "I don't *think,* I *know.*" Maybe he did know, but then again, more likely he didn't—but that was his style of speech. He always knew everything.

Over the course of the fishing season the skipper built up some anger at Herbert because he was too slow. In the end he fired him.

Herbert knew the captain was superstitious and, when they got back to shore and Herbert had packed his bag to depart, he said, "This is all right for you to do, but before I leave, there is one thing I am going to do to you, skipper. I am going to put a curse on you. You won't know when it is going to work but, when it does, think of me." He just said it to him like that; then he turned away and walked up the dock without a word, never looked back to see the reaction.

After that, Herbert went to Portland and got another fishing job. In the meantime, that arrogant skipper backed his vessel onto a ledge in Port Clyde and couldn't get her off. When the tide went out, she rolled over.

One of the Newfoundlanders found Herbert later in a restaurant in Portland and, edging away as if he was facing a witch doctor, pointed his finger at him: "I heard you when you put that curse on the skipper!" To Herbert it was just a joke. He wasn't practicing voodoo, but he sure got his revenge!

Jim Albee

I have never been into any man's house on this Earth that radiated the peace and tranquility that come out of Jim Albee's house. The minute you walked in, you were totally and completely relaxed.

Kids loved him. Kids younger than us, preschoolers, would drop in to visit, but also teenagers. It was a welcoming place.

Jim was born in 1878. "I was sixteen," he told me, "when I ran away from home. I got up before daylight, snuck out of the house while my mother and father were still sleeping, and went down to the harbor. In the harbor there was a ship carrying coal. I went down and got aboard that ship. I wanted to sign on as a crew member. It was just about coming daylight when I could see my father heading my way in a dory, rowing off towards the ship. I was on the fantail when he made her, and he said, 'Have you signed any papers since you have been on that ship?' 'I have been signing them just as fast as I can, and I have just signed the last one!' I told him. My father simply said, 'Well, write to your mother whenever you get to where you are going.' He turned around and rowed right back into the harbor. That is how I started my career."

Everything in Jim's house was old. Everything had its own story to it. That chair, for instance. It came from somewhere. It wasn't from Wal-Mart. It wasn't machine-made. Someone made that by hand and, whoever had sat in it, his or her vibe was in it. In his living room was a big rocker right by the radio that was definitely Jim's chair, where he hand-rolled cigarettes — Bugler Tobacco. It used to come in a light blue package, and it showed a soldier blowing his bugle.

Jim had a ring on his finger that—I don't know if it was the ring that was beautiful or the essence of that man, but my God, it was the most elegant ring I have ever seen! It fit Jim perfectly. They talk about the Bishop's ring—to me it was like that, almost sacred.

On Monday, Wednesday, and Friday nights at seven o'clock sharp *The Lone Ranger* came on the radio. Jim was an avid listener. On winter evenings and stormy nights we'd be up to Jim's indoors listening to "Hiyo, Silver, and away!" On summer days when we'd be out playing, his windows would be open, and all of a sudden at about seven o'clock, you could hear "The William Tell Overture" start up over the town of Bernard. We would laugh: "Grampa Jim is listening to *The Lone Ranger!*"

Jim had a kind, gentle authority. I can remember when we were teenagers and were going through those stages of rebellion we all go through. Jim's grandson Lawrence turned a little balky on him and got told, "You just keep on the present course you are running, Skipper, and you are going to get bumped!"

Once Jim caught us experimenting with cigarettes. Of course our parents were not supposed to know about these things. On this occasion Lawrence had got impatient. He hadn't waited till we got far enough down the road out of sight of his grandfather's house when he lit up. When we got back that night Lawrence's father Myron was over and Jim decided to bring it up. "Lawrence," he said, "when you were going down the road this morning, did I see a cloud of smoke coming out of you?" Of course, Lawrence knew he had him.

Jim was not a rich man; in fact, he was downright poor, getting by on his Social Security check. But that man knew how to enjoy anything. Sitting down to any meal, just to listen to him smack his chops, you would think he was having a banquet in King Solomon's house. By count of worldly riches he may have had none, but something inward about that man was very wealthy; he found out a piece of life most of us missed.

Once in a while, my brother-in-law Chandler, who lived next door to Jim, would go down to Lottie's store and bring back a treat. Jim would be reading the paper or listening to the radio. And Chandler would call out, "Jim, I have a dilemma here. I was down in Lottie's store and I got this box of ice cream, but I haven't got anything to eat it with."

Jim would say, "You just put that right on the table and I'll see if I can take care of the situation." Then something magic happened. That was the best dish of ice cream they ever had in their lives, always.

I can remember the last day Jim ever walked out of that house. I was close to twenty years old then and Lawrence was grown up and married. Jim got so sick he couldn't take care of himself anymore, so Myron came over with two other fellas to help take Jim in a car over to his house. When Jim came out on the doorstep—one fellow on each arm—he was a little unsteady. He saw the car down there and just paused for a moment. "Isn't this a fright?" he said. "I am just an old nuisance."

Myron said, "Look, mister, you have done plenty for us and others in your lifetime. Now it doesn't hurt us any to take our turn. I don't want to hear any more talk like that ever come out of you." They set up a bed over to Myron and Irma's house for him.

I went to see him one last time before he died. He was too sick to talk then. I was sitting in a chair by the foot of his bed when the old man looked up and gave a wave of his hand, like he recognized me and was saying goodbye.

Their Last Days Fishing

On his last day fishing, George Murphy went out lobstering to tend his traps. He was an old man then but a very able-bodied one. He had a prehistoric body, but men grow old and finally have to pack it in. "The last day I went fishing," he said, "a thick fog shut in on me." There was no GPS or radar then, as I have explained, just a pocket watch, a compass, and a tachometer. "That fog shut in and after a while I was entirely lost and befuddled. I didn't know how to get out of the mess I was in; then I came across Bud Jewett." Bud was another lobsterman, much younger than George. "He come by me and I flagged him down. 'What is the problem, George?' Bud said, and I explained that I was completely lost. I hated to ask him, but I said, 'Would you guide me back into the harbor?' 'No problem, George,' Bud told me. 'Don't feel bad a bit about it; you just follow me.'"

When they got back so they could see the harbor they stopped, and Bud said, "You're okay now, George."

"Yes, I am," George said, "I really want to thank you for that, Bud. When a man reaches this point in his life, I think it is time to call it quits."

Towards the end of his life, Herbert Thurston didn't go lobstering but tub trawling. He'd start early in the spring of the year, fish right on through the summer, and then stop in the middle of October. Whenever he finished one of those trips and got his fishing gear put away and stored, he looked down the dock to where my father was and said, "Well, Frank, I am going to den for the winter." It tickled my father, how Herb put it, like a bear crawling in for hibernation.

One summer, maybe in 1959, when Herb was in his seventies,

he'd gotten up to go out fishing around one-thirty in the morning. When he set out, it was clear but, as he entered the deeper ocean, there shut in a thick fog. All Herbert had was the usual compass and pocket watch, so he knew his course and time. But when you are twenty miles or so out in the open ocean, all you have got other than your compass and pocket watch are marker poles and your middle buoys to run for. You either make them or you don't. If it is a dungeonly thick fog, it could be extremely difficult, and you might miss your gear. You might not find it at all. So rather than set his trawls, Herb would come back. This happened three or four times right in a row. After the fourth he said, "When I went out there, the fog settled down again. I turned my trawls upside down into the sea and said, 'Herbert is done. That is the last trip. The ocean can have my fishing gear for good now. I'm finished working the sea.'"

I Enlist

A lot of people in my Pemetic High School class joined the military. Quite a few of the men chose the Coast Guard, which had an enlistment period of four years; that seemed to be the appropriate service for the men who wanted to be located near home. Those ones took their boot camp in Cape May, New Jersey. Other branches that men from my Pemetic class joined were the Air Force and Army. I know of no one who joined the Marine Corps or Navy.

For five years out of high school I just fished. I had no steady girlfriend. I was just enjoying the single life. It was lobstering, trawling, hand-lining, then swimming at Echo Lake after a day of fishing, partying at my friends' homes, and things like that for me. I had no desires to marry or join the military at that time. I was fine with just fishing and partying.

In July of 1961 I was down on Main Street in Ellsworth when I had a premonition about enlistment. I heard a voice say just as clear as day to me, "If you value your life, you will get your military obligation over with as quickly as possible." Without a bit of hesitation I just turned straight around and reversed my course. I walked back down the street that I had just walked up, went into the registration office, and said, "I am here to volunteer for the draft." I never questioned that voice from nowhere. I had heard something that knew more than I did.

The Army had a draft program then that was for two years; once you'd done two active years with them, you got put on standby. "Standby" meant that the first two years after being let go, they could call you back to service. They named it a "manpool." You might be required to do two weeks of summer camp with some branch of the National Guard each year when you were on standby. After six years you would get a discharge from the Army.

In August I got my salutations (my draft notice) from the President, who was Kennedy at the time, and I took my written examinations and physical in Bangor in preparation for boot camp. It was just a general knowledge test. I entered the Army on the twelfth day of September, 1961. A lady from the registration office in Ellsworth used her own car to take a bunch of us—four or five men—to Bangor to be sworn in.

This was right about when they had the Berlin Wall scare, and neither Russia nor America were backing up. It looked like the world was going to be plunged into chaos any day, so the Army decided to change from a peacetime to a wartime army of a million men. It must have been a decision made by the higher-ups because, on the ground, the Army was no more ready for us extra men than the Man in the Moon.

The Army flew new recruits to New York City, where they

had a bus ready to transfer us to Fort Dix, New Jersey. We arrived at Fort Dix about eleven o'clock that night. We were tired, of course, but there were papers to fill out. Finally we got some bedding. It felt good to lie down; I'll put it that way. It felt just as good to go to sleep.

At Fort Dix, the first barracks they put us in was an old wooden two-story building, and we were supposed to be in that reception center for two weeks. They vaccinated us, tested us, and issued us our uniforms: shorts, trousers, dress fatigues. Every man got two wall lockers and a foot locker to stow this stuff in. One of the lockers was for dress and inspection clothes, and the other for working attire.

The barracks was hardly in tiptop working order. To keep its door shut, we had to brace it closed with a board; otherwise it would just fall over. There was a hole right over my bunk in the roof; if I was an astronomer I could have located all of the stars in the Milky Way just by looking up through that hole! There were seventy-two of us men in that building altogether, but the next morning, when we all got up, there were four mirrors to shave by. The Army had rules: no one does nothing until you are shaved! It was comical to see us men lined up in front of the mirrors, each one looking this way and then the other, trying to get a view of himself.

All day for the two weeks we went to movies and lectures about Army life. They would show you how military life compared to civilian life, how you took care of yourself right down to hygiene, diet, place of worship. After they had finished terrifying us to death, any one of us would have to have been the Son of God to behave as good as the Army tried to make you think you'd have to. It was all part of the program.

There was a hurricane coming up our coast one night and they didn't know if our old barracks would hold up. While we were out listening to Major So-and-So rattle on about something or other, they moved us out. They took all the clothes from the lockers and threw them in one great big pile in a new barracks. We didn't get back until nine that night, and there we were, a bunch of new recruits trying to figure out who belongs to what. Thank goodness we had our names stenciled on everything. Then they sent us to the training center.

The hurricane hit the first day of basic training, and it rained, poured, and blowed. Still we were out there, mustered up for our drills. I can remember the first sergeant giving us an orientation and letting us know what a bastard he could be when the wind got hold of papers someone was carrying. While he was yelling and the rain was coming down, hundreds of records were flying hell west and crooked, all over Fort Dix.

I was one of the most naïve soldiers who ever hit the Army. I barely knew my left from my right. I had no knowledge of anything that prepared me to be a soldier; everything was new. The U.S. Army was a completely foreign place to me. I was twenty-three years old, while most of the other men were only about eighteen or nineteen, having joined up right after high school. My own Pemetic friends were out of the Army before I was in. They told me it had taken them six months to adjust, but it took me about twelve. Back home I had owned my own boat for five years, but down in the Army I was just another common soldier.

A Visit from the MP

George Sawyer, a boy I had grown up with, went into the Army right after high school, then got sent to Korea for a thirteen-month tour of duty. When he came back, he had one more year left to serve. The Army stationed him at Fort Dix as a military policeman. I hoped to see him. Sure enough, one

Sunday morning George came to visit me, but on that particular day I had gone out the minute I could escape because it was a free day on base. In the afternoon, when I got back, the other recruits were quite nervous; they thought I'd gotten into some deep shit: "A man from the military police was here looking for you, Seavey. What have you done?"

Later, George came back and we had a good time catching up with each other. Just as George and I were talking, Sergeant Vega, my drill instructor, an ex-Marine who had shifted over to the Army, came by. Jokingly, George said, "Sergeant, can you do anything with him?"

Sergeant Vega was a very serious man, and he replied, "Well, he's gonna get it someday, but Jesus Christ is he slow!"

The Few That Didn't Make It

There was a lot of harassment in the Army. Most men came through it fine, but now and then there's a few that just don't get it. The Army will do everything it can to put them through their paces but sometimes comes to the decision that certain men are not meant to be soldiers. Of course, the military is used to every trick; they know people—they know the games and they know the difference between somebody who is putting it on and someone who is showing their real colors.

Now, of course they are not going to let us recruits know it, but the officers were always watching us like mother hens. They could do this and that and make you think that you were the most despicable piece of shit they ever come across at the same time. A taxi driver on base once told me that around Fort Dix he'd rather hit an officer than a new recruit because the new guys are so closely cared for, he'd be in more trouble for hitting one of us.

We had one man in my platoon that wasn't cut out for the Army. Private Black wanted to be in the Army, but he was not coordinated physically and he got confused under all the harassment. His biggest problem was left and right; they kept getting confused with each other. He gradually became despondent and confused.

Every division had a kind of master sergeant called a Field First, and Sergeant Spar was ours. He oversaw everything we did and, if he didn't like the way something was going, he'd step in and correct it as he saw fit.

Says Sergeant Spar to me, "Black's not trying."

Says I, "Sir, he is doing his best."

Later in the afternoon the Sergeant sent for me to come see him. Private Black was there.

Says the Sergeant, "I gave Black a very simple order, simple enough for him to carry out, and he didn't carry it out. You lied to me."

I say, "He always used to try then, sir."

The Sergeant was having none of that. He said, "See, Black, you made Seavey out to be a liar."

After that Sergeant Spar decided to assign Private Black to write five-hundred-word essays every day, just like the English teacher used to do in school. He'd give Black a fresh subject each time. Then Black would read them out loud for us in the barracks. My God, he would write like you couldn't believe! In our outfit we had a few ex-elementary school and high school teachers and even college professors—all buck privates in the Army now—and they were mighty impressed at how Black could write. Subject after subject would be assigned by Sergeant Spar, and Black'd just keep writing on each like an expert.

One day down at the live range we were firing and something wasn't right. Private Black had a loaded M1 rifle out on the range, and the Company Commander come up behind him and said something to him. Private Black looked like he was kind of in a stupor and spun around like a man on rotating gears with the loaded rifle in the pocket of his shoulder, his left hand on the upper hand guard, and the index finger of his right hand on the trigger. That rifle was pointed right straight at the Commanding Officer's face. If Black had squeezed the trigger, the C.O. was a goner.

Now Private Black didn't mean to threaten or intimidate anybody. He was confused about where he was and forgot himself. The Company Commander told him in a steady voice, "Private Black, turn around and set the rifle down," which he did. "Get him off the firing range" was all the Company Commander said after that, and that was it. Private Black never had to train with us again. All harassment stopped from that moment on, and he was treated with respect. He became the barracks orderly until they could discharge him honorably. I guess they made the decision that he wasn't faking it, or at least that they didn't dare call his bluff. Whether you believe this or not, the Army was capable of deciding some people weren't meant to be soldiers; they didn't try to kick everybody's ass into shape.

Bolo

You have to get a good score to pass basic training. Highest is a hundred; lowest is seventy. Below seventy you have to go through the whole of Basic Training again. Out on the firing range you could gain fifteen points on your score if you shot well. If you got a "bolo," like I always did because I could not hit the target, you flunked. If you got a "marksman," you qualified; if you got a "sharpshooter," that's even better. The best was "expert." As for me, I lost my fifteen points, but I did well at all the other stuff and ended up with a score of eighty-five, which was pretty impressive for the most naïve man in the Army.

For my success, I won a three-day pass. I was not supposed to go beyond New York City on the pass, but I had full intentions of going to Maine. The Army had told us that, right after Basic Training, some of us would be sent home for two weeks' leave but others would be sent on. I didn't know which group I'd be in, and I was homesick as hell. I didn't want to throw the dice, so I made a break for it.

At that time, servicemen could fly standby on all airlines for half price. So I got to La Guardia and found Northeast Airlines. A line of soldiers two hundred feet long was waiting to get on the flight to Maine. Just as I was standing in line, a man came out on the stairs of the plane and said, "That's it; that's all we can take." Most of those men just gave up and walked away, but I was in such a state of despair—to think that I couldn't get on that plane—that I just stood there with all those men falling out around me until there were only three or four of us left. Wouldn't you know, the man came back out of the airplane and put up his finger: one more. I double-timed it up the ramp!

When I got to Bangor, I gave my sister and brother-in-law a call. They drove up and met me and then brought me home that night. My folks didn't know I was coming. I got in about nine o'clock. My father had gone to bed—he always went to bed early—so I went upstairs and I opened up the bedroom door and I said, "Is that you, Dad?"

He leaped right out of bed and said, "Christ! What are you doing here?" I didn't tell him I was supposed to be in New York City. We talked a while, and then I went across the street to see my mother where she was babysitting the neighbors' kids. She was tickled to death to have me home.

I had to be back at Fort Dix by six o'clock Sunday night, so I left Sunday morning to catch Northeast's flight out of Bangor. That part was fine. When I got to Boston, however, I had to switch to Allegheny for a plane to take me to Newark. We were in the air with plenty of time and everything was hunky-dory. Smooth sailing!

Now, I had a window seat right near the left wing, and I looked at the engine and here comes a steady stream of oil right out of it. I called for the airline hostess and I said, "Come here and be very, very quiet. You look at that engine and tell me if what I see is normal."

She whispers, "Oh my god, don't say a word." She went up into the cockpit, and pretty soon the pilot came on to say, "Fasten your safety belts; we have got to go back to Boston." So we turned around midair, landed fine, and a mechanic came out to work on the engine. Needless to say, my time was getting short. If I was not back at the base by six o'clock, I would be AWOL. They were going to raise total hell, lots of harassment. They would work the death out of me, and I'd have to stay confined in the barracks other than training. If they took it to the limit, I could have gotten court-martialed.

So there I was, sweating bullets, angry at myself. The Army scared this young Maine lad shitless anyway, and now I had to go and take a risk, on top of it! It looked like I was going to lose to the clock.

Finally the mechanics got the problem figured out and we left Logan again, but we are talking a margin of minutes now. When we landed in Newark, I got a bus to Fort Dix that took about an hour and a half. I know because I counted every minute.

I got to Fort Dix at 5:45. I hightailed it in as fast as I could to the dayroom and handed the man my pass. "You was lucky, wasn't you?" he said, sizing me up. "You went home."

"No, I went to New York."

"I know you, you bastard. You was lucky!"

A couple of weeks later I graduated from Basic Training, and I found out the Army was going to ship me to Schofield Barracks, Hawaii, for advanced infantry training—but I would get two weeks to go home after all: Thanksgiving dinner at home in Maine—paradise!

I mean, we Downeasters are all for adventure and seeing the world and testing our mettle, but home is home and, once you leave the island, let alone cross the state line, you are in purgatory till you get back. That's a rule I would test yet many times in my life.

Seavey and the Seagulls

The Army decided to ship me directly to the Twenty-Fifth Infantry "Tropical Lightning" Division on Oahu Island, and they gave me travel pay from Maine to San Francisco, California.

In late December, we soldiers going to Oahu Island were eventually loaded on a troop carrier named *General Mann*. She was somewhere around seven hundred feet long, and she was owned and operated by the Navy. We left San Francisco late in the afternoon and sailed all that night down the California coast. In the morning it came up calm as we motored into San Diego. We picked up some more sailors and a bunch of Marines that were going on to Okinawa and Japan. Of course, they wouldn't let any of us on shore, so we were hanging around together on deck. I said, "You boys enjoy this day, because tonight you are not going to like it so much."

"What do you mean?" a man asked.

"Well, you are all going to be very, very seasick tonight."

"How the hell do you know?" another said.

I replied, "Well, we have been sailing close to shore—don't think the open ocean is like this. This here is a storybook ocean. Offshore the water can get very rough, and it's going to tonight."

"Just where do you get all your information, *Mister* Seavey?"

"You look right up in the sky," I say, "See those seagulls up there? They tell me." Well, of course, they laughed.

"Here is a man who talks to the seagulls! Seavey and seagulls—it goes together well. What other things do they tell you, Seavey?" They were teasing me now.

"They tell me that, if you keep this ridicule up, you will regret it very much!"

Now seagulls, when they sense wind coming, go way up high in the sky and circle like vultures. They just go round and round; they glide without flapping. The other men didn't recognize the signs I was picking up but, since I had been a fisherman, I knew such things.

At about six o'clock we left San Diego and, as soon as we cleared the harbor and hit the dark waters, that seven-hundred-foot ship was rolling rail to rail. The storm the gulls predicted was hitting us on the port side, and it pitched us so bad that they couldn't allow us to go up across the deck for fear we'd wash away. You talk about some sick men! We mopped up vomit for three days and three nights. On the fourth day we finally come out of it, just like that. The Pacific Ocean was as peaceful and serene as she could be.

Hawaiian Welcome Party

In back of the bridge they had a great big movie screen mounted right to the spar. On clear nights we'd watch movies, just like going to the drive-in. We'd all sit there in a huddle. The sergeant, the officers, and their families had rights to the nicer spots; the rest of us were like animals huddled up behind the superstructure.

I remember one night we were watching a Western set out in the desert country with cactus and this and that. Two old cowboys rode up on their horses, complaining how they were parched for some water. Well, that ship went down into a roll and hit a wave, sending water flying right across the screen! Someone shouted: "There's some water for you!" It didn't do them much good on the screen, but the whole group of us had a good laugh.

When we finally arrived at the pier in Pearl Harbor, they divided us up. Twenty-five hundred new recruits were coming in on that transport, which meant that they would be discharging 2,500 others. Our arrival that night made some men very happy. It was bedlam when we got to the barracks. The outgoing men were so tickled that we were coming—the replacements—that they were hooting and yelling. Us new recruits just looked at each other like, "My God, what are we in for?" Well, they divided us again and put us in different regiments throughout the division. I got shipped to B Company, Fourteenth Infantry. From there we got broken down into platoons—weapons for me. Weapon platoon's job was to support the three rifle platoons. I was to be in one of the mortar squads that shoot overhead rounds. We also had two anti-tank guns, 106-millimeter recoil-less rifles—they were guns to behold; they could knock a tank out. But at the time, I didn't know any of that—I didn't know shit from shinola. I had a lot to learn.

Two months of advanced infantry training had to be completed before I could do anything else at Schofield. I trained in mortar and the anti-tank guns in the morning, and in the afternoon and evening I had to fall out to take advanced infantry training. Only when I graduated from all that would they let me become a full member of the outfit. The harassment would stop, and I would be treated no worse than any other man.

Until then I learned that if I kept my ears and eyes open and my mouth shut, I got along fine. Get mouthy and you'd be in trouble quick. If there was a problem with discipline in weapons platoon, Sergeant Clark would say, "If you want to behave like an animal, we got three rifle platoons right upstairs where we could put you real quick." Sometimes they even called the rifle platoons the animal platoons because they were more like pack animals; this day and age they call 'em "the grunts." If a man in weapons platoon screwed up too many times, the platoon sergeant roared, "Upstairs with you, buddy. You'll be happier there," and that either straightened him out or up he'd go. They'd keep their word to put you up there.

Trouble in the Field

The first significant mess I got into when I was in the Army was in March of 1962. We were out on Oahu training, and it was big-time maneuvers. Our Company Commander was named David G. Schofield, same as the base. He was an able leader, but he had the two personalities of the nursery rhyme: When he was good, he was very, very good; and when he was mad, he was horrid. I don't think anyone in that company — officers, sergeants, or enlisted men — hadn't been filleted by him at one time or another. There was no doubt he was the Commander.

Captain Schofield liked me for some reason, but he'd ream me out just like anyone else. Whenever he got to me, I'd let it be like water over a duck's back because I knew the man. This particular day, we were on maneuvers against the 27th Wolfhounds, another regiment of the 25th division. It was a round of war games. We were up on steep, muddy hills out on the mountains of Oahu. When it rains there, it gets slick, and driving a truck on that mud is just like steering on ice. I was the driver for the second squad, eighty-one-millimeter mortars. We had a three-quarter-ton truck and trailer in which we carried the mortar and its equipment.

As you might guess, things started going wrong out in the field. The supply truck broke down, so they decided to transfer its cargo onto my mortar truck. Then the truck for the mess hall, another two-and-a-half-ton transport, broke down, so they had to put me on driving for the mess hall. Now I was driving for the mortars and I was driving for supply and I was driving for the mess hall, and I was going non-stop—when my fan belt broke.

An E4, who was about to be discharged, was together with me in the broken truck. I was just a private, E2. Captain Schofield drove by and said, "You men, put a sign on this truck that says it has been burnt up." It was as if it had been destroyed, like it would be in a time of war. The idea was, rather than letting the enemy have the truck and supplies to use against us, we'd have burnt it.

We made the sign and set it. Then, while everyone else went off on maneuvers, we stood guard duty around the truck. When the 27th Wolfhounds came upon us, they wanted to take the truck. "Is there not one of you men can read?" I said, pointing to the sign. "This truck has been destroyed by fire."

"That is true," one of the Wolfhounds snapped back, "your truck and trailer has been burnt to a crisp, but you two haven't, and you are who we want."

Well, the E4 who was with me was a lot more experienced

at soldiering than I was. He whispered to me, "You know what they are going to do, don't you? They are going to take our boots off us so we can't outrun 'em. To hell with them! When I holler you go left, I go right, and then they can't catch us, especially with all their equipment on. You go down over that hill behind us and we'll rendezvous on the other side."

So like a damn fool I listened to him. Well, we broke away while the Wolfhounds scrambled and shouted, and rendezvoused on the other side of the hill and came out on a road and started walking. But who should come along with his entourage in tow but Colonel Muir.

Colonel Muir was no ordinary officer. He wore a blue patch on his right shoulder that went down to his elbow. It was a signifier that he had been one of General Merrill's Marauders in World War Two. General Merrill had led 5,600 volunteers on a suicide mission into Burma. Of the 5,600 Army rangers, only fifty-four came back alive; Colonel Muir was one of them. That man was a real soldier.

Colonel Muir and his driver shot right up to us in his jeep. We told them of our dilemma. Muir announced, "Oh Jesus! Those Wolfhounds are going to steal everything on that truck and trailer. I'll take you back to B Company."

When Captain Schofield found out about our escapade, he was furious. He wanted us to stay right there with the truck because he knew what was going to happen. They were going to steal the supplies off our truck and trailer. He filleted me out right up one side and down the other. He was so mad that at last there were no words coming out of his mouth; his mouth was just moving. He couldn't even speak he got so tongue-tied. I had to haul ass out of there. There was nothing else I could do.

When we got back to where we had left the truck, we found that the Wolfhounds had realized that the engine would start;

it just wouldn't cool. They drove that truck with its broken fan belt into the woods until the engine heated up; then they parked it and stole the supplies off it. Even though it was a war game, I was responsible. That part of it was meant to be real. I suppose the Army could have made me sign a statement of charges to pay for it out of my own pocket, but I was making only seventy-eight dollars a month. I would have had to be in the Army five thousand years to pay the bill.

Another time we were down by an old abandoned World War Two airfield, having bivouacked there for the night. It was near the ocean, so me and some of my buddies went down and took a swim. The rollers were coming in, combing, and there were big swells. It was freeing just to be in that ocean—to let the waves pick me up and ride. It was about seventy degrees, not the North Atlantic, but it made me think of times back home.

When we finally got out and dried off, who should come along but a bunch of sergeants. They were greatly amused. "Seavey," one of them said, "what in hell are you doing to the poor old Company Commander? You are going to drive the poor old man right plum nuts!"

"Whatever I done, Sergeant, I'm sure it isn't enough. I'll try to do more." I guess I am a prankster at heart.

At the bivouac area that night there was a guy from Florida, Alton Rodin. He drove for the mortars, too. He said to me, "You have been through quite a lot today, Seavey. We have got to do something; we have to go out and have some fun tonight. We'll leave right after we eat—they won't suspect a thing. We'll just get in my truck and go to town, you and I."

And we done it. We rode straight out of there just like we were on orders. We went down to the end of the airfield, which was about a mile long, and drove out through the gate. We found this little town with a bar, and the two of us went in there and had a good drink or two. I guess we got fairly drunk.

It must have been about eleven or twelve o'clock when we got back to the airfield. Alton turned the headlights off, and we drove up to the gate quiet as can be, but they had put up a barbed-wire fence right across that runway and even placed a guard at the entry. When we got up to him, he hollered, "Halt!"

"Up your ass!" Alton said and drove back around, making sure to give the guard a wide berth. "You think that barbed-wire fence is going to stop this truck, Seavey? I don't."

We hit the fence doing about fifty miles an hour. The last I saw of the barrier was sparks flying as that barbed wire parted and a picket went rocketing out into the night. Alton sped down the rest of that airfield as fast as he could go and turned in at Company B with the headlights still off. "Make it to your tent and, hopefully, nobody's been looking for either of us. If they do ask, you don't know a damn thing."

Off he went to his tent and I went to mine. I asked my tent-mate if anyone had asked for me. "You are in luck," he said, "no one has."

Not much later we could hear the sergeants outside, yelling, "What was that truck? Who was in that truck that drove in here?"

My squad leader came over to the tent and said, "Seavey? What was that truck?"

I said, "I have no idea. Been sound asleep. It woke me up, Sergeant. I don't know what it was—I heard it, that's all."

The next morning the Platoon Sergeant came up to me: "Seavey. The Company Commander and Executive Officer want you to report to them."

So I go over, and Lieutenant Alexander and Captain Schofield are waiting for me. Captain Schofield is in his T-shirt and he is getting ready to shave.

"Private Seavey reporting, Sir."

"Seavey," the captain says as he is lathering his face up, "May I use your mirror on the truck to shave by?"

"Be my guest, sir."

"Mirror, mirror on the wall, who has the most beautiful Company Commander of all? Is it A company? No. Is it C Company? No. Is it B Company?"

I quickly replied, "It is B Company, sir."

"Goddamn good answer. Now about last night, Seavey. Have you got all that shit out of your system now?"

"Yes, sir."

"About the other day when I chewed you out, I want to apologize to you. I did not have the full story at that time. I was furious with you, but I see that it was not entirely your fault. Now get the hell back to work."

He realized that the other man outranked me and that the Wolfhounds had been underhanded—plus we had forgotten that we were supposed to have been killed in action so it might have been better if we had let them take us than run away. After all, that's when the trouble started.

When the maneuvers were done and we got back to barracks, I told Captain Schofield that I was going to press charges against the 27th infantry. "I want a chance to redeem myself and get our supplies back, sir."

"Won't do you a bit of good," he told me. "Do it if you want to—I won't tie your hands—but you are going to get nowhere."

I went to Supply Sergeant Samuelson, and he offered his help. He said to me, "You know, one of the things I always would have liked to have been is a lawyer. I have always been interested in law. Let's go after the 27th and get 'em for this. It's gonna take a long time, though." He thought about it for a moment. "I'll tell you what you have to do and I'll get you the forms. You'll have to do all the running-around work and you'll have to be persistent. This won't be won overnight, but we are going to try to get all the stuff they stole back."

I took the forms he gave me and I went to every man in the company, asking them if they had anything on my truck or trailer. "Your gas mask? Rifle? Toilet articles? Cigarettes? Anything you can remember, but try and keep it honest: only what you really lost. Fill it out; sign it. I'll be back again."

Well, I had to fill out all these forms and take them to the supply sergeant. He then took them to the Company Commander. After that the Company Commander passed it up to the Colonel; the Colonel sent it to the General; and the General sent it down to the Colonel of the 27th Wolfhounds; each time it ran that gauntlet, back it would all come again. The paperwork went around like this for two months.

I was down to the motor pool working on my truck one afternoon when some men come down from B company and said they had good news: the 27th infantry came over with a two-and-a-half-ton truck loaded with equipment belonging to Company B. Their colonel had to apologize to our colonel. That afternoon I met Captain Schofield standing out in front of the barracks. I gave him a salute and said, "Good afternoon, Sir. I hear we got a few goodies back from the 27th."

"Congratulations. You did it, you little herring choker!"

Big Gun

I came very close to killing a bunch of us when we were on maneuvers. We were doing live fire with the mortar and, by this time, I was no longer the truck driver but an assistant gunner. Now ideally there should be five people for the gun: a squad leader, a gunner, an assistant gunner, an ammo bearer, and a truck driver. Realistically, though, you are going to get four on a gun, the ammo bearer and truck driver combining jobs, and that was how our squad usually was.

This day we were running maneuvers with our troops out in front of us about a half a mile. In a time of war we'd be shooting over their heads to protect them, but this time we were shooting halfway between us and them so no one would be hit by the live rounds. I was on number-two gun, the middle one, which gets the most firing because they line the guns up by the number-two gun. We would aim number two, and then, once that gets on target, the men would set the other two guns into action.

For some reason on this day the squad of mine got even more reduced, to two men; I don't know why, but we had the gunner and the assistant gunner only, and we were also encountering firing problems.

With this kind of a gun it is the gunner who aims and the assistant who shoots. The gunner we had was good, so he told me, "I can handle the gun myself. You just go to work and get the rounds ready." This meant I had to take the safety device off the nose so the round would explode, and I also had to get a certain number of bags of powder off the fin assembly. The powder had to be mathematically plotted so the rocket would hit the target with a great degree of accuracy.

So I am doing this procedure and I pick up a round and take the safety device off the nose to make the live round, when the platoon sergeant hollers at me and gives me hell. He says, "Goddammit, you get on the gun and help the gunner!" I can't disobey him, or tell him what I'm doing; I can only follow his order in the heat of the goddamn thing—so I just put the round down with the ones we were going to shoot. But I forgot to take the bags of powder off the rocket.

We were getting ready to shoot. Ordinarily, what you do is you let the rocket go down the barrel and it hits the firing pin, which sets off the bags of powder—and away the rocket goes. The load we were using was white phosphorus, a big round for us in the mortars. I let one of these rounds go down the tube, but it misfired. Sometimes they won't go down into the firing pins but get lodged in the barrel at the base plate; you can give it a kick with your boot—that usually shakes it free. This time, though, when I kicked the barrel, nothing happened. As the other guns took over, we went to get this round out of the barrel. The platoon sergeant and others were watching us because this round was live and dangerous. I carefully took the barrel out of the base plate and tipped it up while the gunner clasped his hands over the barrel and caught the round as it came out. To his astonishment, the safety device had been removed; the thing was loaded with bags of powder! If it had fired, it would have gone out into our troops and God knows how many would have been killed or hurt and it would have been my fault. I had set the round down and forgot that I hadn't removed the bags of powder.

What had happened that day that saved us all? Talk about a coincidence! A coincidence is when God chooses to make a miracle and remain anonymous. On the round we had just fired, the fin assembly had come off and lodged in the bottom of the barrel and prevented the overloaded rocket from hitting the firing pin. When we tipped the barrel up a little higher, the fin assembly dropped out. That faulty component saved us all.

A Bolo No More

I was a bolo when I went into the Army, which means I didn't get a passing score with the rifle. Even when I was a full-fledged infantryman, I still flunked with the rifle. However, I had a high enough score in everything else that I passed basic training. Now every so often, the whole regiment had to fire for score. When we did this, we first went to the rifle range for two weeks and shot every day for practice. After two weeks each man's shots counted. When you're firing for score, you shoot half your test in the morning and half in the afternoon because of the difference in light; that way, they test you twice.

This one particular time the whole regiment was not shooting very well at all. Our scores were bad, and I wasn't the only one shooting poorly. Captain Schofield called me to his quarters and said, "Seavey, you have never qualified with the rifle, have you?"

"No, sir."

"Why?" he asked.

"I don't have that answer, sir, but not only am I not firing good, a lot of other men are not firing good either."

"And why can't anyone shoot?"

"Sir, do you want me to parrot to you from the Army manual or do you want me to speak my mind?"

"Feel free to speak your mind," he said. "That is why I called you. I figured you were one that would tell me the truth."

So I did. I told him everything that I saw: "A lot of men can't seem to shoot in this outfit. The instructors can shout over the P.A. system all they like, 'There is nothing wrong with these rifles. It's you goddamn men.' The men won't say anything because they'd get in trouble. And, sir, you do have your share of proper bozos in your company, but some of them are intelligent people, only they are not going to say anything. They are just riding it out, but they've got no confidence in these rifles."

Schofield nodded in agreement. "You want to know what the problem is?" he asked.

"Yes, sir."

"The M1 was a good rifle in its day. It was new during the Second World War, but these rifles are getting worn, they are getting old, and they are getting loose. Each day when you get done firing, the platoon sergeant makes you break the weapon down and clean it. When they go back together, they are not going back exactly the same as they were before. Now, I am going to use you for an experiment. You are one of the worst shooters, so I want you to bring your rifle here and we're going to jam a rag in its upper hand guard so it'll be tight when you get done shooting at the end of the day. Don't you break it down to clean. Only clean it by running an oily rod through the bore as far as you can go. I'll tell your platoon sergeant and, if anyone tries to make you break down your rifle, you come see me immediately and they won't again."

"Okay."

I did what he said. I got better in no time and was hitting the target efficiently. Pretty soon Schofield made his whole company do it the same way. Soon Company B was outshooting the whole regiment, head and shoulders. When the colonel figured out what had happened, he put out the order for *everyone* to jam a rag in the upper hand guard and clean it just the way we were. That was the first time I passed. I had become a marksman and, as time went on, I became a sharpshooter with the new M-16 and then an expert with the rifle.

Nightmare

Every January we would go down to Hickam Field. It was a big airbase, connected to the civilian airport. We used to fly out from there on cargo planes, C-130s—tanks, trucks, men, what have you, all of it. We'd go over to the big Hawaiian Island.

We landed in Hilo and then we'd have a forty-mile ride up to Packaloa Valley on Mauna Loa Mountain, which was around seven thousand feet above sea level. We used to call it "going to the moon." It was quite dry up there, and there was a lot of lava rocks from the volcano. Many times you'd be in this material—dust as fine as talcum powder—clean up to your knees. Other times you'd be right on lava fields. It was very similar to training on the moon—so we thought—except that we had some oxygen to breathe. Each January we'd spend three weeks up there and then we'd fly back to Honolulu on the Air Force C-130 cargo planes—planes they still use—and spend the rest of our time on Oahu Island. It was important training because we were meant to be prepared for semi-tropical and mountainous guerrilla warfare.

Things were very tense back in those days. The Russians and the Americans had their stand-off with each other; there was the Berlin Wall and the Bay of Pigs down in Cuba. We were just a hair's breadth from nuclear war. Southeast Asia was breeding its own war, which began in 1965, and I guess it didn't finally end until 1972.

Back in January of 1963, when my division was training up on the moon, I had a premonition. It happened when we were bivouacked two men to a tent. One night I dreamt that my company was in Southeast Asia under combat conditions. We had been reduced to about seven men (down from maybe an original one hundred and fifty or so in the whole company). In the dream the Asian army was coming in full-strength behind us about five hundred yards away. They were at full strength; they were not shot up at all; we were shot up badly; we were practically annihilated. Fighting back would have been ridiculous—just suicidal.

We were running like animals, trying to stay ahead of the

Asians. It was just every man for himself. I remember when I was running I was thinking, "Now I know what a hunted deer must feel like." It was damn scary.

And the smell of it and the fear of it—it was a dream so true that I knew it had to be a premonition. It was something like horrid. The whole huge Asian army was just coming behind us. I jumped out over this bank. Some of the men were going off into the woods to my right. When I cleared that bank, I fell down flat to the ground, hoping no one could see me. I dug out a place where I could hide up under the bank. I was figuring that the enemy would be so intent just moving onward that with a little bit of luck they would leap right over me and not see me as they contended with the bank. As they came past, from up under the bank I could see their combat boots going right out over me, one after another, maybe two hundred men. When the last man cleared the bank and their army passed out of sight, I came out of hiding and went left. I was trotting through the woods, looking for friendly forces to join and hoping I didn't get shot at by either side, when I woke up in my tent on Mauna Loa. My partner was fast asleep.

The dream was too vivid to be just a dream—these were real Asian boots; each enemy soldier had a real uniform; the two hundred or so men were individuals—I can still see them jumping out, one by one. I says to myself, "Jesus, this outfit is going to be annihilated!" I knew I had seen the future.

I had from January until August yet to serve in the Army, and I counted the days, hoping we wouldn't get sent to Southeast Asia. We never did get called to serve in Vietnam while I was on active duty—leastways my outfit didn't. There were some other outfits that got called but ours didn't, and those that did went to Thailand.

Aloha

In my last month in the Army, August of 1963, about three weeks before I left for home, we had a full-dress inspection. The Colonel himself was going to examine us that Saturday morning. Well, back then, if you wanted to go to Southeast Asia, you could volunteer and, if they chose you, you would get six more weeks of intensive training with the M-16 machine gun. You'd then get three months of duty over there before they would return you to your outfit. At the time, the Army had more volunteers than they needed, but they were still asking, and people were still volunteering.

There was a man in weapons platoon with me who wanted to go badly. His name was Hackworth. He was from Arkansas and was a truck driver for the Eighty-One mortar squad. Hackworth wanted to go to Southeast Asia in the worst way. He kept volunteering and would always get turned down. They never give a reason; he just wasn't one they chose.

Now before the Colonel comes to inspect you, the Company Commander goes through first and tries to make sure you know all the right answers. When the Company Commander came before Hackworth this time, Hackworth presented arms; then the Commander grabbed his rifle. He was checking it out, all the time asking him questions.

"Hackworth! Do you still want to go to Southeast Asia?"

"Yes, sir!"

"You know they are not running maneuvers over there. It is the real thing; it is war. They are using live bullets. You still want to go to Southeast Asia?"

"Yes, sir!" says Hackworth.

"When I went through officers' training school, two of my buddies went to Southeast Asia and they are both Captains now. I stayed stateside and I am still a First Lieutenant. But there is a catch to it: they are both dead. Do you still want to go to Southeast Asia?" the Commander asked again.

"Yes, sir!"

The Company Commander said no more and let him take his rifle back. He then went on from man to man, down one rank and the other, just asking them normal questions as you might guess they ask during the inspections. Questions about your rifle and all.

Now, they always seemed to save their off-the-wall questions for me. I don't know why—maybe I amused them. Whatever they asked me, I would tell 'em straight. Sometimes—remember with Schofield—I would ask them first, "Do you want the textbook answer or do you want me to speak my heart, sir?"

They always wanted my heart.

So on that day when the Company Commander came before me, he grabbed my rifle and first thing he said was, "Seavey, why don't you want to go to Southeast Asia?"

I says, "Sir, I am not about ready to take a chance on losing my life in a war that this country may give up as a lost cause at any moment." Now you may think that this is pure hindsight, and I'm saying what I might have said, knowing what I do, knowing in fact what we all do now, about how Vietnam turned out. Well, I swear to God, that's exactly what I said in August, 1963.

Now you've got to have the whole picture. I'm in the third rank of military personnel. There was the Company Commander, the Executive Officer, the Platoon Leader, the Platoon Sergeant, and the First Sergeant. What I said broke all military rank! The Company Commander just turned around and slapped his knee, laughing. Then he said, looking back down the ranks, "Hackworth! Listen to Seavey. He makes a hell of a lot more sense than you do!"

And that was it, exactly how it happened.

A couple of weeks later I was on the *General Walker* (she was a 500-foot-long troop carrier that was owned by the Navy but run by the Merchant Marine). She had just picked up us soldiers from the twenty-fifth division who were going back to California, either to be transferred to other outfits or discharged out of the Army altogether. I felt light-hearted and free.

Back in Oakland, it was nothing more than waiting in line, getting records updated, turning in our uniforms, and collecting our travel pay, which was enough money to get back home. I took a bus to San Francisco, where I caught a flight to New York. Then I took Northeast Airlines to Bangor, Maine.

With two years of full service behind me, I was now on standby for the next two years.

One day about three years after I had gotten out of the Army, I picked up the *Bangor Daily News* in Southwest Harbor. The headline was shocking to me: Company B, Fourteenth Infantry, had been wiped out. I wondered how many of those men I had known so well in Hawaii were still part of that outfit and were now gone. Probably most of them. Maybe some of them were either discharged or transferred to other outfits by that time. The premonition I had in Ellsworth and the dream I had on Mauna Loa—well, I am glad I did not hesitate. They probably saved my life.

Now if you think that's shocking, listen to this. I can tell you that at least three times the dream of 1963 came true, because that is how many times I picked up a different edition of the *Bangor Daily News* and learned that Company B, Fourteenth Infantry, had again been decimated in the Vietnam War.

After each time, all they do is stock it up with new men. Then the new men die.

The Life

I started right back lobsterfishing again when I got home. I had fifty traps that I had saved from before I went into the Army, brand-new traps. I had a punt, I had buoys, but other than that, I had to start right back from scratch again. Gordon Robins gave me fifty more traps as a loan; of course he wanted me to replace them eventually, but it helped to get me started. The punt was solely for getting me to my lobster boat, but I didn't have one at the time so, for a percentage of my catch, I rented a little twenty-eight-footer from Lester Radcliffe, the man I have sold lobsters to all my life. It was very fair. I was happy with the arrangement and it got me going again.

For the uninitiated, let me explain the role of the dealer in the fisherman's life. The dealer makes a big investment in the lobstering operation because he maintains the facilities, and he's also responsible for the fatalities in the lobster population after he takes them from the fishermen and before he can move 'em to the markets. If he buys a thousand pounds of lobsters from boats, that's not what he's going to sell. Some of the lobsters will die. That's shrinkage. It may be from starvation; it may be from a fight; it may be from fresh water—too much fresh water'll kill them. It may also be from sea-fleas; if a sea flea can find a weak point on a lobster's shell where it's been wounded or something, it'll just eat the lobster away.

All that can happen to the lobsters after they're sold off the boat, but the fishermen get paid on the pounds they catch. So I didn't begrudge Lester his share.

I will now describe the lobsterfishing life for you. Back in those days we made our traps on the wharf, during the winter over the woodstove when it was too stormy to fish, or as Thoreau put it, "when the snow was falling hard and the wind was roaring through the trees." We went lobstering then, but not as often, due to the weather. It was a good season to rebuild our gear and to overhaul it, and to share the company of our fellow man.

Now let's pick an imaginary starting point. We've constructed our traps and we first have to load them onto the boat. We might take from fifty to a hundred of them at a time, depending on the size of the boat and what she can handle. Back then we could fish as many traps total as we wanted, and I fished maximum three hundred, a small gang. Some fishermen set as many as six hundred. Nowadays there's a limit; it's eight hundred in this area, roughly Bar Harbor to Swans Island. I think Swans Island has a special law and is limited to four hundred and fifty per boat.

When I fished alone later in life, my routine and all of the work were the same as when I was younger and went out with my dad. I was usually on the grounds about the time that I could see daylight. I timed my day by where I was going to start fishing. We usually like to be on the fishing grounds about a half hour before sunrise, or light enough to see. If I had two hours' running time, I'd leave accordingly and, if I had no distance to run, relatively speaking, then I'd leave later. I would always start by daybreak and be in by three o'clock in the afternoon, except in the winter. Winter fishing, I might not get back until six at night. Shorter days and lots more rope to haul on pairs of traps sunk deep down on winter lobstering grounds would keep me out from daylight till after dark. Long-line trawling, that was a different story. To trawl I had so much farther out to run that I usually started at one-thirty in the morning just to make it back the same day.

On fishing days, there isn't much leisure time. It's home, shower, eat, and to bed by seven; a fisherman works all day on very little sleep. Sometimes my dad and I would be coming back from Vinalhaven or somewhere late in the afternoon, and I'd be listening to the sound of the engine, not concentrating on it or anything, and suddenly it would stop for a second, just a micro-second, total silence. Of course, it wasn't the engine stopping, but the mind. I have come to understand that that's the body's way of taking a brief catnap, and you can do nothing to control it. It just happens. I've tried to stop it and I can't. You wake up as soon as you fall asleep, but that little bit of sleep somehow makes a huge difference in keep the mind and body refreshed and alert. Maybe it's a survival mechanism.

The Territory

So, back to my account of lobstering: it's the start of a new season; I have fifty traps on my boat. I have a wooden bait box of nylon pockets, at least enough for one per trap. Now the box would more likely be fiberglass. I also have to load one tub of bait for fifty traps. If I had a hundred traps, it would be two tubs. I make sure the traps are tied on the boat, so she don't roll them off her. You attach them in blocks of, say, ten, with nylon rope and two half-hitches for your knot. Then you head out to the fishing grounds.

Years ago we used to use landmarks to locate our territories, and I have provided my old landmarks in the appendix to this book. Now we use GPS (global positioning satellite), much more efficient, much less poetic; much more accurate and much less adventuresome.

I mainly got my territory where I fished from my father, and some other men did likewise, but where you fish and where you don't is a matter of custom and fisherman's law, which I'll get into later. It was easy to pick up fishing in the same area that Dad did, and no one was going to dispute my right.

But you shouldn't picture territories as exclusive. All of our buoys, with their different colors marking the different fishermen, are mixed in together at sea, so we share a territory, sort of like a communal garden, though that doesn't mean we'll tolerate just anyone joining the community.

The territory is also not one place or even a continuous region. For that matter, it's not a consistent discontinuous region. I fish from right outside the harbor in the warm months to as much as two hours' running time in the winter, so I have many separate territories where I mingle with both the same and different other fishermen.

When taking a boatload of traps off to set, you want a relatively calm day. You don't want to be setting traps if it's twenty-five miles per hour southeast winds; it would be ridiculous. For one, the boat would be unstable. Even with the traps tied, she's gonna roll them off of her. You can haul 'em up to twenty-five to thirty miles per hour wind if you want to take the punishment, but you can't set 'em. When the wind gets to be ten miles an hour, it's starting to make whitecaps. At twenty-five miles per hour, the ocean is feather white. At fifty miles per hour, the seas are combing. That would be a full storm. You wouldn't consider even fishing on a day like that.

The way you prepare the traps to load them on board, the rope and buoy are coiled neatly in the trap. That's just good housekeeping. Now when you are on the fishing grounds, and the sea is calm enough, you take the rope and buoy out of the trap, make sure the tailer is tied to the head trap with a bowling knot, run out the buoy and the rope, and bait the traps from the barrels of bait on board. You just take handfuls of herring, or whatever you're using, and stuff it in the bait pockets, and hitch one bait pocket to each trap.

You watch your boat's indicator and notice the depth of the water and the type of ocean bottom that's under you, be it rocky, sandy, or muddy. There are times you want to be up on the hard rocky bottom and other times down over the hard bottom in mud. Lobsters migrate. You basically know where they should be tending depending on the season you're fishing. Then, after that, you've got to figure out exactly where they are—up on the bottom, down over the bottom. There's no set law as to where they have to be. You have to figure it out. Experience will teach you that. Intuition comes from experience.

So you want to set your traps in the appropriate territory for the time of year and where you're accustomed to fishing, and then precisely in spots where you have figured out lobsters are likely to be on this particular day, and also not so close to other traps—your own or someone else's—that they'll snarl.

We fish either pairs, two to a line, or singles, one on a line. We run out the buoy and the rope that are attached to a trap or pair of traps, hitch the loaded bait bag in the traps, close the doors, and push it overboard so it will settle on bottom right side up. It takes a trap a matter of a minute or so to reach and settle on the bottom.

You can fish them as close or as far apart as you want, but I usually keep fifty yards between them.

You lobster different territories all at the same time. Your next territory might be two hundred yards away or a mile or more.

When you're setting traps, you're just setting. When you haul and rebait them, then you're fishing them. Either way, it's working the sea.

The Game

Remember, two to three-thirty is my rising time, A.M., of course, depending on where I'm going to fish that day. Then, if we're setting traps, we do that till there are no more on the boat, and then we might go to fishing and rebaiting traps that have been set previously. We do whatever work needs to be done, and we usually keep at it until four in the afternoon. There's not much of the day left to do anything but wash, walk the dog, eat, and go back to sleep.

We let the traps set on the ocean bottom for a few days or so, and then we go out and haul 'em, rebait 'em, and set 'em back again. We have a trap hauler that works hydraulically. These days the machine entirely pulls the traps off the bottom, not the man. When I first went with my father, we used a winch head. A belt from the engine kept it turning, and we wrapped about three turns of rope around the winch head and then pulled the trap in by hand. The engine couldn't pull it in by itself; it needed continuous tension on the rope from the fisherman. The trap hauler substitutes a wheel for the winch, and it pulls the rope by itself.

You'll have more traps out during the season than you can haul in one day. It may take you two or three days to make the round of them all.

When you haul the traps, you take out the lobsters, measure them, check them out to make sure they're legal, and put rubber bands around their claws so they won't bite each other. Of course, when you're hauling, you need to carry these bands in your bait box. The dealer will give you the bands, no charge.

Then you put the catch in bushel baskets or crates, a hundred pounds to a crate.

A trap's yield will vary from nothing to a dozen or more. It varies from trap to trap. Just because one trap is empty doesn't mean the one next to it is. The other might have a number of lobsters in it. Lobster traps also fill with many other species—urchins, hermit crabs, whelks, starfish—and we put those back in the water. There could also be fish in them—cusk, cod, flounder, different types of sculpins like horned and sea ravens. We save a lot of those fish to eat, but we'd throw back horned sculpins and sea ravens. There are also plenty of sea fleas, but they just run off on the washboard, the side of the boat.

Fishing alone, the most lobsters I ever got was 524 pounds. At my worst I never got nothing, but I've come back with only twenty to show.

If the traps are fishing good, we may well leave'm where they are, but, if they're doing poorly, we may shift them to another piece of bottom. That means we'll keep 'em on board and let the rest of the day's fishing, successful or not, determine where they best go. Usually we relocate them as we go along.

There's no hard and fast rule about trap positioning. Fisherman's logic defies logic. Harve Moore used to say, "It's best not to let the lobster know what you're up to"—and that about expresses it, presuming one could read what passes for a lobster's mind. I may move some traps if they're not catching well, or I may just leave them till they start catching. If I have a trap that's fishing well, I'll probably leave it where it is; I'll tell myself, "Why move a trap that's doing well?" On the other hand, it's not good to let the traps get lazy, as silly as that sounds. I suppose it's no sillier than trying to outsmart a lobster.

The Dealer

At the end of a fishing day, we bring our catch to the wharf. I've always sold to Thurston's Wharf, first Lester Radcliffe, now his son Mike. Lester didn't own my boat anymore once the *Wolfhound* was constructed, but that didn't make us any less close or mutually dependent. Of course, when you're going in a dealer's boat, you sell to him. Just common sense.

I have had many a laugh about my friend Richard Grossinger, who I'll introduce later. When he was writing his thesis on fishermen and didn't know shit from shinola at the beginning, on his first day at the wharf he asked Lester what would happen if a fisherman going in one of his boats tried to sell elsewhere. Lester couldn't believe the question. He first said, "I should hope they would sell here."

Then Richard asked, "If they don't?"

And Lester replied, "If they don't! Well, I'd think they'd find themselves walking on water."

Lester had a way of summing it up pretty good.

Having a dealer means having a home wharf; it is beneficial to both parties. While I'm willing to sell all my lobsters to Lester, he's willing to donate to me a little corner of his wharf to keep my stuff. And he does that with each and every one of his fishermen. It's convenient to me to have a place to stow my gear. The wharf space is tit for tat among the dealer and his fishermen; it comes out even. We all have a little agreement—this will be my turf, this will be your turf; and I stay out of your area, I don't go piling my stuff in it, and you don't in mine. It works out pretty good that way. Now and then there's a little chew among the fishermen, over each little section of the wharf, you know, but it doesn't usually amount to anything serious.

If you want to be an independent fisherman and not have a home wharf, you use the town pier to load and unload, and you pay a rental fee to use the wharf.

Price

B ack then, when I started up again out of the Army, the dealer paid a dollar, a dollar a half a pound or so for lobster. Right now it's $3.50 a pound for softshells, around $5.50 for the hardshells. Over the years the price has been up and down, and it's set by the markets, supply and demand.

I have sold lobsters for as low as thirty to thirty-five cents a pound—that was back when I fished from a skiff with an outboard back in 1953. The price would go up somewhat in the winter. It was in the fall of 1957 that there was the first dramatic effort to get the price of lobsters up. The Maine Lobstermen's Association called a strike. They said that the tradition of rock-bottom pricing had gone on long enough: we needed more money. Many of the boats tied up and didn't go fishing for a period of time. The federal government proclaimed that the Association didn't have the power of a union and could not legally call a strike. I guess they were hauled into court and their hands were slapped a little bit and they were told not to do it again. So instead of continuing the strike, they held voluntary tie-ups whenever they wanted better prices for their catch. The first time I ever knew lobsters to go to a dollar a pound was in the winter of 1958.

Now we have ship-to-shore telephones in our boats, so we know when the price goes up or down anywheres along the coast 'cause the fishermen get talking, you know, and if we find out that someone's getting a dime more than we are, then we're going to do a whole lot of bitching and griping. We make it disagreeable that way for a day or two and the price'll come up.

I remember once Lester got in a grumpy mood and said to a few of us fishermen who were grumbling about price fluctuations, "You know what I should do. I should lower the price to 70 cents right now and keep it there all season; then there wouldn't be these ups and downs and complainings."

I turned to Fillmore Turner and said loud enough for everyone to hear, "Should we send him flowers or donations?"

That got a laugh.

In the '50s into the late '60s, the dealer used to pay in cash daily. Now he has an itemized account of what you owe the wharf for supplies you got from him like rope, bait, salt for the herring, fuel, oil, gloves, oilcloths, cleaning materials, and so forth, which he deducts, and then he pays you the amount of money he owes you above that, once a week, by check. The IRS really likes those checks. It gives them a better paper trail. They didn't think too much of the cash, but the older fishermen sure liked it; I'll let you guess why. It was part of the custom then, and no snooping at the wharf by outsiders.

Lobsterfishing Seasons

Let's start out right in January. We might as well start at the first of the year. It's cold weather and we're in 40 to 60 fathoms of water; that's where we set our traps. Some fisherman say there's no money in winter lobsterfishing. I disagree, but I remember a few years ago at the wharf there was a heated discussion about this topic. It had been windy and snowy for eight days, and men were getting a bit stir-crazy. One man who had all his traps set said that, if the weather was better, he could be making good money. Another man who never fished in the winter said, "That's not saying what it's costing you." The first man boasted, "I can haul four or five hundred pounds a day." "No, not a day," the second man said, "because you ain't been out for a week that I know of."

I think I'd rather haul my traps in the winter and not worry about whether it's costing me more than I'm making. When I fish, somehow the bills get paid and food ends up on the table.

As the season gets warmer—we'll say the later part of March or first of April—the lobsters will start working in, up to 10 fathoms of water. In the summer they'll crawl away to shed. About the main thing lobsters are sensitive to is the temperature of the water. In July, August, September, October, they're in fairly close, 5 to 25 fathoms' warp of rope, as I explained. The water's fairly warm, and we fish in close—in shoal water, we call it. But as the sea gets colder, we keep moving off into deeper water. So if we, let's say, started out in 15, 20, 25 fathoms' warp, then 'long in November we'd be up to 40 to 80 fathoms of warp.

What really cools your water off the quickest of anything is snow; snow'll really chill your water. So you get two or three good Northeast snowstorms, as you will, and of course these lobsters that were in close are crawling for deeper waters. And so you keep going off. That's how we follow them along.

We fish islands in the bays during warm weather for the shallow water around them: Black, Placentia, Gotts, the two Duck Islands, Little and Big—you can see them from Seawall—and Green Island. These islands are lobstering territory during the summer and early fall, but after that the prey leaves for deeper water.

Of course, the boys in Augusta from the Fisheries department, who come lecture us on the wharves, have their own theory; they say the lobsters aren't migrating, but the warming water wakes up ones that were sluggish and sets them into activity. When the water gets cooler, the lobsters inshore go into inactivity, but out deeper, the water that's a hundred, two hundred feet down doesn't change so much. They say we are chasing a thermocline, not lobsters, but, since we don't care which lobsters we catch, it hardly matters whether it's lobsters traveling or lobsters waking up. We find 'em where they are—they crawl into our traps after the bait all the same. I prefer "moving lobsters" to a thermocline, 'cause that's how fishermen talk. They seem to me to travel about half a mile a day when on the move. But I guess you could put me in the class of people, way back when, who thought the sun moved around the Earth.

Lobster Biology and Conservation

A lobster grows by shedding its shells. And when they come out of this shell, they're just as soft as a piece of rubber or a piece of jelly; they can't protect themselves at all, so they hide, you know, under rocks and things like that, and they stay there until this shell of theirs starts toughening up. As it gets harder they come out, but when they first come out, they're still soft—and that's what they call a shedder (or softshell). It will take numerous weeks before it will turn into a hardshell.

Lobsters are scavengers; they clean the ocean bottom. Now what they eat, and what we use to catch 'em by, are sardine or salted herring—it's the same thing. If they can it, it's a sardine; if we use it for bait, it's a herring. Lobsters seem to like herring the best, and herring's easy to use, to fill into the bait bags. I've used flounder, mackerel, and redfish. I'd use mackerel if I couldn't get herring.

Now we have conservation laws in Maine. Maine used to produce between 18 and 24 million pounds of lobsters a year that were caught, and that catch was protected by rules and wardens enforcing the rules at the wharves. Fishermen carry a device, a measure, which reads 3 1/4 inches on the small end, and you take it and stick it right in the socket of the eye of the lobster, not touching the eyeball intentionally, of course. Then, if that small measure will go down over the back shell of the animal, it's too short—but if the small measure will not go down over the back of the shell, then you can sell it. So that way it makes it that the smallest lobster you can sell will weigh about one pound.

Now for the big size, it measures five inches on the back of your measure, and when you put the measure in the socket of the eye, if the shell of the lobster is too big so that the measure won't go down over it, that is considered too big a lobster, so we throw that one back for breeding purposes.

The low end of the measurement is not exactly for breeding purposes, but so that small ones'll reach a bigger size. A lobster is no bigger than an ant when born. You throw your small ones in so they'll grow. You throw the big ones in just so you make sure there's enough of those size lobsters left. You depend on your big ones for breeding. If we cleaned up all the little ones, it wouldn't be long 'fore we'd be looking for a new business. And if we didn't throw back the big ones, it'd be likewise.

If they're really soft, you throw 'em back because they'll get harder as time goes by. If female lobsters have eggs on them under their tails, that's another status of animal you can't sell; you return them to the sea as breeders. To make sure the egg-carrying female survives, you punch a V in the flipper of her tail right-of-the-middle one, and that way she can never be sold as long as that V-notch is in her tail. You put it in the right-of-the-middle flipper, and then there is no question as to it's legal. One of the other flippers on her tail could be marked up, and that don't count. It's that right-of-the-middle one. Now back when I started fishing, it was the middle flipper, but they realized that the middle flipper is right under the anus, so they changed it to the flipper next to that so as to do less harm to the animal. It also used to have to be a heavy notch; now it's a "no tolerance" law—any little nick, no matter how fine, and the lobster is illegal.

The cut is made so somebody low enough couldn't get away with scraping those seeds off. If an unethical fisherman catches her, and it's the first time, and she's got eggs, and she's got no notch in the tail, then there's nothing you can do if he's going to brush those eggs off and sell her. However, when you find one with seeds on it, you make a notch and throw her back in. That way you protect her from some convict catching her and brushing the seeds off. And she's protected as long as that V is in there, even after she's done bearing seeds. If she keeps it till she gets over the big measure, then that's the charm as far as she's concerned; she's protected for life.

An unethical fisherman might also try to cut around a V, eliminate it. To overcome that, the law reads that a mutilated tail—it could be from a bite from another lobster—means it's no dice; you don't sell it and you have to throw it back in. A lobster whose right-of-the-middle flipper has been mutilated in a fight, if she's female, is protected too, till it sheds out. That's a lucky lobster, though she might not know it. A fisherman who catches her has to put her back in the sea. He may think it's unfair to have to return her when it's nature that put the notch in, but the law protects the lobster industry first. You can't worry about the few lobsters a fisherman might lose because of chance mutilation because, if you did, you might not have an enforceable law protecting the vast majority of egg-bearers.

I don't know how many try and cheat, but it's like anything.

Fishermen are the same as any other group of men; there are so many rotten apples in any barrel. Biggest percentage of them are fine, but it's very easy to get tempted, so you got to make sure there's a law.

Uneducated fishermen who scrape the eggs off female lobsters are actually killing their own business. They're aborting thousands of lobsters because a big female'll definitely have a lot of eggs on her. Scraping seeds off a pregnant lobster would be like not planting the garden in the spring and then standing around disappointed because you haven't got any crops in the fall. You can't kill your young. You can't have your cake and eat it too. I mean, in some ways you've got to leave the ingredients for future purposes.

No one who wants to go lobsterfishing for a living is against conservation laws, not if they want to keep it up. Of course, if they want to get out of it and don't give a damn, then they might be the type to say I'd rather have my dollar today than two dollars after I'm dead. Eat, drink, and be merry! Now that's been said before. Make all you can today and to hell with tomorrow. But sometimes, you know, you live to see your business die before you do—you've outlived your livelihood, and you're looking for another trade.

Wars

When you bought a license in those days when I was just out of the Army, it said you could lobsterfish anywhere on the Maine coast. Nowadays it's divided into zones. Either way, though, there seems to be a moral and a legal law. There is sort of an agreement amongst the fellows that you don't go over in a territory that another harbor's noted for fishing. Like I wouldn't take my traps and go to Swans Island with them, or

Long Island either, and they wouldn't come to Bass Harbor's territory.

Tradition sets the rules. Lobstermen generally fish in peace. You can only place your traps close enough to another man's traps so they won't snarl. Everyone knows how far that is. Sure, there are mistakes made every day, but as long as they're not deliberate, you just overlook it and they do likewise. Some people have a lot of trouble, but overall the people that fish year after year work together. Yet there is a darker side to lobster fishing.

If folks are aggressive, whether they are defending their own territory or invading someone else's, they will come and cut off other men's traps or the heads of the traps—the nets that keep the lobsters in. If a fisherman thinks you are fishing where you don't belong, he might just give you a warning by driving a knife down into your buoy—or sometimes he'll haul your traps and leave the doors open for a warning. If you don't take your traps and depart, there is going to be some cutting done. Some people take the warning and clear out, and some people fight back. A fisherman who goes against community sentiment might not find his gear. He can fish where he wants, legally, but it'd prove expensive after a while. Are you going to fight, or are you going to run? If you are going to fight, you'd better mean it. You are taking a risk of your livelihood.

At sea, geographical location is the convenience to us to get to it. Mainly Bass Harbor fishes Duck Island and Blue Hill Bay, but Southwest and Bass Harbor can mingle at the Duck Islands without too much difficulty. I wouldn't fish Johns Island out by Swans because that's too close to both Swans and Long; it's right 'tween the two. On the other hand, neither would they take their traps and go off to Duck Island. Now they've got a legal right to go there, just like I've got the right to go down in their territory. But I'm not ignorant of the fact that if I done it, I wouldn't expect to find 'em. There would be some harassing incident done to them.

Sometimes lobstermen are overly territorial and have difficulties fishing in peace with one another. Back when I was young, I imagined myself getting involved in cutting; it seemed part of the job. I thought, if someone was disturbing my traps, then I'd bait him up, lay a trap for him, try and catch 'im. Then I'd go over, talk to him, tell him I saw him and, if that didn't do nothing, then I'd talk to the warden and, if we couldn't prove nothing in court, then I'd take it into my own hands. It'd be just like guerrilla warfare. I'd do whatever'd hurt him, bleed him enough until he stopped bothering me. That's how a lot of fishermen talk even now.

But, as good fortune would have it, forty years have passed since then and I have been cut, but I have never cut.

Now, if I had to cut your trap peacefully because it snarled in my lines or in a propeller or whatever, I'd repair it with a water knot, a good clean knot. To keep good relations, I might also tell a man that I had done it. Most times it is best to be magnanimous and cut your own trap to undo the snarl. That keeps things easier. I have returned lost traps, and I have not been bothered much by trap wars. I have sometimes gotten what we call "ugly knots." If you cut a man's rope, take the two ends and tuck them through, or put the rope into a square knot with two long loose ends—that is an "ugly knot." If a fisherman was rip-roaring mad with someone, he might put an overhand knot in the offending rope, or a cow's tail. I wouldn't do that myself, but some will.

Certainly there's macho fisherman talk, and even occasionally action to back it up. Once in a while, there are cutting wars; the fleet out of a harbor will cut the living hell out of someone.

What triggers it? I don't know.

There have been some shootings out to Isle Au Haut and one by Seawall. I remember a fisherman at Lester's—I won't name him—announced one day, "If I think someone's hauling or cutting my traps, I'm gonna keep watch, settle it down to one or two men, ask them if they want to die; most often they don't."

The most extreme case I ever heard of came from my brother Frank some forty-odd years ago. I cannot tell you if it is true or a folk tale, but Frank felt it was true. Frank said there were a couple of lobstermen that got into a hell of a problem over hauling traps, maybe even stealing traps. One man ended up shooting another man and killing him. It was such a trauma for the one that killed the other one that his hair turned white overnight.

Another story came from my father's uncle, Arthur Norwood, my grandmother's brother who was born in 1878. Arthur told me that when he was lobsterfishing, another man was hauling his traps. "I seen him hauling my traps," he said, "I spoke to him about it, but he didn't see to stop hauling them. Well, I had a rifle that would not shoot a long distance, but it carried a very big chunk of lead—it could be very damaging. I went down around the shore and hid in the woods, and I watched him. There he was, hauling one trap right after the other and all of them mine. When he came in front of me, I opened fire. I fired seventeen shots at his boat. I put four shots in his engine, which ruined it. I never aimed at him or intended to hurt him— I just wanted to teach him a lesson. Needless to say, he never bothered me again."

People have stolen traps and added them to their own gang to fish. A warden could go out and under-run the gear—haul the traps up, see if the buoys and the traps correspond—but the crime would be difficult to prove in a court of law. For instance, he could claim you framed him. If you could catch the thief pulling the trap and setting it, then you have a case, although it would be one man's word against another. The only way you could really catch them would be to have a witness— best if the witness was a warden.

Now I know, in one case a man was hauling on a foggy day, and he came running through the mist to a new location where he had left his traps. It was one of those days where you can have mist on the water and then come out of it instantaneously—into blue skies and sun shining—like the curtain was pulled on a theater show. He came right out of the fog near his end trap where he wanted to start hauling, and there was another man cutting off his buoy. When he saw the owner coming, he just cut it off and threw it and headed in another direction—took off and hightailed it.

"To hell with it," said the first man. "I know who he is. I seen him do it. I am not going to waste my time chasing him." So he went up to the cutter's traps and cut off his end one. The next day the cutter lopped off another one of the first man's traps in retaliation. The first man took revenge and cut off ten pairs of the cutting man's traps. The guy lost twenty traps that day. The first man had no intentions of backing off. They left each other alone after that, but they never spoke again.

Another time a fellow went to fish a new area and, when he went to haul his traps, the two end ones were missing. The next day two more pair of end traps were gone. He didn't know who it was, so he said, "If I can't fish here, nobody will fish here." Tit for tat. He told a friend who he knew was innocent, "The cutting's about to start and, if you want to clear out of the area before it happens, I'll give you a half hour."

The guy said, "Thank you."

Then the first fellow cut four pair off every man who fished that area. The message got across.

Now wardens can't tell you *not* to cut; they know it's the best means of enforcement and makes their job easier; it has to be done. Unspoken law. They're not going to tell you to cut, either—no way! If you get caught cutting, you lose your license.

The Wolfhound

The first boat that was really mine, *The Wolfhound,* was started on the first day of December, 1964. By then I had made enough money fishing that I was able to afford it. The price of lobster was high, and the lobsters themselves were plentiful.

Ralph Stanley and Tucker Spurling were *The Wolfhound's* builders. Today Ralph's a national treasure—officially. Hillary Clinton gave him that recognition at the White House itself. Back then, though, he was just a boat-builder and a fiddler. When the boat came to a certain point, I did all the sanding and painting myself. On the sixth day of May, 1965, we launched her. She was thirty-five feet long and ten feet wide.

My father and I went fishing together from *The Wolfhound,* and I must say, the fishing was excellent. We went hand-lining and lobsterfishing in May and June. Hand-lining, we would get from three to six thousand pounds of codfish and pollock a day. It was on the 24th day of May that year we got the 12,747 pounds of pollock, hand-lining. During that summer we'd go tub trawling, and we often got between 5,000 and 10,000 pounds of fish a day. I do not know if young people today would even believe me, those amounts of fish, compared to the devastation that the fisheries are in. But, once upon a time it was possible to haul that much fish in one day within twenty miles of the harbor. You couldn't make a new dollar for an old doing that type of fishing today. Remember the summer of 1965; it won't be back, at least not before another heaven and earth have passed.

"The No Good Boyo"

The U.S. Army still required me to be available for the "manpool"—two weeks of camp with some National Guard outfit every summer. You might be chosen or not; lucky me, I was chosen both summers. The first one I served with the 220th tank regiment from Portland, Maine, and then the second, I think, it was the 120th infantry regiment from New Haven, Connecticut.

One of the things I loved to do in the winter, when the fishing was slow, was take a one- or two-week vacation down the east coast. My travels could lead me all the way from Maine to Florida, but they always included a stop-off in New York City. I planned to spend a week there each winter.

I used to stay at the Hotel Dixie on Forty-Second Street and go sight-seeing and enjoy the pleasures of the city. (The Dixie, by the way, doesn't even exist today.) I liked to visit the Hayden Planetarium and hear their lecture about the stars and that there was such a thing as time and how they could break time down, say into leap years, and still never get it right, so they were losing a few seconds every three hundred years or so. Other favorite spots of mine were Madison Square Garden, Radio City Music Hall, and some of the television broadcasting companies like NBC where you could sit in the studio audience. I saw a big circus once at Madison Square Garden, and I watched the Gary Moore Show live. I saw Sammy Davis, Jr., starring in *Golden Boy*. It was about black people living up off 127th Street in New York and their way of life. I'd also take in some of the new movies when they first came out and the shows off Broadway.

During both 1964 and '65, when I was participating in the short reserve sessions, the World's Fair was playing at the Polo Grounds in New York. I was back in uniform again and had my papers, so I went to the servicemen's YMCA in New York City. For about three dollars a night I had a room and public showers—what I needed for home sweet home. I used to go down a few days in advance of the start of camp and stay at the servicemen's Y and then go to the Fair for a few days. I drank a lot of Hofbrau beer. My favorite was the German Beer Garden. The drinks were delicious, the music was fun and, while the Americans merely clapped, the Germans hooted and whistled, which pleased the band leader. That was the life then— fishing, beer, New York City, the Guard, swimming, partying, and women. I was a hard-working fisherman but, for my exploits, I was also known as "The No Good Boyo." The name fit me to a "T." That just about rounds it out.

The Late-Night Woman

One particular January, which I think was 1965, after spending a number of days in New York City, I decided I was going to go on to Washington, D.C., for some more sightseeing. Though I was planning to leave the next morning, I was in no hurry—I was on vacation. I thought to myself, probably I'll leave the Dixie around nine o'clock or so and go over to the Port Authority bus terminal. I traveled by Greyhound in those days.

At the Dixie that night, however, a person in the room next to me turned their television up high at about three A.M. If whoever it was was trying to be obnoxious, he really succeeded as far as I was concerned. Sleep was impossible. So I says, "Well, the hell with it. I know the Port Authority will have a bus going

to Washington, D.C., even at this time of night. I'll leave now."
By four o'clock I had checked out of the Hotel Dixie and was
headed to the bus station.

It was very quiet. Not much was going on, it seemed. I was
just walking by myself, nobody about, and then I saw this lady
wearing a trench coat, running towards me. As she got up to
me, she said, "Where are you going?"

"Port Authority."

She says, "Don't go! The police are over there and they are
having a gunfight. You'll walk right into it!"

I says, "Thank you very much for telling me!"

We did an about face and, as chance would have it, started in
the opposite direction together. She and I began talking small
talk as we walked along the streets of New York, four A.M., kind
of quiet. Then we saw a restaurant. Just the cook was in at that
hour. Through the window he was getting the stoves warmed
up and preparing for breakfast. I says to her, "Have you eaten?"
Obviously she was very poor, probably homeless. "Let's go down
and see if he'll let us in." The door was open. We asked him if it
was all right if we came in.

"Yeah. Come on in. Take a table. When I get ready I'll cook
your breakfast for you." She and I sat at the table and talked
away, just about life, everyday sort of stuff. Eventually we had
our eggs, bacon, toast, and coffee.

"Have you got a room here?" she asked me.

"No, I just checked out of the Hotel Dixie."

She says, "You have been very good to me so if you want to
get a cheap room, I will reward you for this breakfast." The only
thing she had to give was herself.

"No, my dear," I says. "It is I who am indebted to you—you
saved me from walking right into a gunfight! Breakfast is my
way of thanking you."

When we were done, I says, "Well, I am going to assume now the gun battle is over and I am going to the Port Authority to catch a bus." We went out of the restaurant together, up onto the street, and said goodbye to each other. She went her way and I went mine.

There was a special connection between us. I know that to this day. Beyond that, she owed me nothing.

It was still dark, and it wasn't but a short time later I was on the New Jersey side looking at the skyline of Manhattan from a Greyhound headed towards Washington D.C. When I got there, I went to Arlington Cemetery and the Smithsonian Museum and toured the White House. I saw the changing of the guard at Arlington.

It was about ten years later—I was married with three young children by then—when I met that lady from New York City again.

One of the things my wife and I used to do with our kids to make each child feel special was to take them on little trips, just one of them and just one of us, a two-night/three-day excursion together. Sometimes my wife would take Mary; sometimes I would. Sometimes I'd take Frank or vice versa. I always took Wayne because Wayne wanted to go to Holden and do freshwater fishing. Mary and Frank always wanted to go to the Holiday Inn in Ellsworth and go swimming, see the movies, eat out at the restaurant, go shopping, and things like that.

This particular trip, Frank and I went to Ellsworth. He was very young; I don't think he was even in kindergarten at the time. We were in the hotel in the double bed together, and I had all the drapes pulled in the room. It was as dark as a dungeon.

Somewhere between three and four in the morning I woke up. Frank was sound asleep. I had this feeling that somebody was in our bedroom. I thought to myself, "How did anyone ever get into this room?" So I just lay there perfectly still, trying to get my eyes adjusted to the night so I could spot where they was.

Now at the foot of our bed across the room were a dresser and a mirror. I was scanning through that area when all of a sudden the woman from New York illuminated up in color, just as she had been ten years earlier in New York City. I recognized her instantly. She was making direct eye contact with me, and I was just staring back, looking at her right in her eyes. When she'd made sure she had my undivided attention, I heard her say, "I want to thank you for that breakfast we shared in New York City. I have come to say goodbye." That was the whole of her message and, as soon as she had said it, once again she faded. I knew full well she came to me then at the hour of her death. Yes, we had had some sort of spiritual connection, whatever you want to call it.

The thing that amazed me was that, once we parted ways in New York City, I know I could have scoured that city with a fine-toothed comb and never seen her again. Then ten years later, at the hour of her death, I was in some hotel up in eastern Maine and she had no problem locating me, none whatsoever.

Marriage

Back on Mount Desert Island in the summer of 1965, there were two new women in town: Susan Tibbits and Betty Hall. Betty was from Manchester, New Hampshire, and Sue was from Lynn, Massachusetts. After they had taken nurses' training together, they both became RNs in the Lynn hospital.

Well, they had taken the summer off to get away from city life and were renting a little cottage down on the Old Point Road— off what we all call the "Back Beach." I would see them driving 'round in their little red Buick convertible with their dog, Butch.

One day I was outside the post office, waiting for the mail, when their dog came up, cocked his leg, and took a leak on the rock I was sitting on! Because of that, we had to exchange a few words, but they were pleasant ones.

That summer we had a long foggy spell and it had been a few days since my father and I had been out fishing. One night in particular the fog was in close, dungeonly thick with no signs whatsoever of clearing. I was down on the Back Beach and ran into Betty and Susan. We got talking and it became a good conversation; we all three of us liked each other. I had lots of girlfriends then, but no one I was steady with.

They asked me if I drank and I says, "Yeah, I drink sociably."

They says, "Want to come up to the cottage for a drink?"

Well, I didn't know that I was being experimented on. It seems that any man they had ever seen before couldn't hold his Southern Comfort so, glass by glass, as I thought we were shooting the breeze about fishing and our way of life and their way of life and where they were from, they filled me solid full of Southern Comfort. About twelve-thirty I walked out of the cottage completely pie-eyed and looked up. Every star there ever was was out in the sky, God's whole universe. The weather had cleared. Father would be ready to go fishing at one-thirty, so I says, "Well, girls, you have got to excuse me, I have got to go fishing now."

They didn't say nothing, but I could see they thought it was just the alcohol talking.

There was a fence with a gate that ran right across their property. I headed out in the direction of what I thought was the gate. I didn't make any gate. I made the fence, but I had too much pride to admit I didn't make the gate, so I climbed up the fence and then fell head over heels into the woods, hollering as I went, acting as though it was what I intended. They shouted out to ask if I was okay, and the pie-eyed boyo replied, "I am just fine."

I went back home, woke my father up, and said, "Dad, the weather's cleared."

And we went fishing. I was sick all day long, just like I was seasick. I guess I got through that day, but just barely.

Sue, Betty, and I spent the rest of that summer and the fall sightseeing, swimming, eating all the lobsters and fish we could, and talking about religion because they were both Catholic. They didn't have much money, so I kept them supplied in seafood. That was probably a courting ritual the Abnaki Indians who lived on Mount Desert before the white man would have approved of.

After a couple of months Sue and I got romantically involved. It was mostly about being good friends. That's the way the relationship with each other got started.

Betty was going back to Lynn to resume her teaching position at the hospital, and Sue stayed in Maine. In September, Sue and I were still romantically inclined, so we went to Massachusetts and I met her family. Right from the get-go we had a playful standoff; I guess they were a little resistant to someone taking their daughter. Her mother tried to rib me. She said, "You don't have to pretend to be that nice around me because I know you lobsterfishermen eat short lobsters, haul each other's traps, and do all sorts of illegal things."

I replied, "You surely have room to talk because all you're doing is insinuating things, and I know you are a real thief."

She looked at me quite shocked and said, "What do you mean?"

"Well, look right on your garage. Haven't you got lots of lobster buoys from the State of Maine? Do you have a written receipt from all those fishermen for all those buoys?"

"No, we picked them up off the beach."

"Don't you realize those buoys belonged to other men and you had no right to take them? Look at that black and white buoy over there. Pick it up and see if it doesn't say H. Smith."

Sue's father picked it up. "Mary, he's right. It says H. Smith."

I says, "Look at the red and white buoy. Does that not say M. Albee?"

Once again Sue's dad said, "Mary, he's right."

I says, "I could go on and on, but have I not now made my point? If I was a lobster warden, I'd have you locked up and throw away the key. Ignorance of the law is no excuse."

We became instant friends.

When Betty came back to visit Sue, I introduced her to my best friend Tucker Spurling, and they liked each other and started dating.

I married Sue on February 12, Lincoln's Birthday, 1966, at St. Pius Church, Lynn, Massachusetts. Just before getting married, I did convert to Catholicism. I took catechism classes from Father Bellafontaine in Northeast Harbor.

I liked the Catholic faith because it was run by men, no women at the helm like with the Baptist or the Congregational. Men don't get fanatic or hysterical about religion. You see the priest and talk to him and work things out. That's that. None of this "death on your soul" business. There's no one to keep examining you and nagging you.

A few years later Father Gower became my pastor. The man showed a very sensible attitude towards God. From the beginning he was fair and used me well.

I did the best I could to change my beliefs according to Catholicism, but it really didn't affect me; it was not the answer for me. As a child, I had gone to Sunday school at the Congregational Church at the head of the harbor in McKinley, but that didn't have much effect on me either. I never belonged to any religion, and my parents left it up to us kids what we wanted to do.

Betty and Tucker got married a year after we did, and they are still married today.

For our honeymoon Sue and I took the train to New York City and stayed at the Hotel Dixie. When we got home, we rented the Jones cottage on Old Point Road, right across from the spot she and Betty lived when we met. We lived there only until June because it was a winter rental. The Joneses came back, and we got a cottage in Bernard. We lived there for a year and a half until we bought a house on the High Road in Southwest Harbor.

Dad Passes On

My father's last fishing trip was in the middle of April of 1966, only he didn't know it at the time. One day my father and I were going to go hand-lining, just the two of us. I went up to his house about two o'clock in the morning, and my father said, "I don't think I am going to be able to go today. I have tightness across my chest and I am short of breath…. Well, maybe I might be able to go and, if I can't fish, I'll just lay down on the locker."

"No, Dad," I said, "If you are sick, you are not going." I went down and got my wife Sue, who was a nurse, to have a look at him.

"Frank," she says, "you have to go to the doctor and get examined. No way can you go out fishing today." So we took my dad to the doctor, and they put him in the hospital. He'd had a heart attack. He insisted up and down that he had indigestion. He was seventy.

On the last day of my father's life I was out fishing. My sister was over visiting him that day and, when I stopped by, she came out crying.

She said, "He is going to die."

I said, "We don't know these things, Olive."

"I talked to the doctor. He says he acts like someone who has had rheumatic fever. He is not recovering. The doctor thinks he's dying."

Sue and I went over to see him that night and he said, "I feel like there is a bubble in my head, right between my ears." He wanted to be alone, by himself, and we respected that.

That night, May 4, 1966, Sue and I were lying in bed when we both popped right up, looked at each other. As I said, "Dad is here," she simultaneously said, without a split-second difference, "Your father is here."

You could feel his essence, just like he was sitting in that room. I know full well when a person dies, whatever the presence is, that soul, that essence, it still exists; it is just that its dimensions change. You couldn't see his shape, but you could feel it, and I said, "My God, can you—it's like he is here in person! Let's see how long it takes the hospital to tell us."

Fifteen minutes later, at a quarter past nine, the telephone rang. Sue answered it and came back and stood in the bedroom doorway. I said, "He has died, hasn't he?" She nodded. We got dressed and his presence was still there, following us as we went out of the house. Then, as I closed the door, we both said at the same time, "He's gone," just like that.

My oldest brother, Frank, who was forty-eight at that time, had been working in a machine shop in Ellsworth because his wife was from there and didn't want to leave. But Frank had always thought of coming home and fishing with Dad. He had gone out with him before World War Two and then again for a brief period after the war. When Father died, Frank came back home. He couldn't wait to get out of Ellsworth. He took over my father's boat and traps, which was all right with my mother and the rest of the family. We brothers and sisters never fought with each other over Father's boat; it was fine with us that Frank had it. As for his leaving his wife's home town, I don't know what it was like for her, but she kept quiet about it in public.

A UFO Visits Maine

The spring that Dad died, I went fishing with Frank often. It was in August 1966 that Frank and I left the harbor at our usual time, about one-thirty in the morning. We were trawling and had a two-hour or so run out into the ocean before we could set our trawls. Somewhere around a quarter of two, as we were coming between Black Island and Placentia, planning to run right out between the two islands and down into Green Island Channel, something unexpected happened.

It was a dark night, clear. Whoever or whatever it was could certainly see us coming. We had four running lights on: one red, one green, two white. We were the only boat traveling out from Bass Harbor at that time, all alone out there. Frank was standing in the companionway on the port side of the boat and I was steering on the starboard side, so he didn't see what I saw at first. I looked out over top of Placentia, and I can't say just how high, but maybe 1,000 feet up, maybe 1,500 into the sky, I saw—knowing not what else to call it—a spaceship.

This spaceship—if you have seen *Close Encounters of the Third Kind*—whatever they designed up for that spaceship was the size of this one. It was gigantic. It had no lights around the outer perimeter of it like it did in the movie. The ship was in total darkness and silhouetted beautifully in the sky. We could see it just grand!

Right out of the center of the bottom of it, there came a big shaft of light—a spotlight—and they were shining that light down on the island of Placentia. Now Placentia is quite large, about five miles around the perimeter. The spaceship was radiating light on the island in a circle of fifteen feet diameter.

I called for my brother and said, "Frank, come over here a minute and take a look and tell me what you see...."

"Jesus!" he says, "What is it?"

"Is that a figment of our imagination?"

"No."

"Do you *really* see it?"

"Yes."

"You sure you're not imagining this, Frank, or are you seeing it like I am?"

"I am seeing it, Wendell; I am seeing it!"

"If you reported that to the Air Force, they'd tell you that you never saw it or that that light has always been there. Frank, have you ever seen anything like it?"

"Never," he says.

"Obviously there's things up there that we don't know about."

"I'd say we know about it now!"

We watched the show in the sky for five minutes or so. The lights themselves I'd seen a few times before 1965, but I had never seen the object that made the lights like this time. Sometimes, on these earlier ones, the lights would go on all at once and go off all at once; they'd come on in sequence and go off in sequence. They'd go horizontal and then they'd go vertical. But not this one; it just stayed lighted in the sky.

Our boat engine was running, but I could hear no sound

coming from a ship engine. Like a damn fool, rather than stay there and watch and study and observe it, I had to get smart. Thinking about what I had done on previous occasions and unable to resist showing off, I said to Frank, "You want to see your little brother make them shut down that light?"

"I'd like to know what in the hell you are going to do about it!" he replied.

"Watch." I headed the boat straight for it and I flipped the running lights on and off three or four times and, sure enough, they shut the light right off up there in that spaceship. The whole ship just disappeared.

Frank looked at me and said, "How did you know that they were gonna do that?"

"I didn't know one hundred percent, but I had a pretty good idea because I'd played around with others before—unidentified flying lights. If you flash your lights at 'em, they'll shut 'em off! I have never seen what's made the light before this one, and I've certainly never seen a light quite like the one we just saw, but I have seen others just as strange. I figured they would turn their lights off when they knew we could see them."

We kept on going down Green Island Channel and by the time we had gotten about two miles out down the channel, I turned around and looked. "Frank!" I said, "They have stayed right put! They have the light back on again!"

Needless to say, if I ran across such a spaceship again, I would not be so hasty and foolish. I would not put boasting before trying to learn something about a great mystery. Maybe I'd be considered more of a fool, though. I'd do everything I could do to watch that spaceship, make contact. If I had someone like my brother there again to help me, I would try to inch the boat up in towards the shore. I'd go ashore and up through the woods and I would get right under that spotlight! Whether it would be my last mistake or not, I don't know. I'd take my chances.

The Sardine Factory

My brother and I finished out the summer fishing together. When September came, he went lobstering in Father's boat. He got very sick in October and had a heart attack just like Father did. In January of 1967, the same month and year my daughter Mary was born, Frank passed away. He was forty-nine years old.

Sue and I settled into married life. She dropped the nursing and became a mother and housewife. Wayne was born February 22, 1969, and Frank was born February 5, 1970. That, along with Mary, was our family.

When I was single, I used to start lobstering around the 20th of March, and then I'd combine it with hand-lining and trawling, and my working year went to about the end of December. During January, February, and March I'd take my vacation down the East Coast, usually including New York City. Then I'd spend the rest of that time rebuilding or repairing my fishing gear for the following year.

Once I was married, I saw that I would have to work twelve months a year to support a family, so that first year I got a job at the sardine factory in McKinley. I worked there for only thirty-six hours before deciding the factory life was not for me.

Men had the helping roles as far as preparing sardines for the market. Women did all the packing, and they got paid by what they had done, not the hour—so they wanted to be working at all times. It was piecework. If you had the job of supplying them, you had to keep their tables full of fish so that they didn't lose time. You had to be on your toes, make sure you didn't leave anyone's table empty.

You also had to be careful you didn't play favorites, that you didn't favor one over the other, that you didn't give one a better rack of fish than another. See, if the size of the fish was larger, you could make faster time packing the cans. They could look in a minute and see if a rack was lacking in any way. If a woman got a tray of smaller fish one time, you better make sure she had larger ones the next time.

I'd hear, "I guess Wendell doesn't want me to have any fish just now." Not rude or anything, just enough to keep you on your toes. They would not tolerate a second of you slowing them down. They didn't want to go slack. They took great pride in how many years they had worked at one particular table. A woman would tell you she had worked forty or fifty years at the same table, and she had a track record she wanted to maintain.

I liked the women, but they were strict about how they worked. That's just the way it was. The sardine factory was fair; they treated me well; I had no bitching or complaints. I was just not created to be a factory worker. Of course, if you work at a job for thirty-six hours, you can hardly call it a career.

Occupation: Fisherman

I decided that I wanted to make a living with my boat, so I took a scallop drag and went scalloping for the remainder of that winter. That took me through to the spring of the next year, when I set my traps out around the 20th of March. For the next eighteen years when it became winter, I lengthened my traps out for deeper water and went winter lobstering, and then I'd take my traps up in March. Even though the scalloping was successful, I felt the lobsterfishing made more money and, unlike scallop-dragging, I didn't have to do it every day, and that gave me more time to repair my equipment during the winter.

I usually lobstered from the 20th of March until early June. I'd start hand-lining for codfish and pollock as well as continue lobstering in May and somewhat in June, but no later than July. Then I took up my traps and hauled out my boat for two weeks to dry her out, sand her, paint her, and do any major maintenance that needed to be done on her. After that I would go tub trawling for hake, haddock, and cod from early July to early September. Then I'd set my lobster traps again and fish until late February. Sometimes I'd drag for scallops in Blue Hill Bay at the same time I was lobstering, and one winter I went shrimping with Merton Rich out of Bass Harbor to Duck Island, Long Island, and Spoon Island up off Isle Au Haut.

Most days I went fishing, and Sue kept the house and cooked the meals. I gave her some of my best Maine recipes, like one for tongues and cheeks of cod. The lower chin part of the under jaw of the fish is called the tongue even though it's not actually the tongue of the fish, and the cheeks are right in the hollow of the jaw, making two round pieces of meat shaped like scallops. You dip 'em in an egg batter, put 'em in a bag with flour and salt and pepper, and shake it, then salt and pepper and fry them in a frying pan. They sound gross, but they're delicious.

Sue, I, and the children used to take hikes together as a family—Wonderland, Ship Harbor, Sand Beach and, as the kids got older, we went up on the mountains. They are plenty of them on Mount Desert; that's how it got its name—Champlain called it "the isle of barren hills," of course in French, so the "desert" and the "hill" was reversed. The tallest, Cadillac, is the tallest on the whole East Coast, not counting inland mountains like Katahdin or Mount Washington. Some of the others we hiked were Sargent, Parkman, Western, Beech Mountain, Saint Sauveur,

Flying Mountain, Acadia, Norumbega, Pemetic, the Bubbles overlooking Jordan Pond, Champlain, and Gorham. We'd go swimming in Echo Lake, Long Pond, and Somes Pond, and in the pool in the Holiday Inn over to Ellsworth and the YMCA in Bar Harbor in the wintertime.

We also would go to the theater together—*Cinderella, Grizzly Adams*—Walt Disney movies were popular with us.

Sometimes we would take my boat and go with a picnic to an uninhabited island, Pond Island, Black Island, or Ship Island, all in Blue Hill Bay, and we'd have the place all to ourselves. As Mary, and then Wayne and Frank, got old enough, we let them explore—watch birds, pick berries, scale or skip rocks over the water.

We also sometimes would go out in the boat and observe the seals or take a ride with no goal, just a boat ride. I took the kids lobstering with me since they were toddlers, but only one at a time for safety's sake.

One of our closest friends was Father Gower; he used to come over for spiritual and ecological discussions. About that time, Father Gower met Ed Kaelber, who I think had been a professor at Harvard, and these two men got the idea of starting a college over to Bar Harbor. When they were planning, they would meet in our kitchen in Bernard and talk about fundraising. Between Jim Gower and Ed Kaelber getting donations from the wealthy people and businesses on the island, College of the Atlantic was born, just as they hoped. Where the college stands today, there used to be an Oblate Seminary belonging to the Catholics. But it was no longer being used as such, and my understanding of it is that Father Jim did his utmost as a Catholic priest to get this to become an environmental college. Ed Kaelber gave up his teaching job and came here to run the new school.

Soon Sue and I began to see that we were two different types of people, and we each began to gravitate towards other people who were more on our wavelength. We were opposites in how we done life. She being a nurse, she'd chart life. It seemed to me that she'd plot it right down perfectly: you are either right or you're wrong. I was more philosophical and very breezy. I used to say she was like the infantry: you either hit the target or you miss it. I was more like the artillery: if we came within fifty yards of the target, we'd call it a bull's eye.

East is east and west is west, and the twain should never meet. We never did get it together, but we felt the kids should have both a mother and a father, and the kids came first. The relationship certainly made for a good family—no problem there. I felt the kids needed their mother to be home when they were young, and I worked hard to provide that. We stayed married for twenty-two and a half years.

A Local Psychic

Sue and I both liked to read religion and philosophy, and we made friends with lots of interesting people. Our circle included Jesuit priests, school teachers, nurses, and college students. One friend of ours was Bernice Damon, a psychic in Brewer; we used to go to her house for sessions and courses. I may have some abilities, but I don't have any of her gifts—none whatsoever.

She could read letters blindfolded and, when the spirits required, she could write foreign languages that she didn't understand. We had séances, and sometimes she would get a message in another language, and a person there would say, "That's okay. I'm French. I can make it out." The person would understand, and Bernice would write the words, but *she* didn't understand any of them. They just came through her.

Sometimes when she was doing a reading a certain odor would go through the house. It would be the scent of lilacs or lavender. Somehow the spirits were able to make a particular smell. She told me she could take a book and put it under her pillow and sleep on it and be able to absorb the content of the book that way. So it would come to her through her psychic gifts.

She was a very strong woman, physically very tough. When we'd have her and her husband Irving to our house on the island for dinner, I'd serve lobsters, and she'd crack the shell with her hand by hitting it. Wham! She could split it like it was nothing. It wouldn't hurt her a bit. It was like a martial artist preparing lobsters for dining. I told Irving, "If you two ever have a fight, I hope you keep it verbal because she'll kill you."

A Premonition—Mother Passes On

In the month of August 1967, my oldest sister Phyllis and my mother were down in the state of New Jersey visiting Phyllis' daughter Kay and, while they were down there, I was lobstering back home. One day I was running down the east side of Big Gott's Island, not expecting anything unusual, when something *very* unusual happened. I saw, fifty feet ahead of the boat, a coffin loom right up above the water. The coffin was open: my mother was lying there in state, dressed in a pink dress. The vision faded as quickly as it had come. I thought, "Oh my God, Mother is gonna die."

Phyllis and my mother got back a little later from New Jersey with no problems. I went to visit Mother, and she said, "Wendell, there is something wrong with that sister of yours!"

"What do you mean?"

"Phyllis could not wait to get me home from New Jersey. I know what her problem is: she thinks I am going to die."

"Well, Phyllis, she is a little bit different," I replied. "We'll just have to go with that, huh?" The truth was, though: I may have been psychic, but Phyllis was *very* psychic.

As soon as I got back home I called my sister: "Phyllis, I have got to tell you something. When you and Mother was down to New Jersey, I had a premonition in the boat. I saw a coffin with Mother inside and she was dressed in a pink dress!"

Phyllis said, "I had the same premonition."

"Exactly?"

"Exactly."

"She is going to die, isn't she? "

"Yes. Wendell, I am afraid she is."

I was in the barbershop a few days later, over in Southwest, having my hair cut when I heard the ambulance go through town. When I got home, my wife Sue said that they had just taken Mother to the hospital. They thought she had a heart attack. About ten days later she died.

Now Phyllis and I had nothing to do with the funeral arrangements on purpose, but our youngest sister Olive did. She never asked for my advice and I never volunteered any, but Olive did ask advice from Phyllis, and Phyllis said, "Olive, I cannot help you. Do whatever you want, make any decision you need to. It will be fine. I will explain it to you later."

Olive did as much, and the night we went to view my mother's body, Phyllis and I met outside the funeral home and went in together, arm in arm. We walked up to where the coffin was and there was our mother, lying in a coffin the color we had seen in our premonitions and in a pink dress.

"Is this what you saw, Phyllis?"

She said, "Exactly."

I Learn about Ecology

In September 1969, Father Gower sent an anthropology graduate student to see me and Sue. We invited him over to dinner—Richard Grossinger and his wife Lindy. They arrived around 5 P.M. with their baby son Robin, about Wayne's age. We had two big dogs then, a one hundred-pound golden retriever named Joe and a sixty-pound mutt named Butch. No sooner than Richard and Lindy got in the door, those dogs were jumping all over them. The record player had clown music going, and Sue was preparing at least five dishes in the kitchen, so she waved hello from around the corner. They must have thought they entered the madhouse.

We greeted each other, introduced ourselves, and Richard explained that Father Jim had sent him over to pursue his study of our local fishing customs. It was hippie years, and Richard, coming from out of Maine, had long hair and a beard. I decided to play professor, so I put my thumbs in my suspenders and told him to go ahead and fire away. We were pretty deep into territory, gear, and finding directions at sea when Sue signaled me from the kitchen. I says, "Sue and I thought we'd serve you our famous tongues and cheeks of cod as an introduction to our way of eating."

After dinner I told Richard he should come down to the wharf and meet some of the other men. I was there early the next day and told Lester Radcliffe to be hospitable, and I've already mentioned one of the results of his first conversation with Lester! I also told some of the other fishermen—Merton Rich, Fillmore Turner, Bill Sargent, Harve Moore, and Jasper Rich—to talk to him. I said that I thought he was okay.

I almost changed my mind quickly, though. Richard and I had an argument that winter about ecology. He had the advantage because he interviewed me for his magazine *Io,* and then, without telling me or me expecting it, took issue with me in the following pages. The topic was nature. Richard had new ideas about the environment and our place in it. I said, back then, that man was meant to subdue nature, and Richard took my statement and put it in a piece about the damage we were doing to the planet. The way the pieces were positioned, I was the bad example.

Well, I have got to admit, his philosophy was different from what I was used to on the wharf and very different from anything I had ever seen in the Army. I would say that up to that time I was a fisherman with a fisherman's ideas. I had the same philosophy of probably most working people. I was into the writings of Eric Hoffer, who had been a stevedore on the docks of San Francisco. Hoffer made the working man feel good about himself. He spoke of how we were meant to control nature. Even though I was for conservation, I didn't really think it through. I thought man was still in charge. People talked about global warming even back then and how the melting of the ice caps would cause the whole East Coast to go underwater. I thought, "Men'll do something to prevent it. They'll build something against it." Now I'm not so sure.

I came to a new viewpoint only gradually over many years. It was a time of change on the Maine coast as well as the country as a whole. I came to realize that I agreed with Richard. As a fisherman I started looking at the ocean more carefully—what we had done to the sea. Factory trawling, pair trawling, purse seining, and such have substantially eliminated the fish.

My father and I could pull in more fish with a handline back in the mid 1960s in a day than some of the large ocean-going boats catch today in a week. We have devastated the oceans. I turned against dragging and became an even stronger opponent later when I learned from people like Jacques Cousteau, who put cameras on the wing boards of a drag and demonstrated what the new fishing technology does to damage the ocean floor, the home of the fish.

My God, the new industrial boats are so much larger than the fishing fleet of my youth. Once they entered local territory, they used to fish right around the clock. Over a twenty-five or thirty-year period they decimated the fishing stock. Those foreign ships were the worst; the mother ships were floating factories, six, seven hundred feet long, whole cities really. They ground everything from the ocean—the bottom itself, the shells, the sculpins, pogges, and other trashfish—into meal right there. The vessels off the mother ship themselves were two hundred, three hundred feet long, and they went out each day and brought their catch back to the factory. The crew was changed every few months, but the boats stayed out there fishing—if you'd call it that—for six years, and the only thing that brought them back home was the life of the engine. They were governments, and we were competing for our Mom-and-Pop outlets. We were like the old Indians with flint hooks compared to their moon-rocket technology. But the Indians never fished the sea out, and the factory trawlers certainly did. You can't tell people about the danger of overfishing when they're catching them. They say there's an unlimited supply of everything; you couldn't begin to catch all of them. But after a few years go by and they have done it, then they're quite willing to find some sort of conservation.

Gradually I began to speak with people who I thought would be interested or at least open, and I found some agreed with me and some did not. I was too far out there for most of my fisherman friends. The way of life of these new people like Richard was not quite what the people 'round here was used to.

A Heavy Wind off Great Duck

In November of 1969 I encountered the heaviest breeze that I ever met fishing. On the morning of the great wind I was out in the boat whose name I had changed from *The Wolfhound* to *Gramp* in honor of my father. It was a questionable day; there were gusts blowing to the southeast at fifteen knots, and most of the other boats stayed in. I can't say why I chose to go when so many fishermen sat it out. "You have to choose a way," I said to myself, as I sometimes do. "So we'll go this way."

I hauled outside the Duck Islands, and I baited traps out there until nine or nine-thirty with no problem. Yet the wind kept gradually increasing. I came inside Great Duck and hauled down the west side of the island next. That gave me a lee from the southeast wind that was coming right out of the ocean. Then I went over to Little Duck and hauled on the west side of the small island, once more in a lee, and when I got done around eleven o'clock, I washed the boat up and had my sandwich. That was a mistake. By the time I got done with lunch and all, which was about eleven-thirty, the southeast winds had increased to about twenty-five knots.

The ocean was all feathery whitecaps, but still it was no problem; my little boat could handle it well. I started from Little Duck Island headed for Bass Harbor Head. I got about a mile inside the island when something happened that was very extraordinary. The winds, in the twinkling of an eye—and when I say twinkling of an eye I am talking literally, not figuratively—increased from twenty-five to fifty-five knots. I was used to fishing in west-northwest winds up to thirty knots and, if the wind was coming southeast, by the time it got to twenty-five knots it was time to come home because, when the wind comes southeast it is coming right out of the ocean, not from the shore. This time the tide was ebb, so it was going right against the wind, making the ocean a combing sea. They were no longer choppy waves; they were breaking just as you can see down to Seawall or along Ocean Drive, or any place where the open ocean comes right in on the hard shore in a storm.

I saw I had made a mistake. There was no way I was going to get back to Little Duck because if I had faced the boat into the wind the seas would have just rim-racked her. The waves were way too much for my boat now, but going with the sea I stood a fighting chance. I realized that once I got into Bass Harbor Bar with the tide ebb and the winds southeast, the water might be breaking right clear to the bottom. If it was and I got in there I couldn't reverse my mistake, so I shifted course and went to the outside of Great Gott's Island. I was well outside the west side of Big Gott's, a place I figured there would not be breaking clean to bottom, giving me plenty of water to come in through.

I closed the cabin door, just in case the sea crashed aboard the boat, so that it wouldn't go down into the cabin and flush the engine out. I had no time to get a life jacket. They were up forward in the bow. As the sea would cockle and break, I would have the boat running along about fifteen hundred revolutions just to keep up with the waves somewhat and, as soon as each wave broke, it would come crashing down behind the stern of the boat. *Gramp* would start lifting like a sea duck then. The water would just pick her right up. When she was caught in the trough of the sea I took her right out of gear, put her completely in neutral, and let her go at the mercy of the wave. When finally the crest of the wave went and I was coming down the other side, I'd put her in gear and start the whole process over again. She had enough wood in her that she would have remained floating but, if I could have kept her going or not after a wave came aboard, I don't know. If just one wave had crashed aboard of her, it wouldn't have likely sunk the boat. Without the engine, the waves would eventually just crash down on her and stave her up and that would be it. Another danger was that when the boat was on the crest of the wave—right up on top of it—she could get going too fast. I was afraid if she was caught up there the wave could pitchpole her right over. The whole boat would broach and that would have been the end of the story too. But fate was with me.

I was approaching the west side of Little Gott's Island, and I had only another thousand feet to go. Out where the tide was rushing from the bay into the ocean, the waves were still maintaining their full strength but, where the tide no longer had an effect on the ocean, there were suddenly calm waters. It was just as calm as the sheet of paper on which this is written. Where it changed, it changed instantly, as if a sorcerer was laying out a papyrus.

The home stretch was a very long one thousand feet, a long time to wonder whether I'd make it or not when the next wave would have been my last. But *Gramp* came skating right out of those combing seas into calm water, and I knew I was home safe. I came across Blue Hill Bay, which was a piece of cake, and was back at the dock.

It was obviously a damn fool thing I done, staying out there or maybe even going out in the first place. Lester Radcliffe was so mad with me he couldn't even speak. He wouldn't say a word. I unloaded my lobsters, and he weighed them while I fueled the boat up. He handed my tubs back to me and I figured we had better break the ice sometime, so I says, "Lester, Jesus, what can I say? I got caught."

Now Lester was my dealer through thick and thin over all my years of fishing. Lester was also the house mother, godfather, proprietor, captain, head honcho, the minister of the place—"the man," as they like to say nowadays.

His dead silence was just his way of showing concern for me. He never expected to see me again. It was a silence out of caring for me. It wasn't about the boat, God knows. I was no longer renting his boat—I had my own now.

I checked out three reliable sources as to what the wind had done that day. One was a lobsterfisherman named Harry Smith, who was an honest man. He said he clocked winds at fifty-five knots. Halsey Pettigrew used to go on a sardine carrier for the Underwood's factory in McKinley, and he told me he clocked the winds at fifty-five knots also. The Coast Guard in Southwest Harbor also clocked winds at fifty-five knots. *Gramp* had been out in a full storm, not just a gust but a continuous fifty-five-knot wind. Ralph Stanley built a very good boat, and she brought me home.

A New Kind of Education

All my life I have had a spiritual feeling and a psychic sense. It has nothing to do with religion. For all I know it is connected with my being born with a caul around me. Or maybe it ran in the family, since my sister Phyllis was even more psychic than I. As for my sense of the environment and nature, some of that comes from fishing itself. The ocean I knew growing up was teeming with fish and lobsters, whales and seals, and it felt like a very good, natural, rounded world to be in. There was something magical, even spiritual, about taking a line of steam-tarred cotton with steel hooks and a lead weight, rather primitive equipment, dropping it into this frothy ocean that spread to all horizons, so much bigger than the human imagination, and pulling it in and finding it loaded with these huge, amazing creatures, weighing on the average thirty pounds—cod and pollock, but also such an amazing variety: dogfish, skates, sculpins, silver hake, slime eels.

When we got the slime eels, we would just cut the whole gangion off (the line that holds the hook to the ground line). We'd sacrifice it, because they're a creature you don't want to deal with. They're dark, a foot to a foot and a half long, and they lay down this web of slime. They just form it instantaneously. It goes over everything. If one of them gets into a fish, through the gills, it'll just clean it all out. You have to throw the fish away. They're a disgusting thing to catch on your hook, but they're part of nature and have a use and a place in the sea, even if not to humans.

The difference in me was between the old Wendell, the traditional fisherman, just cutting the gangions in irritation, and Wendell, the newborn naturalist, still irritated at the slime and the lifestyle of the creature, but appreciating the bounty, diversity, and resourcefulness of nature.

The penned-off area of the boat, which we called the kidboards, would be loaded with marketable fish. It could hold up to 5,400 pounds before they would begin falling off in back of the boat. One can think of them as just fish you catch, but each one of them had to be born from an egg and grow up to that size and get hungry enough to bite the hook. We were fishing in God's pond, catching the creatures he put in there eons ago, with a method for continuing their generations.

One sees lobsters crawling on ice in a restaurant and doesn't picture that they had to go into a trap that someone constructed out of wood in such a design that they couldn't figure their way out of it and stocked with bait that would interest them and entice them into it. If we could see the ocean bottom, these strange and wonderful creatures would be like the insects working their way through the soil, shellfish that evolved millions of years ago. This gave some perspective on the lobsterfishing industry and made fishing less like factory work and more like prayer. Science, in a way, led me back into religion.

I newly appreciated our fishermen's custom of setting the odd creatures that chanced upon our traps back in their homes so they could continue to maintain the health of the ecosystem and also live out their God-given lives.

My environmental education came mainly from the sea itself, though maybe I didn't recognize it at first. The pace of fishing taught me about the pace of nature. The mechanics of fishing taught me about the ecology I was working in.

I did have a bit of formal environmental teaching in sixth grade, though you would be surprised to hear who gave it to me. Admiral Richard Byrd, the explorer, came to the Casino Hall in Bar Harbor in 1948 and lectured and showed a silent movie about his journeys in the Arctic to all the elementary-school children on Mount Desert Island. At the end of his talk he said, "Many of you kids are reaching the age where you are wanting to go out into nature and hunt. I would like to give you a piece of advice. Go and hunt with a camera and not a gun. Shoot nature all you want to, and study her. If you do this, she will teach you many things."

I never forgot what he said.

Of course, if you are a commercial fisherman, as I have been, you might lapse a bit in these lessons. I guess Richard Grossinger caught me lapsing when he did that interview. I remember a time a few years after that, when he and his wife Lindy went out fishing with me for a day. That evening Sue cooked dinner for us, and we made it a hearty gathering with Father Gower as our guest. After the meal he, Richard, and I were sitting around with glasses of wine, shooting the breeze. The women, Sue and Lindy—well, maybe they were shooting their own breeze in another room. In any case, we were in the living room.

I asked Richard what he thought about me out there on the ocean, catching and killing fish. I suspected that he disapproved—at least part of him did. My suspicion turned out to be correct. He described me from his viewpoint in a piece of writing he published, and I still have it and can quote from it. It takes me back to that very day, but through someone else's eyes:

"Wendell lifts the fish, one by one, his hands in the eye-sockets, cuts open the mouth, tosses the innards into a bucket, and throws each body into a pile down by our end of the boat. Bright yellow oilcoat of Wendell, red blood on the deck, brilliant and rich like grenadine or ruby, spilled from creatures who were just living. Absolutely glowing. So bright the gulls are going crazy to get at it, following the boat in a mad ragtag army, until Wendell dumps a bucketload overboard, and they plummet, pecking away at each other, tearing the organs from the surface and flying off, while a new group joins us, eagerly waiting for Wendell to discard some more."

It goes to show how you do something your whole life and have no idea what it looks like to an outsider. I no longer saw the deaths of creatures or the blood or myself covered in red. I didn't even see my yellow slicker. I was just a fisherman doing his job.

"So, Richard," I said that night with Father Jim right there listening as if to a confession (and I have the exact words because Richard wrote them all down too, later that night before he went to bed), "do you consign me to some yogi or Hindu hell? Or do I have to go through endless transmigrations? Am I going to be reborn a cod or a lobster as my punishment?"

Richard said, "No, I don't want to have hired killers. We're all implicated. Yes, I empathize with the fish, and I feel sad about the spilling of life and the pain in the universe, but I don't know what to do about it. Anything else would be worse."

I responded to Richard by saying, "At least I don't rip the hell out of the bottom like some fishermen dragging. I can't keep from taking their lives, but I can keep from destroying their homes. Right, Father?"

Father Gower said that, according to his understanding of things, we're not part of the same spiritual cycle as fish and lobsters. That's more the Tibetan or American Indian way of thinking. I don't remember his exact words, but I believe he said, "Christ died so we could be fishermen."

It was good to know that we weren't doomed to having to be lobsters, caught in traps, and cooked in pots to pay for our livelihoods this time around. Anyway, I can't be a lobster the next time around because I've made up my mind I'm going to be a master aikidoist and Japanese tea pourer. But I'm getting ahead of myself here because I didn't change to that position until I had had a lot more experiences.

It was really a wonderful evening, and we three continued to discuss philosophy, ecology, and the fate of man and nature for another hour or two. I enjoyed the talk so much I kept pouring more and more red wine. I must have drunk quite a bit by the time we were getting sleepy because I spoke very openly when I said, "Right here is the closest that men can ever become, saying what's in their hearts. I've heard tell that a man and a woman in intercourse is the closest, but I'll have to question that. I doubt if any human beings are closer than we are now."

"Amen," the Father added.

Soon after that evening, Sue and I sold the house in Southwest Harbor and moved back to my home town of Bernard so as to be closer to Lester Radcliffe's wharf. We got a place on Columbia Street, right above the harbor. Not that Southwest was much of a commute, a few miles or so, but in Bernard I could see the scales for weighing lobsters from my kitchen window and just about hear Lester complaining to the fishermen.

Meeting the Nearings

I discovered Scott and Helen Nearing about that time. By then they were an elderly couple who were, as far as I can tell, the father and mother of modern organic farming. They had written a number of books; *Living the Good Life* was the one I read. It discussed leaving society and living off the land. The approach impressed both Sue and me.

Once in a while, we would give each other a free day. That meant that when she had a free day, I would watch the kids and, of course, when I would have a free day, it was vice versa. It'd give us each one of us a chance to go off and do whatever we wanted.

One of my free days back in March of 1971, I was driving around and I got as far as Ellsworth and thought, "I ain't interested in going to Bangor for nothing, for just a meal and a movie. I am going to Harborside to see if I can meet Helen and Scott Nearing." Harborside was only about an hour's drive from Ellsworth, hardly more than Bangor. I didn't call or nothing, just went unannounced. I had no trouble finding their homestead because Harborside was so small and the farm was just to the left, off the main road.

When I got there, real as life, looking like his picture, very weather-beaten, Scott was hauling wood with a sled down from a shed they had up across the field. He was in his nineties then; Helen was about twenty years younger. They were active, hard-working people and both very healthy. You would have never guessed their ages. Scott did look older, there is no denying that, but he was in good shape.

They made me feel that I wasn't intruding on them. In fact, I ended up helping Scott with his wood all that morning. We got along just fine. We worked well together, and we would chat as we worked. He explained that they broke their day down into four-hour time blocks—four hours for bread labor, so they called it, working for your livelihood, farming, gardening, or growing crops that they could sell, like strawberries; four hours for study and reading and intellectual pursuits; and four hours for writing. When they took time off, they called it a free day, and you had to follow *none* of the disciplined schedule—oddly the same name that Sue and I gave to the way of organizing our life that let me come there in the first place.

Scott also discussed the principles of organic farming and self-sufficiency. He said that chemical farming was like a person taking drugs to get a high; you keep it up and you'll deplete your body without giving it any nourishment back. Organic farming was like going with the natural flow of life. The land feeds you and then, in turn, you feed the land. You take something from the soil, and you give something back. That way you could farm the same piece of land for five thousand years, and the earth would be in better shape than what it was when you started. He said, "It's the same way that nature feeds herself. In this location it takes nature three hundred years to grow one inch of topsoil. Compared to a human life, that seems like a long period of time, but if you ask the rocks and the stars, they would tell you that was just a mere flash."

When it came to be lunchtime, Scott invited me to come on in and break bread with him and Helen. They only ate vegetarian food. Doing hard physical labor you can work up a good appetite, and I am not a vegetarian. I wasn't used to the food, so I was eating a lot of bread. Helen said, "What you want is protein," so she cut up slices of apple and put lots of peanut butter on it for me.

Later, I took my wife Sue and Father Gower and some of the College of the Atlantic students down there and introduced them to the Nearings. Of course, they just went nip and tuck with each other. Eventually Helen and Scott gave lectures at the college. One time, with Father Jim in the audience, Scott thought he should preach his own sermon: "Farmer Green was working out in his garden when the minister came by. The minister said, 'That's a very good-looking garden you and the Lord are growing.' The farmer replied, 'That may very well be so, but you should have seen what it looked like when the Lord was doing it by Himself.'"

Working a Different Sea

There was an interesting thing developing out on Great Duck Island. A psychiatrist named George Cloutier owned a property on Big Duck, and he started up what he called the Gestalt Institute of Maine out there. There were a lot of COA students that used to go off there to participate in Gestalt workshops. I provided transportation for that, and I did it for five years. I even attended some of the workshops and learned a lot about interacting.

When you are angry about something, the Gestalt therapists let you vent your rage. One of the ways they do it is that some people hold up a mattress and you can just punch it and name-call until you have released all your anger. I did that more than once. Before I did it the first time, George went and showed the group, mainly me, how to do it, by participating himself in expressing his rage at someone. Then I did it. I punched the mattress and hit it with all my strength and voiced what I thought about this particular person while I was punching. That's not something I would have imagined doing back in the old days in Bernard or in the Army. I'm sure none of my classmates or regiment buddies would have imagined it either.

George also tried to bring out the fact that you had to have closure on things. One afternoon at a workshop that I was participating in, he got news that an old friend of his, a bush pilot, had just died, so George suddenly started talking to this man as though he was right there with us, recalling some of the experiences that they had gone through together such as making an emergency landing in New Hampshire in a farmer's field. Right in the middle of the field was a stone wall. As they were coming down, they gunned the plane just enough to get over the wall, then started braking the plane down and, when she finally stopped, the propeller had smashed into the farmer's barn. When George got finished with the story, he bade his friend good-bye. Then he told us, "You need to say good-bye when people pass over."

My friend Billy Murphy was killed in an automobile accident on Long Hill in 1975. Billy and I had been close since childhood. In the workshop I got a chance to talk to him, and I broke down and wept. During that session, George instructed me to be sure to say good-bye. "You need that closure." So I did.

I said: "How comical you were as a kid. I always enjoyed your sense of humor. You were a great mechanic. You installed the engines in my boat. You pulled maintenance on 'em and my truck. You took my father places while I was in the Army. We played with each other as kids, and then I used your working abilities when we were adults. Your death came so quickly as an accident that I was just not prepared for it. I hate losing you. Thank you, and good-bye."

I will always be grateful to George for teaching me this practice and, when I go to funerals now and there is the opportunity to speak, I always speak to the person who has died and not the people attending.

Back in those days, College of the Atlantic was very small. In the summer, its Allied Whale Watch would travel to Mount Desert Rock, a research station run by the Coast Guard for observing whales and their migrations. Allied Whale used to hire me as a ferryman to take students there and back. Those were days I didn't go fishing.

I took another COA group to Ship Island in Blue Hill Bay for bird-watching and tagging the cormorants. There's quite a population out there. One of the cormorants raked a student's arms with his webbed feet, the claws in 'em, and gave him some wicked scratches. You get close to the little birds and, to protect themselves, they'll projectile-vomit at you. Of course, the cormorants didn't know that these were just COA students trying to look out for their interests. Nature is nature.

So I was spending my time with environmentalists, dealing with Gestalt therapists, visiting the Nearings, talking about reincarnation, and—you know—Holy God! this blew people's minds! One fisherman, who I won't name, came up to me and tried to reason with me because he felt I was getting in a situation that I didn't completely understand. Given the free thinking of the Gestalt therapists, there was a lot of open sex on the island and the fishermen knew it; in fact, the place had become known as Great Fuck Island instead of Great Duck.

This lobsterman said, "Don't you know, Wendell, that psychiatrists are crazy? I've dealt with those people before." When he found out I did know and didn't care and likewise had no intentions of letting go, he laughed at me in a ridiculing way. That laugh was his reply back to me.

I always thought that, for a working lobsterfisherman, I may have carried the greatest diversity of personalities on my boat that you can imagine from 1970 to 1978, and that counts the shellfish and the fish.

I also began working at the Oceanarium in Southwest Harbor during these years. I lectured in the lobster and fishing rooms from May into August on days I didn't fish. It was here, with David and Audrey Mills, that I learned about the biology of the lobster. I already knew about the fishing of them, and that's the subject I lectured on at first. Once I learned about their biology, I lectured on that too. I made the point that we needed a two-hundred-mile fishing limit and needed to enforce it—but the discussion came too late. The damage, in my opinion, was done. Unfortunately, I could never get the Oceanarium to take a strong enough stand on that for my satisfaction.

One of greatest compliments I was ever paid was in the lobster room when a marine biologist brought his son. He thought the talk would be on a very elementary level and that it would just be geared to his son's understanding—ten years old. He told David later, "As I listened to Wendell lecture on the biology of the lobster, I had to attend at every second to comprehend what he was telling the people."

Lester Radcliffe and I had always been good friends but, once I got to carting students around and ferrying folks out to Duck Island, that was a different ball of wax. One time, during a summer when the market price was high and lobsters were in such demand the dealers could never have enough of them, Lester expected lobsters from *Gramp* and me, and instead

I was bringing back people who'd been out to have Gestalt therapy. I was stopping by Thurston's for gas only, no lobster crates aboard. Lester was so exasperated that he said, "You, you, you, you … bird!" Then he thought about where I had been and added, "You, you … duck!"

Gill Netting with Merton Rich

For a few summers I went gill-netting with Merton Rich and his son Bruce. This was to replace hand-lining and trawling. These gill nets we had were fifty fathoms long, and we'd tie one net right upon the other. We had a marker pole, a keg, and a buoy, the same way we did trawling, and we ran out the anchor line and, once the line went to bottom, we had two fin assemblies over the stern of the boat with a fiberglass pipe connecting them, and we ran the nets out from it as the boat was going at high speed. Now there were two lines to gill nets, a lead line and float line, and as the nets settled to the bottom of the ocean, the float line would float the net up and the lead line would weigh nets down and, when they would go down and settle, it would be like a gigantic volleyball net under the sea. The net itself was made out of clear plastic monofilament that fish couldn't see. The fish would swim into the net and get caught by the gills.

Out within a five-mile radius of Mount Desert Rock is where we mainly fished. We would leave our nets setting overnight and haul them once a day and take the fish out while they were fresh. We caught hake, haddock, and pollock mainly; we also caught dogfish, which we did not save.

Merton would haul the nets while Bruce and I picked the fish out of them. We had one other man to dress and clean the fish while we were hauling. In the pen we would wash them off with a salt-water hose to cool their body temperature down quick. That kept our fish very fresh by the time we sold them on the market. The buyers were very happy with our catch.

At certain points while we were fishing this way our nets got into a grape-sized jellyfish called siphonophore. They'd come in unbelievably large numbers. This would make a very brown muddy slime in the nets, and the net would not fish because the fish would be able to see our strategy. The slime ultimately covered all our oilcloths. After a few days Merton started to get very sick. We had never known about this stuff before. You wouldn't notice it lobstering; you wouldn't notice it hand-lining; you wouldn't notice it trawling—but it would plug your gill nets full of the slime.

We called some marine biologists, and they told us what it was and said, "There's no one that won't get sick if they fish in it for a long time." So we would have to tie up until the siphonophore had passed, and then we'd fish again.

An Invitation to New Mexico

I met a lot of good people from the Gestalt group on Great Duck. One was a woman named Kim Lesser who was doing therapy there. She came from Albuquerque, New Mexico, with her husband Matthew and their teenage sons and young daughter. She worked with George Cloutier for a while and then, after six months, she and her family left and went back to Albuquerque.

In the winter of 1978 I got a phone call from her. "Wendell," she said, "come on out to Albuquerque for a two-week vacation on me." I showed some interest and, a few days later, I got a letter from her with a check to buy my plane ticket. I called and said I was coming but I wanted to haul my traps one more time and get 'em baited up.

New Mexico is as opposite from Maine as you can get; Wendell Seavey going there was like the northeast meets the southwest! It was dry, high elevation, Spanish and Pueblo Indian-oriented, different vegetation like cactuses and unusual flowers. The rocks were more colored and worn, and the landscape had these wide panoramas where you could see everything, almost as though you were on Mars. When the sun set and hit the Sandia Mountains east of Albuquerque, you could see three different colors—the top, the middle, and the bottom of the mountains like shades of watermelon, which is what the name means.

When I got back and described what I saw, my wife Sue said, "That is wonderful you had a trip, but how about us?!"

"Well," I said, "how about next winter I have the boat hauled out instead of winter lobster fishing and we'll go to Albuquerque all together?"

Stan and Ruth Grearson

Stan Grearson used to teach environmental education in the school system in the state of New York, and he also was a zoologist for the Museum of Natural History in New York City. Both he and his wife Ruth were knowledgeable about birds and natural history.

The first time I met Stan and Ruth was before I went into the Army, when I was fishing with my father. They saw me standing at the head of the wharf and came up to me and asked if I would take them out to the islands. They said that they had completed all the programs that Acadia National Park had to offer on the subject over a four-year period and wanted to branch off on their own in the three weeks' time they had. In particular, they wanted to film the bird life and seals out on Little Duck Island. Well, they picked the right fisherman because someone else might have barked, "Not interested." I offered to work a few trips in around my fishing schedule. It was as Admiral Byrd said—these were people who wanted to shoot nature with a camera and learn the lessons she had to teach.

The first day I called them to go, it was foggy and, despite the poor visibility, they were game. They brought all their cameras and sound-recording equipment, another couple, a toddler, a dog named Lady Bug who immediately shat on my platform, and Ruth's father—quite a menagerie. We packed everything, put everyone aboard, and off we went.

In the harbor we saw some cormorants, and Stan told me how he helped pass a law in New York to protect this species. This began my environmental lessons from him. He explained that nature makes things for a reason. The plankton in the ocean is fed when water pours over the shore, the wetlands and marshes, and spews into the sea, making up a broth, so much of the land's debris is food for the ocean. The ocean is also fed, in part, by the excrement of the birds.

"You notice the cormorant," is how Stan introduced this story, "when it takes off, there is a great stream of droppings come out of that bird, and that feeds the plankton. In turn, the plankton works its way up four stages, and then gets to the sea fleas, which the fish feed from, then whales and other mammals." So it is a recycled chain like on the Nearings' farm. Cormorants are like organic farmers. Even though it isn't obvious to the sight, seafood that we fishermen catch is linked to cormorants and their compost heaps. Before Stan pointed that out to me, I was like other fishermen. It was an indifferent ocean bird. It didn't hold my interest.

When we got down to Bass Harbor Bar, there was a solid wall of fog. All I had for navigation was a pocket watch and compass. I didn't even have a tachometer but, like my father before me, I knew how to navigate. Once we were underway, I got down in the cabin and came back up. No one noticed it but Stan; he asked me what I was up to. I said, "I was listening to the sound of the engine to see how fast she was turning. I have to shoot a compass course for Little Duck and estimate a time we are going to get there."

Ten years later he told me how impressed he was with my navigation. He was a fanatic on time, and he timed me that day. He said I was off a mere twenty-seven seconds from what I had said the journey would be, going to Little Duck Island from Bass Harbor Head—then he knew he could trust me.

We got to the island fine, and the Grearsons and crew went ashore and took pictures and made recordings of the birds. The equipment could magnify sound and pick up a conversation a half-mile off.

We went out many times that summer, and they kept coming back over the years.

I used to go listen to their lectures on birds and the environment at the college. Stan could mimic a bird's calls perfectly. He told me that he was out rowing one night with another man and his calls were so convincing that a heron came down and landed on the other man's head. Another time, at night, he was outdoors in camouflage clothes and by blowing into his fist, he could make the sound of a mouse, a quick squeak using his lips and fist. He would kiss the hole made by his first two rounded fingers, sort of the way we would make a farting sound as children. An owl who was looking to hunt mice came down and smashed him in the head and knocked him unconscious.

He was also quite psychic. In the early 1960s, as a zoologist with an expedition, he went down to Australia and New Guinea. He used to have dreams and visions that showed him caves that the natives didn't even know were there.

Stan would always look for harm from pollution. In one place in New York State he noticed that the grass and trees were not right; the leaves were limp, and the grass was thin. He went right into the head office of the factory that was causing it and announced to the surprised managers, "You people are not doing what you agreed to do to protect the environment." He turned towards this file in their office and declared, "In the third drawer of that cabinet is the paper that proves it, and I am going to tell you what it says."

He had the ability to read that paper word for word remotely. They were in awe or shock or maybe both.

"You are either going to correct these things," he continued, "or I am going to report you to the federal government."

Back then the government might have cared to correct the violations; nowadays, who knows? Stan had never seen that paper himself, but it was there; he was right.

It was as if you were sitting reading my book in a store, and then you looked up at the shelf and were able to say, "On page 127 in this other book, there's something very interesting." I can't do any of that, but I guess there's something about me that attracts people who can. After all, Stan's most dramatic psychic event I witnessed was when he walked right up to me on the dock that first time and picked me out, a regular old fisherman for all he knew, to be his guide.

When Stan heard about my plan to take the family to Albuquerque, he was concerned. "How are you going to support yourself when you get out there?" he asked me.

"I don't know, Stan, maybe shovel shit on a pony farm." It was a flip response.

Stan said, "I think you would be good at talking."

I said, "I'm not good at much else."

He said, "If you take me around the docks and show me the ins and outs of lobsterfishing, I will make up a slide show. I can mix lobster fishing and the sea-bird life in this area. I'll make you up your own carousel of slides. You can take it around and use it to give lectures. It can be one of the means by which you earn your way on your trip."

At that time, Stan was teaching a course on environmental studies to all the elementary-school teachers on Mount Desert Island, and he set it up so I could present my first lecture to this group. He called it "getting my feet wet."

"I will advise you that, when you start giving lectures, you are going to get nervous and you'll forget what you wanted to say. Rely on your memory; don't take notes. Just wing it the best you can."

Adventures in New Mexico

On December 18, 1978, Sue and I and the kids left for Albuquerque and arrived the day after Christmas. We rented an unfurnished apartment. In fact, we never did furnish it — we ate sitting on the floor the whole time. The guest of honor got an ice cooler to recline on; that was the closest thing we had to a chair. We slept on mattresses and sponge foam. The kids loved it.

New Mexico is very dry. As one visitor once said, "It's so dry you even have to prime yourself to spit here." I had to keep a half-gallon jug of water by my bed; I'd wake up just parched. I'd guzzle it right down. Coming from New England, you have to acclimate yourself to the parchedness and dryness of the land and its elevation above sea level. After a while I adapted to it.

I got a job working forty hours a week at a seafood market

on Eubank Street called The Fishnet. Then one day I attended a meeting of the board of directors of the Albuquerque school district for the middle, elementary, and high school and made my proposal for their approval. At the time, it was the seventh largest school district in the country. During the meeting, the superintendent asked me if I was a certified lecturer.

"No," says I.

He says, "I won't let you in the schools till I see what you have to offer." Then he told me he'd give me a half hour to show my slides to the three members of the board. I replied, "That's not fair to me or to the school system."

So he asked, "How much time do you want?"

"Oh, a couple of hours."

He said, "Okay, we'll split the difference at an hour."

When the time came, I ran through the carousel and the school-board members enjoyed it so much that I was there two hours anyway while I did my thing for them. Afterwards, the superintendent said, "Here's the deal. We have got no money appropriated for you since we didn't know you were going to show up. So, if some teacher needs to take some time off, we'll hire you to come in to look out for the class that day and show your slide show. Or, if some teacher can—fat chance—talk her class out of doing a field trip, then we'll invite you again."

After the meeting, they ran a notice on their bulletin boards for the teachers in the district to read: I was available. Well, I got all kinds of invitations and, whenever I would get a chance to do slide shows for the school system, I'd jump at it. Once I started presenting my bird and lobster show from Maine to the children of New Mexico, word of mouth spread across the state. That may sound egotistical, but it's true; it's the way it went. Through a friend I got a chance to do two showings at the Santo Domingo Pueblo reservation, one for the children in the morning and one for the adults in the afternoon. The Sebola Forest rangers also invited me, and for the life of me, I don't know how they found out about it. I also did nursing homes and people's private houses. Sometimes I would do a lecture for money and sometimes for free. Sometimes I would get gifts instead of money. I got a bolo tie and turquoise belt buckle for one of my private talks for a family.

During the spring around planting time, the Pueblos at Santo Domingo invited the public to their dances. These dances were done by all age groups, from the young kids to the parents to the grandparents; all participated. It was for getting rain for their crops. They were in their proper clothing attire for this dance; they had on their feathers and head gear. The little ones were being taught all the time. If one of them was out of line, an elder would guide him back into place. It was taken very seriously.

When they were doing the dances that afternoon, it was a beautiful sunny day with no clouds in the sky. After the dances were over and we were headed back to Albuquerque, we noticed a big dark cloud forming. It looked like it was filled with rain. That impressed all of us greatly. I said, "My God, it worked." There was no indication of rain prior to that.

The Albuquerque school system offered that if I would stay another year, they would appropriate money for me. I said no, it was time to go home to Maine. I needed to put my kids back in school, and we wanted to live with furniture again. We returned on the tenth day of May, just in time to take up spring lobstering.

From the Boatyard to Boston

I had fished straight from the time I got out of the Army until 1982. There were not many lobsters that year. A plague of stone crabs come right over the bottom; it was just a great invasion of crabs. Around February I was getting low on funds and approaching the March hill. With a family relying on me, I had to climb the hill, so I went for a steady job at Bass Harbor Marine.

The foreman asked me if I had carpentry skills and I said no. He asked me if I had rigging skills and I said no. He asked me if I had mechanical skills and I said no. He said, "Well, you tell us what you think you can do for us."

I knew their moorings were poorly rigged; a lot of them were parting and the boats were coming ashore, doing great damage, so I said, "I can rig your moorings so they're safe for you and you don't lose any more boats."

They hired me to re-rig the moorings and then assigned me to the yard crew. The job included painting the bottoms of the boats, waxing their hulls, pulling the boats out of the water with the travel lift to store them, relaunching them later, and filling the buildings with firewood. In the winter it would take three cords of wood once a week to heat two buildings; we had such big stoves that they would take a four-foot log. It was hard work, physically almost as demanding as fishing.

As it turned out, I stayed at the boatyard all the way until July of 1985. I sold *Gramp* in June of 1983 while I was working there. The lobsterfishing was so bad that it was not worth going back out to sea. In fact, the whole of it was bad, all the fishing— I guess one could say the ocean was finally all fished out.

During those three years I worked five or six days a week, whatever the season was, and never took a vacation. I simply needed to make the money for Sue and the kids, and the plague of stone crabs meant no lobsters worth talking about. I took a jacket and a pair of shoes out of the company dumpster to save money, and I wore those everyday. The jacket got so pitted that one day Steve Keiser, who worked there, asked me if I couldn't afford a better one.

I told him, "I hope life never puts you into a position where you have to do the same to keep the boat afloat."

In the spring of '85 I decided I wanted different work than I had at the boatyard, so in March I went to Boston looking for a job as a lecturer on lobster fishing, carrying my Albuquerque credentials. My wife's home town, remember, was Lynn, Massachusetts, and her mom, dad, brother, and sister-in-law were still living there. They gave me a place to stay at their house just on the outskirts of Boston, about a half-hour ride. I wanted to invent a new version of my New Mexico tour, lecturing on both lobsterfishing and fin fishing (hake, haddock, pollock, and so forth), and I wanted to talk about it from Maine's point of view.

I thought, "If I can get with some museum, I will be in like Flynn." So I decided to go to the Boston Aquarium to talk to the curator. I went in there right off the street with my resumé and I says to him, "Here's what I'd like to do: I'd like to set up a lobster and fishing room at the aquarium here, lecture on these things, and," I added, "I also have slide shows and other teaching aids that I can take into the school system if desired."

"Well," he said, "we are not interested in having a lobster-fishing room here at the Aquarium and, besides, we have a show of our own we take into the school system, which we think is very good so we don't need your show."

I went on to my next destination, which was the Children's Museum in Boston. Although I didn't land a job there, they were somewhat interested. So, onward I went to the Museum of Science. As it turned out, they *really* wanted me, but they told me that there was a problem with my timing. Apparently, on the first floor they were tearing the whole space up to put in an exhibit from China that would run for a full six months.

The curator told me, "Come back in the early fall because we will be ready to dismantle the exhibition. After that we will be looking for new displays and will likely hire you in a minute."

My daughter and two sons were still in high school, and a job in the fall would have meant I would have to leave the island and go to Boston for six months or so. I didn't want to be away from my kids, so I didn't pursue my lecturing career any more. We packed up in Lynn went back to Mount Desert. I took up my job at the boatyard once again.

Activities Director Par Excellence

My wife Sue had gone back to work herself and gotten a job as a charge nurse on the first floor at the Summit House Nursing Home. My father's sister, Millie, resided there. I went to visit Sue one day, and she said, "I'll take you down to Millie's room, but she hasn't recognized anybody for three weeks, not even her own two sons, so don't be surprised if she hasn't a clue who you are."

I thought I'd go down and try anyway.

Sue and I marched through the door, and there was Millie lying in the bed. She looked up as Sue said, "Millie, there is somebody here to visit you. Do you know who this person is?"

Millie just looked at Sue like "You idiot!" Then she exclaimed, "Of course I know who that is. It's Frank's boy." She identified me just as plain as day, and we got talking about my dad, who had been dead then for nineteen years. Suddenly she said, "Frank hasn't been in to visit me lately."

I realized that, in Millie's mind anyway, we had gone back to the glorious days of yesteryear, so I followed right along and took our conversation to before World War One. "Well, Millie," I says, "Frank is over to Portland now fishing with Clarence Turner, so he won't be back for a while."

"Of course," she says, "of course, that's right! How are Clarence and Abbey?" So now, you see, we were back eighty years ago, talking just as good as could be.

Later in the day, the director of nurses, Phyllis Brown, said to me, "You know, Wendell, based on what you were able to accomplish today, I think you would be a good activities director." I thought nothing of it at the time, except I took it as a compliment rather than an insult, as some fishermen might. But, lo and behold, about three months later their activities director resigned, and Sue said to me, "You want to get out of the boatyard? Put your name in." I did.

Well, they had two assistants working with the activities director, but in order to be director you had to be certified by the state of Maine. Neither of those two assistants wanted to take the Activity Director's course. Phyllis told me, "There is a good chance you can get the job, but you've got to be willing to go into Bangor to the Department of Human Services and get yourself certified." She added that the Summit House would pay for the classes.

"Okay," says I, "let's give it a shot."

They hired me on the basis that I would take the certification course and pass it, but they started me immediately. I went in as the boss of a job that my two assistants had to teach me. I got $8 an hour, which was fine by me.

Soon enough I discovered that the activities director before me had kept a very tight rein on things. He did all the book-keeping and the paperwork himself. He didn't allow his assistants to do any of that. He also treated the residents of Summit like they needed to be pampered and protected, the way a parent would act towards a child. I thought, "Well, we're going to make a couple of changes right off quick. The residents here are not children, and I am not going to treat 'em like children. Life has its risks. Sometimes you make it, sometimes you don't. We are going to take our risks here just like we do in life. It is the way they lived their whole lives until they got old and ill."

"If you want to do the paperwork," I informed my two assistants, "you can have the whole of it. I just want to be on the floor with the residents."

The administrator wasn't going to hear about it. "You are the activities director," he said. "You are going to do the paperwork and all this stuff."

"That's all right," I told my two assistants. "You wait till they work with me two months and see my paperwork; they'll be begging you to do it. Let's play this hand of cards out." I was computer-illiterate and, if you have got no skills in computers today, you are a dinosaur. My assistant Allison was happy doing all the computer stuff, and I was happy engaging with the residents. It worked out fine.

When I first started to attempt things with the residents, I found them lethargic and depressed. They didn't do anything; they didn't go anywhere. They'd just lay on their beds: "I ain't gonna get off my bed. I had my dinner; that is enough. Now I am going to sleep, excuse me."

These people needed to be let out—they had to get out of this place. It was putting them in a trance. I made my views clear, but Allison and Gloria said, "We tried all that. We planned trips, we hired a bus for them, and, oh yes, they all signed up for it, but the day the bus came none of them wanted to go."

"Aha," I said, "they need some other kind of approach. This Mr. Nice Guy stuff is over. What I am going to do is I am going to piss them off. I'm going to make 'em mad and find out if there is any life left in this place. If they get mad back, then life means something to them."

Acute care was on the first floor. These people were really sick. Those on the second floor could do a lot for themselves; they were nowhere near as ill. We held our activities in the first- and second-floor dining rooms, and everyone from both floors who was able came. I decided I would try to get two good entertainers from outside the nursing home to perform, one on each floor. I would put folk music on one floor and a glass harmonica on the other at the same time. I created a conflict on purpose; I wanted them to have to make a decision. Just as I had hoped, the residents started coming to me and wondering aloud, "Which one am I going to?"

"I can't make that decision for you," I would say. "You have got to make it yourself."

"Well, I want to see both!"

"You can watch one a while," I said, "then go down and watch the other."

"Well, which one should I watch first?"

"I don't care which one you watch, that is up to your personal likes and tastes. There are two good movies playing at the same time, and they ain't coming back. Which one are you going to see?"

"I can't . . ."

"It is up to you," I cut in before they could finish.

"Well I don't want to get up from one and go see the other. That would spoil this and that . . ."

So finally I says, "We have choices now, don't we?" I had really pissed them off, more than I thought that a simple conflict between guitars and harmonicas would do. I guess they were ready to be irritated; it was just beneath the surface.

Within a month of my starting, one old gentleman in a wheelchair grabbed me by the shirt, slammed me up against the wall, and shouted, "I have had it with you!" And he was just the first to have an outburst of temper with yours truly being the cause.

"My God," I thought, "there *is* a spark of life!"

Of course, I was not telling anyone higher up what I was doing. Still, we had our weekly administrative meetings and stuff like that, and I had to go. At one of these meetings, after word had filtered upstairs, the administrator said to me, "You are creating chaos in this place. Jesus, you have got everybody mad! We can't have you doing this; you have got to stop it."

"Look," I said, "there is a plan to my madness. I don't intend to keep it up. All I wanted to do was get 'em out of their beds! Now they are angry and they are going to get up, so we can run it normal."

Another program I started around this time was van riding. I said to the residents, "We are getting out of this damn place. We are going out to meet the world. And we ain't hiring no fancy bus; we are going to take the Summit van and ride ourselves."

The outings I reserved for Saturdays, when I was there by myself without the two other assistants. We would take two rides in the morning and one in the afternoon. As with the entertainment, I made the residents sign up for the rides themselves.

We would go to flower shops, and the florists would give the old folks flowers. We would go to bakeries, and the baker would give them cookies. Soon the Summit House van was getting to be well known, as were its passengers. People throughout the island began to welcome them.

The trip wasn't easy for everyone. Dot Lawson had MS, multiple sclerosis, but she still wanted to come. It was hard for her to keep her head up. I noticed that she seemed to do okay up to about twenty miles, usually around Ellsworth. That's when her head began slumping. The first time I saw that happening, I made do with the resources at hand. I took off my belt and put it around her forehead and buckled it at the back of the bucket seat, so she wouldn't flop over.

"Careful your pants don't fall off," she said.

That's the kind of merriment we had.

One lady, though—Bertha Howell was her name—had sat in her room for three years, mostly with her arms folded, glaring at the wall. You talk about perseverance! You talk about obstinacy! She had a son living in Ellsworth and a married daughter in New York, who would get up to Maine during the month of August to stay at a camp they owned right across the road by Echo Lake. When Bertha's children would send her flowers, she'd say, "Take 'em out. Get them out of here; I don't want them. I don't want them in my room. Give them to anybody who wants them." They'd send her a fruit basket and it was the same: "I don't want it. I don't want to eat it. Give it to the nurses!" She'd sit there stoic in a chair with her blanket wrapped around her, glowering out there at whatever, not moving at all. She wouldn't even come out of her room for her meals. They had to bring them to her.

This charade went on about six months, and it got to the point where the thing I wanted most in that job was to blast her out of her cave, smoke her out of that damn cell! "Bertha," I said, "your husband used to be a fisherman, didn't he?"

"Uh-huh."

"You used to go out with him once in a while, didn't you?"

"Yes, I did."

"You wouldn't happen to like the taste of lobster, would you?"

"I love it!" Bertha told me. She actually got a warm look in her face at the sound of the word "lobster."

"Okay," I said, "next Wednesday there is going to be a lobster feed in the activities room. If you don't want to eat it, you'll be served the regular food the Home provides for you, but if you want lobster, one of the obligations is you have to come to the activities room to get it yourself."

"Order one," she says. "I'll be there."

That Wednesday, after three years, the mountain moved. Bertha came down and not only did she partake of lobster; she turned out to be queen of the day. She was drinking toasts to people, cheering, laughing for the first time in three years.

I said, "Bertha, you pulled the wool over my eyes. I thought you were an isolated hermit, but you are a regular damned old socialite, ain't ya? I've got news for you: there is more to this place than just lobster feeds. I want you to take van rides with me Saturdays."

"I'll think about it. I am not going this week, but don't you give up on me."

"I ain't going to give up on you. I'll be here a while."

"One of these Saturdays I am going to surprise you and do it."

And guess what? After she done it the first time, she continued to do it. Then she began to come to sing-a-longs and other events too. She would poke out of her room and inch into the hallway. She was a large lady and, wherever she sat, she had a commanding presence. It was like being with the Queen Mother.

When it came to be summer, I knew her daughter and son-in-law were up from New York. "Bertha," I announced one day, "Saturday I want to make sure you go with me on the van ride because I have got a treat for you, a big surprise."

"What is it?"

"If I told you, it wouldn't be a surprise, so I am going to make you guess. If you will come, though, I will guarantee you will be very happy."

I never even called her daughter or husband, I just took a chance they'd be home. As we started driving, I thought to myself, "Lord, if you want this to work, let them be there or I have struck out."

"Where's he going, where *is* he going?" she would ask the other residents. As I pulled right up into her daughter's driveway, she exclaimed, "But this is her place, this is Jackie's place!"

I went to the house and knocked on the door. Out came Jackie and her husband. I said, "Come on out to the van; somebody wants to meet you."

There was Mother. Oh my god, you talk about happy! They were as happy as could be. They brought out a bag of cookies and shared it with the residents.

The administrator and I were having a little tiff at the time, but that day when I got back, he said, "My God, you must be doing something right. Bertha's daughter and son-in-law called, and they were tickled to see her not only out of bed but in an agreeable mood and coming for a visit."

That doesn't mean things stayed absolutely smooth between Bertha and me for as long as I worked at Summit. In fact, when I was getting ready to leave and they were showing the new activities director how things were, Bertha was acting up again and refusing to go on a van ride. Maybe she was just showing off, but I could play that game too. I walked up to her, held my right hand out, and said, "See the velvet glove on my hand." Of course, I was just play-acting. There was no glove. "Inside that velvet glove," I said, "is an iron fist and, if you don't come on this van ride, I'm gonna smash you on the jaw with that iron fist."

She put up both arms with her own clenched fists and said, "Don't you dare threaten me!"

I said, "Are you now coming?"

She said, "Yes."

My old friend Betty Spurling, the assistant director of nurses, looked at the new activities director and said, "God, he is a master of bullshit!"

Well, maybe and maybe not, but I was the best activities director they ever had, maybe the best in the state of Maine. In fact, being activities director at a health-care facility was the best I ever was at anything. But enough is enough. Time to move on.

Road Trip Blues

I quit April 15, 1987, after twenty-two months. I realized that I needed to be outdoors doing physical work. Sue and I were arguing worse than ever, so I decided to move into an apartment in Southwest Harbor. We were separating. Meanwhile I had gotten my old job back at Bass Harbor Marine Boatyard, and I ended up working there a year and a half to see my sons through high school. Wayne was now completing his senior year; Frank was a junior. Once Wayne was out of school, he wanted to go lobsterfishing; he had been a cook at the Brick Oven Restaurant in Bar Harbor. I got him a job on a lobsterboat out of Southwest Harbor with Tommy Lawson, and he became a full-time fisherman. The following year, Frank graduated from high school and joined the Navy. He took his boot camp at the Great Lakes Naval Training Center in Waukegan, Illinois.

Sue and I finalized our divorce on September 7, 1988. I am a very breezy, philosophical sort of man. It is awfully hard to get me to pinpoint and stay right in one position. I am kind of evasive. Sue was always very precise about everything. She had been a nurse before we met. Our two different styles just did not blend. I was the one that applied for the divorce and she went along with it. The day we finalized our divorce, we ended up driving to Don's Shop & Save and going grocery shopping, and that was the last thing we did together as husband and wife, something we had done a thousand or so times before.

I bought Frank's 1978 Dodge pickup truck from him when he enlisted. I was now free in a way I hadn't been since the years after I got out of the Army. It was maybe my last best chance to travel.

I decided to set off and explore this country and see if there was any other place I wanted to live or another type of work I wanted to do. Was I a dyed-in-the-wool Atlantic person, not a Pacific person? Well, I intended to find out.

I got rid of all my earthly possessions, except what belongings I could load onto my new half-ton, slant-six Dodge. I loaded the back and even the cab. People gave me different things for good luck—a dollar bill, a string of paper cranes a friend made with his daughters, a notebook for writing in, a rock from Sargent Mountain. I left on the 5th of October, 1988. You would have thought I was going to the moon.

I set out across America starting from the far Downeast— Maine. Even as I left, there was a problem with the universal joint in the truck. It was going to go at any time but, universal joint or not, I was ready to move on. Now, this truck had around a hundred and forty thousand-odd miles on it, so I wasn't going to push it hard. I made an agreement with myself that I wouldn't drive at any time over forty-five miles an hour. Unbeknown to me, my former co-workers at the boatyard were taking bets on how far I could get. The conservative bet was that I might make Brewer or Bangor, about fifty miles away. The farthest place anyone bet I'd make was the state of Vermont.

I put up a brave front, but I was feeling lonely and empty from Orono onward. While riding through the mountains at twilight time, through rain and mist, I asked myself this question, "What is this trip for anyways?" Then I got very quiet. The answer was, "This is a spiritual pilgrimage." All fear and emptiness and loneliness left. I knew I was well.

I camped in my truck under the cap, the first night in a shopping center in Glenn Falls, New York. My bed was a big foam sponge for a mattress with a cover on it parallel to my tailgate. I could sleep there perfectly fine. Sometimes I would stop in parking lots and sometimes just off the side of the road. I used truck stops as my base camps because they had laundry and showers and a good meal and were safe places to stay. A friend of mine at the boatyard, Patty Tierney, gave me a whole book of tickets to McDonalds. That was often my lunch—nothing that would have passed muster with Scott or Helen Nearing. I would drive for about three hours, and then I'd pull off into the next truck stop.

Time was not of the essence on this trip. I was in no hurry. I might get up and travel in the night or I might travel in the day. Usually I slept through the night and traveled in the hours of daylight.

Driving with the Geese

I went across Vermont and came through Albany, New York, then ran along a beautiful valley where they had horses on rolling hills for miles and miles, Schoharic County, and then I continued through flatlands. All the while I was going along at forty-five miles an hour. Along about Ohio's border with western New York I came in with a flock of migrating birds in a huge "V" formation, headed west, the way I was going. We ran side by side with each other for two hours nonstop. My speed was their speed, forty-five miles an hour. I didn't have to slow down or speed up to stay with them. We kept wingtip to wingtip. When they reached their pivot point, they took a ninety-degree turn to the south. That was the last I saw of them.

I was impressed that I was going across the country at the same speed as birds migrate. Back when the settlers went across the country, they would have thought that forty-five miles an hour was breakneck speed.

It was the journey that was important, not the destination. Still, I am sure I irritated some people. I got a few horn blasts and more than a few fingers, but I wasn't that fragile; it didn't bother me a bit. I finally found one vehicle that was driving slower than I was, and I passed it!

Lost in Chicago

In the East and Midwest the truck stops were big, very noisy places: dishes clanking, everybody talking with everybody else, perfect strangers holding conversations. Some of them fed hundreds of people all at once. I was impressed by the drivers that would conduct little questions and answers with each other: "How far is it to Tallahassee from Buffalo?" The fellow who was asked would name it to the mile.

As I got into Indiana, I formulated a plan to go see Frank. He had just graduated from boot camp and was sent for three months to electronics school at the same base. In order to get there, I had to go through Chicago. I thought if I made it clean through before the city was up and about, I'd have a better chance.

I woke at a truck stop in Gary, Indiana, about four o'clock in the morning and started my approach. On the map I saw that Route 90 would take me right through Chicago and up to Waukegan but, when I got to where it should be, much to my surprise they had torn Route 90 down, ramp and all. They were doing a complete renovation job. There was a detour with signs to point you here or point you there, but more often than not I'd miss the signs that pertained to me. I got completely lost. It did me no good to look at a map because I didn't understand what I was looking at.

At last, around seven o'clock or so, I pulled into a restaurant and had my breakfast. By the time I came back out, the sun was rising. From then on, I followed the compass. I said to myself, if you go any one direction long enough, you have got to come out of anyplace, no matter how big it is. I wanted to go north, so if I kept the sun on my right-hand side, I was heading north. That is all I did to get out of that mess. When I come to a street where I no longer could go north, I took the next major street I could find to keep the sun on my right.

At last I started coming to expressways. I was doing forty-five still, and I put on my warning lights so that the other expressway drivers would think, "Well, that is a piece of shit going down the highway. I'll just steer around it." No one ever gave me the horn, the finger, or nothing that day. They just completely ignored me, and I kept going my merry way.

When I finally got out of Chicago, I was in the country. I never did see a sign, but I figured I was still heading north. I had been using my truck like a boat. I had driven for forty-five minutes or an hour, and I guessed it was about time to stop and take a reality check, maybe see if I was anywhere near where I was going. I pulled into this station to fill my truck with gas, and I asked the attendant, "Am I anywhere near Waukegan?"

He said, "You are right on course. Go another nine miles and you are there."

The Great Lakes Naval Training Center

The Great Lakes Naval Training Center is a major base, humongous big. The Navy only had two recruit training centers at the time, and that was one of them. When I got on base, I went to the last address that I had for Frank, the place he had been at boot camp. They had no trace of him. "We pay real close attention to them while they are here," an enlisted man told me, "but once they leave, we pay no more attention."

I said, "He is somewhere on this base." Then I called back home to get ahold of Sue. "If he phones," I told her, "tell him I am on the base looking for him."

At last an idea dawned on me. I said to myself, you fool, why do you look for a needle in a haystack? Go to the military police and find out if they know what they are doing.

I located where the police headquarters were and I told the MPs, "Here is his service number; here is his name. Consider him AWOL. Can you locate him now?" They tracked him down in about five minutes and put him on the phone.

"Frank," I said, "you come find me. I am over at the military police station."

Frank looked really sharp in his uniform, all Navy. His commanding officer knew his dad was coming and let him have the weekend off. "Have a good time with your father," he snapped, "and report back here at three o'clock Sunday afternoon."

Frank and I went off together in his old Dodge and spent two beautiful days with each other in the Great Lakes area, doing simple things like skipping stones, walking around beaches, collecting interesting rocks, a drink or two at the bar. We stayed in a motel, just like in the old days, watched some TV, and slept like two logs.

Westward Again

The next day we drove around, shooting the breeze. We went shopping at the commissary, and he insisted on buying me things. He even filled my tank with gas, patted his old Dodge, wished us well, and gave me $10 for the road.

After I left Frank on Sunday afternoon, I headed west towards the prairie.

The first night out I stayed in La Salle-Peru, Illinois. I had breakfast with the locals early; they were really talkative among themselves but not interested in conversing with a stranger. I had gone from the fast-paced city to the laid-back country. The city doesn't care who you are or where you are from; it is like "Welcome, make yourself at home." Rural places say, "Eat your meal, keep your ideas to yourself, foreigner, and then hit the road." There is an outer toughness and aggressiveness to the city, but there is a closed-offness and exclusivity to the rural areas.

I stayed with some relatives of a friend of mine for three nights in Oskaloosa, Iowa. They took me to a breakfast place where a man named Hugh had been in the restaurant business for fifty-seven years. He walked with a limp from an injury forty-seven years ago, and his hands shook so bad, it's a wonder that the coffee all made it into the cup. He had a quick wit about him and was, overall, a happy man. There was a stool at the counter that was his, and no one sat on that but Hugh. His customers loved him. They enjoyed putting the shit to him, and he enjoyed returning it. In Oskaloosa, I got my first haircut on the trip, and I learned about the soft-coal mining that was done there in its day and got the town growing.

My first day out of Oskaloosa I drove to Sioux Falls and made nightfall at Larry's Truck Stop there, slept like a log from 10 to 5, was up, washed, shaved, ate breakfast, and got on my way at the crack of dawn. It was another beautiful patch of sunshine, but the wind was cold, dry, and piercing. I thought, "I am surely going through America's heartland"—farms, ranches, flatland, rolling hills. I was beginning to wonder if there ever was such a place as the ocean, or did I just dream there was?

Gradually the land formation to my left on I-90 changed abruptly way off in the distance. It was the start of the Badlands, twenty-eight miles of looping, winding roads through land being eroded by wind and water. The Ogallala Sioux live there. If I had the power to do such, I would redirect the jet planes fifty miles either side of this great parkland so that travelers would not have to listen to those engines as they passed. It would be a stretch of country with peace and just the sound of the world and wind (and, yes, the auto traffic). I spent the night at a truck stop in Rapid City, South Dakota.

I detoured through the Black Hills to Mount Rushmore. Then I continued into Wyoming. Wyoming is what you would expected the West to be, a very rugged, beautiful state in places and very stark and bleak in others. I would not care to live there, and I believe a lot of others feel the same way, for the land is sparsely populated. I did have a feeling that those who call it home really love it.

Four days after leaving Oskaloosa, around two or three o'clock in the afternoon, I came into the town of Gillette, Wyoming, and stopped in a little restaurant. Inside were four men at one table. Other than that, I was the only one there. I went to the bar and sat on one of the stools to have my lunch. I asked the waitress how far was it from Gillette to Buffalo, and she looked at me and said, "I don't know. I don't travel that much. I work most of the time, you know." She seemed proud of the fact that she worked hard, like her job was the highlight of her life. "Maybe those fellas over there at the table would know." She hollered over, "Any of you know how far it is from here to Buffalo?"

It turned out to be only sixty miles, and yet this woman had no clue whether it was sixty or six hundred.

The Sound of a Teaspoon

Out west, going into a truck stop was like visiting a library. Nobody was saying nothing to nobody. All you could hear was the clink of the silverware. There was no conversation. It was so tranquil that you could hear a teaspoon hit the floor at twenty miles. In the big eastern truck stops it was bedlam, but out here each person was eating in their own silence. Even the people that lived in the area and stopped in were quiet. In Buffalo this truck driver came into the restaurant and announced, "My God almighty, isn't it quiet here!" Everybody just stared at him like he'd said something wrong.

I slept in my truck, and the next morning I got up and ate breakfast. I was leaving fairly early, but the local people were already coming into the restaurant for breakfast. This woman

and her husband took a table. I was impressed with the magnitude of his build; he looked like a Greek statue. They sat down
to eat and never spoke one earthly word to each other. She
looked entirely bored, as if to say, "I am so tired of this guy. If
any of you would like to have him, he is yours." They ordered
their breakfasts, and the waitress brought their plates, heaped
with bacon and eggs.

His had home fries. He said to the waitress, "You know I do
not need these. These potatoes are extra. I don't eat that much."

"It comes with your order, so I brought it. If you don't want
to eat them, just leave them aside. " I could see that he was a
man who measured life by an eyedropper.

Looking for a Friend in Montana

When I reached the state of Montana, I went looking for
the old Gestalt therapist from Great Duck Island, George
Cloutier. He had moved to Montana some years before, and I
wanted to find him. He supposedly lived in a small town called
Clancy, where I had written many letters to him. He always
wrote back, so I knew I had his address correct. Since I hadn't
heard that he had moved or anything recently, I thought I'd
hunt him down, no problem. Around mid-afternoon, on my
way to Helena, I pulled off at an Exxon gas station and filled
up my truck. I asked the attendant how far it was from there
to Helena, and she said, "I don't know. I don't travel that much.
I work most of the time, you know."

I thought, "Just a minute! Back in Gillette I accepted that
line, but this woman said the exact same thing; she parroted it
too close! There is some hidden meaning behind this. I haven't
figured it out yet, but I will before this trip is over!"

I continued on and I got to Clancy, where I expected to find

George. It was a little small town—I mean tiny—and so I went to the post office and asked, "Could you tell me where George Cloutier lives?"

"Never heard of him," the postmaster told me.

"Really? I wrote letters and sent them to this post office for years. I know he has received them, yet you tell me you don't know him? This is a town of population what, one hundred?"

The postmaster said, "Sorry can't help you. Never heard of him. Don't know him. Maybe he is in Montana City, four miles from here."

So I continued to Montana City, which was a city only in name. I went into the general store. It was a real old cracker-barrel place with a round woodstove in the middle and a bunch of geezers sitting around, talking. I said, "I am looking for George Cloutier. Do any of you people know him?"

"Never heard tell of him."

"Nobody knows him in Clancy, either, but they sent me here. Then I come over here to this little town and now none of you people claim to know him!" I was frustrated. I could tell by their expressions that something was up. "I *know* you know him, and I know you won't tell me where he is, but I do not know why. I am going to the police. I'll find him yet. Have a good day, fellas." I turned 'round and walked out of the store.

Just as I was at the threshold, one elderly man called out, "Just a minute. How do you know George Cloutier?" I told him.

Then the man said, "You are two months too late. He just moved to Billings. He has some kind of ranch there, raising deer. I have a feeling he may also work at the Montana State Hospital, but I don't know."

Montana is a big state, and I'd already gone through Billings at daybreak that morning. I had made an agreement with myself that I would never backtrack. So after all that I continued through Helena to the Idaho border.

It wasn't until many years later that a little blip in the *Bangor Daily News* reported that George Cloutier, living in Billings, Montana, had died. That is all it said. I asked his former wife, Lee Longnecker, down to Portland, "Did you realize George is dead?" She hadn't heard the news.

Later I met someone from the old Duck Island days and he told me the story: "He was an inmate at the Montana State Hospital. It was not a voluntary choice. He got into a fistfight with one of the other inmates and had a heart attack and died right there."

What really happened in Montana and how he ended up in the mental hospital, I don't know—but it must have been disturbing because the people in the neighborhood certainly wouldn't discuss anything about George Cloutier with me.

Journey's End

I had only eighty miles of Idaho, but it rained all the way through them. Three deer ran out in front of me, going through one of the passes. I blew the horn. Two got across; one turned back.

My first stop in Washington was Spokane for lunch. At a place called Matthew's Restaurant I had codfish, potatoes, and cole slaw, topped off with some blueberry pie. Then I headed for the town of Bellingham. I stopped at Chelan Lake, which is fifty-five miles long with mountains coming down both sides. I continued through miles upon miles of rugged, snow-capped mountains with many waterfalls. I never had a ride like that.

Twelve days out of Mount Desert Island I got into Bellingham; it was around 4 P.M. I looked up my friend Kit and her son. I had met her originally at the Civic Center in Augusta in

1985 at a New England workshop for social-service workers and activities directors. She was in my training session and class; then I hung out with her in the evenings. A lot of us would meet at the bar. I guess I did a bit of storytelling and holding forth. I became a sort of celebrity there and, according to the administrator David Waldron, I really put Summit House on the map. The representative of a band that was playing at the Civic Center, AC/DC, enjoyed me so much at the bar that he invited me to come to New York and introduce their performance there. He said, "People seem to like you."

I can't explain it. It was just a strange thing in my life that happened down there. In the class people would clap and cheer when I spoke, no matter what it was I said. They even cheered when I walked into the room. I was real popular, and I don't think it was just my brogue.

Anyway, I turned him down. I said, "No, I've got kids in school." (I should add: those kids were thoroughly disgusted with me for not doing it.)

Kit and I became friends after that, and we wrote to each other over a three-year period during which she moved from New England to Washington. So now I was looking her up. I'll say right away, so there is no misunderstanding—it wasn't a romantic thing, just a friendship.

She took me to the harbor to see the boats, and we went down to the ocean where I dumped part of the canning jar of water I had brought from the Atlantic to put in the Pacific. Then we watched the sunset.

I spent a full day being shown Bellingham, and then she took me to see Vancouver, British Columbia. It is a beautiful, international city, and covers a large area. After touring the Vancouver Aquarium, we went to Whitehead on the coast for dinner.

My goal starting out was to stay away from Maine long enough that I could make a decision on what I wanted to do with my life, whether it was to be more fishing or not, and whether I was to return to Maine for good or take up elsewhere. I guess I had undertaken this trip throughout the country for many of the basic reasons that Thoreau went to Walden Pond, to ask the questions he asked, to find out what people live by, to reduce life to what it is really about. I was glad I gave up everything back in Maine and took few belongings with me. It gave me the option of making any place along the way my home. I wasn't on vacation visiting places, wearing rose-colored glasses. I was in it for real.

I figured to do most of the exploring in Washington, partly because I had a friend there and partly because it is a coastal state like Maine—in fact, the opposite corner of the United States.

Seattle was the state's biggest city, so I spent two whole days getting ready to go check it out. Anyway my truck had a flat tire with a large nail in it I needed to get fixed. I handled that, and then I got some papers copied off. Finally I left at eight-thirty the next morning. I went to the aquarium in Pike Place Market and found the director straight off. I tried to get myself hired showing my slides and lecturing on lobstering and fishing, but they had a small budget and wanted to spend what they did have on West Coast sea life. I found out in one day in Seattle how the ball game is run. It would probably not be better in San Francisco or anywhere else on the coast. I decided to go back to Bellingham and try to rent a place for a few months.

I began searching for an apartment the next day, but I found that people didn't want to rent to you unless you committed to a year, so the next day I went down to the docks, the Sunny-brook Fish Wharf, and introduced myself to some of the fishermen. I got right into the swing of things and helped them load their gill nets. I almost got a chance to go out on one of the boats. They fish for crabs, and they gill-net, purse-seine, and drag for salmon out of Bellingham. The fishermen go up and down the West Coast, even as far north as Alaska.

The next day I called on apartments advertised throughout Bellingham with no luck. Bellingham actually has a cycle. During the summer and fall the men are out on boats fishing, often far away and then, as the season draws to a close, they pile ashore looking for rents. Since the fishing season's end cut out most jobs for me, I decided to move on. I called the real-estate people and the fish wharf I had contacted to tell them to forget me because I was leaving. I was also realizing that I didn't like the West Coast as much as I thought I would. It wasn't Maine. Back in Maine I was a local boy, and they'd look out for me; they'd hire me first. Here I was an outsider.

The weather was foggy in Bellingham when I left. Fog, rain, and a heavily oppressive, overcast sky seemed to be half of the city's weather during the time I was there. With that Japanese current running by, I doubted if there could be any hope of it ever changing. The sun came out after I got forty miles or so away, and it followed me right into Oregon.

I stayed on the coast. Astoria was the place that most made me think of Maine, a little like Bath. I loved the feeling of a little city of maybe 10,000, and the Columbia River is beautiful. I spoke to some fishermen and found that they were having success catching salmon, but I didn't see a chance of getting on any of their boats. I continued on to Canon Beach.

In Maine you would see islands and bays along the coast; here it was just open ocean with some large rocks jutting up and broad sandy beaches, quaint little towns and mountains along the way. At Newport I talked with Kirk Jones, owner of a longliner trawler named *Sea Hulk;* he was tied up with engine trouble and hoped to get going by early the next week, to squeeze in some fishing before he had a back operation. For a moment I thought about going on his boat but, as we talked, the moment passed. The back operation made him reluctant to take on any more crew.

I went on to Medford and Ashland. Ashland was a great cultural town, with a theater and college. I surprised old friends from Albuquerque there, Matthew and his wife Jay. They were gracious and took me in. The next day she drove me to a Zen monastery nestled in the mountains and, after that, an herb farm run by a husband and wife, Rising Sun; it was something like the Nearings' place, except a moneymaking operation.

Yeshe Nyngpo, the head of the local Zen temple, was out of town. Jay must have been speaking for him when she told me, "You don't have to do anything with your life but live it and live it peacefully."

I thanked her and said it was worth the whole trip across the country just for that.

She added, "But you could have phoned."

I told her that even a meal is no good unless you are hungry for it. She gave me a funny look because that didn't really follow. Then I laughed and said I guessed the Oregon mountains were turning me a too Zen and I better get out of town before I did any more damage.

However, before I left, I got in a few more adventures. We went to the Ashland Hills Inn for a musical, *Jacques Brel is Alive and Living in Paris.* Then the next day Matthew took me on a flight in a plane he and two other guys owned together. We were soaring above mountains and lakes. I had no nervousness about being in the plane with him. After we landed I ate ripe figs off a tree, first I ever had like that.

In sunny weather I headed down through northern California and the redwood forests, stopping at Crescent City to look at the fishing fleet. I talked with a guy who was rigging up for crab fishing, and he told me that, once the season started, he could get up to forty pounds a trap at about 80 cents a pound. As the season wears on, the catch drops to more like ten pounds per trap, price around $1.80 per pound. The Crescent City fleet was idle except for draggers, with other boats rigging up for crabbing; the season started in December.

The fishing talk made me think of Maine. I was beginning to realize I belonged on the East Coast, not the West Coast. New England was home to me. I had found that out firsthand and from real-life experiences. I was getting myself ready to head back.

I had thought in particular once to live in San Francisco. It was the place I thought I most wanted to go. I could remember it from my Army days, and I had always kicked myself that I didn't stop and stay there longer after I had gotten out of the service. I thought it would be the highlight of my trip, but when I got there, it was so different from what I remembered from 1961 that I couldn't wait to move on. Smoke and gas filled the air; hubbub of traffic was everywhere. Radio and TVs blared in the restaurant I chose, and people were not friendly. My whole system seemed to be telling me to hightail it out of town. As I looked in the canyons of the city streets, I had no other urge than to pass right on through. It made me almost vomit to think of stopping. I bought a newspaper anyway and looked at the price of rents and job offers, and it made me feel like I was in a science-fiction story and had gone to another universe. After that I stopped only for traffic lights and people. I just drove right on through. I made my destination Monterey, and the aquarium there didn't disappoint me. It was the greatest I'd ever seen.

Big Sur is pretty nice—rustic, peaceful, rugged, beautiful as they say—and I wouldn't have wanted to miss it. I stopped at the Nepenthe Restaurant for breakfast at 7:30 A.M. I had heard good things about it from a friend back in Maine, but the sign on the door said they don't open until 11:30. The Downeast part of me was affronted. I thought, "Even the birds don't get up here till 8 A.M." Breakfast would have to be elsewhere.

I left Highway 1 and took Route 101 to Route 58. It was hilly and winding country, made mostly for ranching, I guess. The more I headed south down the West Coast, the more anger I could feel in the air from the inhabitants. I could sense the collision between wealth and power, the tension of too many people. I didn't think to blame the people themselves. We are complex, interesting creatures, actors and actresses with different masks and costumes for different scenes, and we sometimes get in over our heads, but not for lack of trying.

When I got to Bakersfield, I told myself I had to make a decision about what I was going to do. Was I going to stay on the West Coast longer or go back east? Since I decided I hadn't seen anything any better than what I had left or that I couldn't live without, I called my sister and said, "Olive, I'll be back in about two weeks and I'll need a job on a fishing boat, lobster boat, or a scallop boat. I don't care which." Now I realized late November was not exactly the time to go job-hunting in the state of Maine, so I added, "Let me know if there even is such a thing when I get back."

I drove through the desert country of California and came to a little settlement named Ludlow. It was settled originally as a water-stop for steam engines. Time had turned it into a gas and diesel station for cars and trucks. The mood inside the restaurant was surly, and that included not only customers and waitresses but the notices posted all over. The waitresses didn't talk at all; they were very pinch-faced and only joked among themselves. None of the customers were laughing or conversing; they just had fixed stares; men gawked at women who walked in and didn't take their gaze off them. The debate on the restroom wall said it all: "You people are nothing but desert rats, a pack of rats that's what you amount to." Someone answered it, "You others are nothing but liberal motherfuckers. We believe in 1. Right to life. 2. The American flag. 3. We don't love fags. All fags should be killed."

Southern California may have been Happyland to some, but it was the last place I'd care to live.

I drove through the Mojave into Arizona, crossed Arizona into New Mexico, and arrived back in Albuquerque. I never expected to greet it almost like home. I spent a week there, visiting with my friends, and then continued east.

In an Amarillo coffee shop, a waitress asked me where I was from. I told her, "Maine." She said she thought that was another country, and I said, "Or maybe another solar system."

Back to Maine

I reached Maine in mid-November of 1988. I stayed with my sister Phyllis in Ellsworth that night and called Olive from there. "Give me a list of the boats you've found," I said to her. She read me the list. Out of all the names on the list, I liked the sound of Ronald Johnson the best. He'd just lost his stern man, so I gave him a call. "Ronald, I hear you don't have a stern man anymore. Are you looking for one?"

"To tell you the truth, I have got an ocean full of traps, my man quit me without any notice, and I have been so depressed I haven't even thought about doing anything about it!"

I said, "Look at it this way, if you are looking for a stern man,

I am looking for a job. Are you still having breakfast at the Deacon Seat Restaurant at five o'clock in the morning? I'll meet you there and we can talk it over."

We had breakfast together the next day. It was storming and the boats didn't fish, so we went for a ride in his truck. He told me how it had been good lobstering, but it wasn't going to last "'cause it's approaching early winter."

I said, "I haven't been so far away that I've forgotten everything. I've been in this business a long time, and I know how it works. That doesn't worry me. I just want to get started again."

Ronald said, "You are hired. You can start Monday."

So that is how I got back into fishing.

I moved into a single-bedroom apartment in Southwest Harbor. I was happy but out of money. I had just enough to pay the deposit and a month's rent. My total belongings were on the truck. A month later I had enough money to buy a box spring and a mattress. My furniture consisted solely of a rocking chair that I had taken across the country and back.

My first day lobstering in seven years, November 23, was sunny and clear with the wind northwest in the morning. The wind hauled out to the west by afternoon. Ronnie had the new wire traps that were much lighter and easier to handle than the old-fashioned wooden ones. My hands were weak, and my back was lame, but it felt as though, with a couple of weeks' hauling, I could get to where I was. We brought back 540 pounds, not bad for my homecoming. "Good-bye, Betsy," I thought, in answer to that song "Sweet Betsy from Pike." "I'm an Atlantic person, and I'll go by myself if I do."

So I was living one day at a time, and each day was full.

On November 27 we baited up a few traps, shifted a gang, and took about eighty up. The wind was warmer out of the south. I was in better shape than the first day. I felt good.

By late November the lobsters had dropped off, down to 200 pounds a day. In fact, we found quite a few more scallops than lobsters in our traps. Maybe that was a sign. We began to rig for winter scalloping.

By February I could afford curtains. One night I was hanging them, and a lady named Ann just walked in. We had been good friends back in the '70s when she was Ann De Cleene, and living in Somesville. She had three sons, Don, Steve, and Jeff, that were the same age, within months, of my kids, and they had played together when they were children. She had been living in Canada for eleven years and was now Ann Murphy. We had been corresponding over the years, and I definitely had an old flame for her. She was in town staying with a friend, while trying to buy a bed and breakfast to run, since her home in Canada had burned down. The friend said to her, "You know who's back in town? Wendell." I had been writing to her just before I went on my trip, so she knew I was single, and she knew I was traveling, but she didn't know I was back. She'd been living in Canada for the last eleven years. As she came into the apartment, before even greeting me, she exclaimed in astonishment, "What are you doing?"

I said, "What does it look like? I am hanging curtains."

"Well," she says, "this isn't the way you do it. You don't strangle them with a bowline knot!" She swept me aside, took over, strung my curtains for me, and then we went out for a drink. She told me she wanted to move back to Mount Desert, that she loved the island.

Later, when we were getting romantic, I told her, "If you come back here, you come back because you love Mount Desert Island, not because you love Wendell Seavey. The island'll never let you down, but Wendell may. I've been fickle before."

For a period of six months she became the dorm manager

for the college kids at the Jordan Pond House of Acadia Park, but she was mainly a stained-glass artist, so she gathered up her savings and rented a storefront in Southwest Harbor and started Hot Flash Anny's. She made a retail business, selling her own art and others' on commission. She also repaired stained-glass windows and made them from scratch. She's done work for Martha Stewart, St. Savior's Episcopal Church in Bar Harbor, and Nedda Casei, a retired Metropolitan Opera star in New York City, and, to make a long story short, Hot Flash and I fancied each other. After living together four and a half years, we took a chance and got married.

Adventures with Chris Kaiser

Ann and I made friends with an interesting couple, Mary Carol and Chris Kaiser. She was a Reiki teacher, and Chris did odd jobs around the island. He had been a pharmaceutical salesman as a profession, but I guess you could say he dropped out. I've heard he was a maverick from the time he was young; he never walked the mainstream way.

I took Mary Carol's course just for interest. I'd always had a good experience laying on hands because my hands are warm and I can generate energy. I can take away headaches. I didn't really adopt the traditional Reiki techniques, but the class helped me understand energy healing better.

Chris was a different story. He was more than a close friend; we became each other's teachers and colleagues, and we stayed that way long after Mary Carol and he split up and she moved to Colorado. He'd come up to my house, or I'd go over to his house, and we'd share a meal together and have our conversations that way. His favorite topics included earth energy, vision quests, and American Indian spirituality, and he liked to discuss these things along with his approach to life. These subjects were compatible for me, and we went at it pretty good sometimes. He was much more New Age than I was, whereas I had an old-fashioned spiritualist background. He would find messengers and spirits in the Mount Desert landscape and attribute them to pagan or Indian sources. One time he brought a group together on the Winter solstice and had me lead the chant. The lights actually dimmed and came back.

Chris and I would hike together. Even though I was native to Mount Desert, he would show me the sacred sites he found that I knew nothing of—power centers on the island, particular rocks and pools in Acadia Park. One of these great boulders left by the glaciers was particularly special to him as a healing rock. It was out of Blackwoods Campground as you start up the southern trail of Cadillac, and he said it was the base chakra of the entire power grid of mountains and rocks and lakes on Mount Desert. Because it looked to Chris both wise and innocent, he named it after his son—it was called Wolfie's Rock or the Wolfie Rock. He had named his son after an Apache chief, Stalking Wolf, because he believed that Wolfie was a reincarnation of the medicine man.

The Wolfie Rock is about the size of four automobiles put together; it has a face with a receding chin that looks like the face of a giant turtle. Its eyes are covered with moss and lichen. Chris thought that the chinline showed that the rock was free of arrogance, and he believed the boulder itself was part of a larger medicine wheel of rocks in the area. To be more specific, it was the part of a stone circle that could slow brainwave cycles down. He also thought that if you stared into its left eye, you saw an endless parade of other images and faces.

During this same time I got involved in other native American rituals. I went on a firewalk over to Salisbury Cove. My friend Ed Lueddeke arranged it. We burned a lot of wood that night, and we raked coals over it, so they made an area of maybe about six feet wide and ten feet long of hot coals. Ed told us that before you walk, you should make sure it is okay with your ancestors. If you get a message or a shock up your leg, you probably will not burn. To get us into a meditative state, to raise energy up, he played a tape of drumming music.

When it came for me to walk, I stood right up to the coals on my bare feet; I paused and directed my energy between my eyebrows. My father and my oldest brother Frank suddenly appeared to me in an apparition. I could see them in front of me. My father was in the background, and my brother, who was a short man, was about to his chest. My father was looking very stoic, and my brother had a grin on his face and nodded to me. At that moment an electrical shock went up the back of my legs, just like Ed had described, and I knew then that I had received a message from my ancestors. Without a moment's hesitation, I walked over the hot coals slowly. As I walked, I watched my feet on the coals, and sparks were flying out from under them. The coals felt like I was working on that packaging stuff they called "peanuts"; that's what it felt like under my feet. I was amazed that I was doing this and not burning at all.

When I got across the coals, different people in the crowd said, "Good job, Wendell."

Dana Mitchell, an elder of the Penobscot Nation, attended the firewalk but didn't participate. He told me that they have other ways of reaching that state in their culture, but he did not elaborate on what those were. I pressed it no farther than that.

Since then we've become very close, almost like brothers. We've taken many hikes and walks together and canoed across

Blue Hill Bay. He's gone lobstering and fishing with me. Our families spend every New Year's Eve with each other.

Mary's Story

My daughter Mary went to a business college in Manchester, New Hampshire, for three months in 1986, but I don't think she was meant to be a businessperson. She considered getting into playing and teaching music, but before she could do that, she got pregnant and had a son, Brian. The baby's father was one of these deadbeat dads; he never put two cents into the boy financially or emotionally.

It was a rough haul for a while.

In 1994, when Brian was six and she was a single mother living in Bar Harbor, Mary wanted to get off of state aid, so she went to school at Eastern Maine Hospital in Bangor. She became a nurse, an LPN. She went right to work and planned to study to become an RN, like her mother. Meanwhile she had been going out for a number of years with a decent guy named Jay who worked in a convenience store in Hull's Cove. They finally got married in June of 1994, and Jay adopted Brian. Only two weeks after her marriage she got diagnosed with a brain tumor. In Bangor, they opened her skull and discovered they were unable to operate, so they sent her to Brighamand Women's Hospital in Boston, and Dr. Black there was able to remove 85% of the tumor. He couldn't remove the whole of it because a blood vessel went right through its center, but he went after the other part with radiation.

She was no longer physically or mentally capable of driving or working as a nurse, so she stayed at home and took care of Brian.

Chris Kaiser didn't think too much of the Western approach

to medicine. He considered it very male and aggressive, and he thought that Mary's inner male was calling her shots and held her female side in a death grip—that that was part of the reason she was sick. He wanted to take her to the Wolfie Rock in order to slow her down. He said she was in super beta, and he meant to put her into theta so that she would be in touch with her healing feminine side and start dealing with the tumor. To our surprise, Mary was very open to going to see the rock.

On a Tuesday in 1994, before her surgery in Boston, Mary, Chris, Sue, and Jay went on a pilgrimage to the Wolfie Rock, and Mary returned to it a number of times after surgery. I used to take her there too. She came for its energy and comfort. In Chris' view of it, she became buddies with the rock. The night before her checkup to see how she was progressing after the surgery, the rock came to her in a dream. She told me that she found herself approaching its face when a bear appeared. Jay grabbed her, but she told him she had nothing to fear. The bear picked her up and carried her to the rock and laid her on it. She felt a healing energy pass through her body. Then she awoke, knowing that things were going to be all right.

Whether it was because of the rock or not, Mary lived five years after she was diagnosed with an inoperable tumor, but then a second tumor formed at the site of the old one; it was type four and malignant.

They operated on her in March 1999, and when she came out of the operation, she had her long-term memory but no short-term memory. She stayed at a nursing home in Bar Harbor until she passed away on December 8 at about three in the morning.

I'm at peace with it. I'm okay on the day of her death each year, but I get very depressed on her birthday.

Nowadays

Nowadays I don't own a boat of my own. I go as a stern man, just as I did with Ronald Johnson when I started back up in '89. I fished with Ronald for six years and two months, and then one spring it was time for a change. I wanted to go halibut fishing as well as lobstering, so I joined up with Billy Soukup, while having a boat of my own built, which was possible because Ann's mother had died and left her some money. Roland Stanley and another man made the hull, and Tim Butler finished the construction off. It was a very small boat, a twenty-foot Mitchell Cove skiff named *Great Balls of Fire*.

About a year later, Hot Flash decided to do a little nautical home improvement, and she removed two side windows in *Great Balls of Fire* and replaced them with stained-glass ones. It was a newsworthy event at the time; *Downeast Magazine* had an article on it. I heard tell by the rumor mill some distant cousin of mine named Mike Seavey was commenting about it to another man. The other man was telling him I was married again, and Mike was surprised. The guy said, "He married Hot Flash Anny, you know the store in town."

Mike said, "No shit?"

Then the second man said, "Not only that, but she put stained-glass windows in his lobsterboat. It's a fucking floating chapel out there."

I kept *Great Balls of Fire* for about five years, but I couldn't fish the way I wanted to. She wasn't big enough.

I knew I was never going to be able to afford a real lobsterboat—a thirty-footer with a diesel engine and all the rigmarole it would take. So I sold my little boat and my traps and went back to being a stern man again.

That is what I have done ever since, and hopefully that is how I can round out my working life. I joined up with Stan Wass in his boat late July 1999, and went with him until April 2001. Then I went for a while with my son Wayne in his boat until late September 2001; after that I went back to fishing with Stan.

One afternoon I found myself sitting around my deck with Tucker Spurling, Warren Goodwin, and some of my other long-time buddies, drinking Bar Harbor home-brewed beer and slapping away the mosquitoes because that year was a bumper crop. Warren says to Tucker, "How many traps you got down this year?"

"One hundred," he says.

"Good. Put down another hundred and maybe you'll catch yourself something."

My goodness, we were now the old-timers!

Arthur Bunker's Story

I met Arthur Bunker in September of 1952 when we went to Pemetic High School together. In our senior year we stayed at the Hotel Dixie on 42nd Street one night on our week-long class trip. I guess Arthur meant to put some itching powder in *my* bunk, but he came in tipsy and took the powdered bed by mistake and I took what was available, his bunk. He got the powder, but we remained good friends.

When we were in high school, his mother lived on Isleford (Little Cranberry Island) and his sister lived on Great Cranberry. Quite often on weekends I would go down to Isleford and stay with him. In the winter we'd go bird hunting or whatever. Well, one night when I was staying with him in the dead of the winter, we went over to Big Cranberry Island with his sister. She had children there and, being a bit irresponsible, we never told her I was coming, so to make room they had to take one of the kids to bed with them while Arthur and I shared a child's bed. We slept together that night, and I can remember his sister giving him hell about it in the morning. She said, "Arthur, don't you ever do this again. You tell me when you're coming."

Anyway, it was that Saturday night on Great Cranberry before Arthur's bawling out that we went up to the firehouse to play cards. There was this crotchety old geezer there—I can't remember his name, but he was the janitor—and he had the stove all cranked up because the firemen were having a meeting that night. This janitor was a little deaf, so he had got the television wound right up, and us boys went and started playing the eighty-three card game. This game takes four to play and you play in couples. Well, Arthur had enough so he just went over, big as Billy-be-damned, and shut the television off. That didn't go over too good. "Turn that goddamn television on just the way I had it!" the geezer said.

Arthur said, "You have got to turn it down." Then he thought for a second and added, "All right, we'll come to a compromise. We'll go halfway." He set the dial accordingly, and the old man at least tolerated it.

Then in come the other fellas. We were all there, everybody from the island, a big social event, having a good time, and then the firemen had to have their meeting (it's why they came in the first place). They didn't let official business get in the way; they managed to hold it in fifteen minutes, pretty much record time, meeting called to order, meeting adjourned, and then we all go back to playing.

Now, the janitor had a 1930-odd coupe—one of the old factory cars, rumbleseat and the works. About 10 o'clock the old guy decides he is going home; he had all he wanted of our ruckus. A bit later, though, in he comes through the door. The hall is full of people, and he is livid! He looks at us four teenagers over there playing cards and starts calling us every piece of profanity he can think of. Arthur just looks up and says, "I appreciate it if you didn't call us your family names. What is your damn problem, anyway?"

Well, someone had gone out and shoveled his little car right solid full of snow and, of course, he thought it was us young folks. When it boiled down to it weeks later, his own son, it turned out, had opened up the door and done it. But anyway, that was one happy Saturday night on Cranberry Island.

Arthur went into the Air Force right after high school. He made a career of it too, stayed in for twenty-two years. He took his boot camp at some big Air Force base in Texas and, as a recruit, unlike me, he shot the highest score with a rifle of any man that had ever gone through that facility. No one ever topped his score, so far as I know. Arthur was like a computer when it came to rifles, handguns, and carbines. He knew the bullets; he knew the speed of a bullet; he knew the grains of powder in it; he knew how the lead was made—anything there was about a weapon he was simply a genius at it. The Air Force let him set up the rifle range and gave him free rein because there wasn't anyone who knew what they were doing better than Arthur. He taught there eleven years.

After the Vietnam fighting started, Arthur transferred to California. His ambition was to be a tail gunner on a B52 bomber. He had to take special training for the guns on that aircraft. There was a pair of them for defending the bomber and, during his training, Arthur figured out a way to perfect the gun better than anyone had before him, to make it shoot more efficiently than the way the government had them set up.

So they allowed Arthur, on his planes, to alter the gun the way he wanted it to make it perform at its maximum. Arthur did that in combat for another eleven years.

One time he was in a group flying in squadron formation returning from a bombing mission over Southeast Asia, and the pilot of the plane directly to the rear was coming right up too close. Arthur was sitting in the tail of the plane as usual; he could see there was an accident waiting to happen—the pilot was too close for safety—so he radioed his own pilot and said, "This fellow on your tail is too close. Tell him to back off just a little bit, would ya? There could be an accident here."

When he heard the message, the pilot of the other plane got mad. He said, "You tell your tail gunner to mind his own damn business, please! I am flying the plane, not him." And that pilot kept right there. Well, Arthur took those guns—of course he didn't aim at the plane itself—but he let go a burst of fire. Soon, the other pilot called Arthur's pilot and said, "Your tail gunner is shooting at me!"

Our pilot said to Arthur, "What in hell is going on back there? Can you explain? The other plane says you fired at him."

"Now you tell that son of a bitch," Arthur replied, "if I had fired at him he'd be a ball of fire heading for the earth right now. That was just a warning shot but, by the way, I am noticing he has backed off."

"Well," our pilot says, "don't do it again, please."

That was Arthur.

In his later years, Arthur was retired and living in Abilene, Texas. One night he was installing refrigeration in a restaurant and, when he came out, about 10 o'clock, three or four guys walked by him as he was going towards his vehicle. He paid no attention to them and just kept on his way, but one came up and used a lead pipe to smash him in the head. Not a robbery or anything, no rhyme or reason, just one of those crazy things that happens. Arthur came to three weeks later in a military hospital. He'd lost his taste; he'd lost his smell; and he never was quite right after that. They didn't even know if he was going to come out of it, but he did; only now he was slower. He'd had brain damage because they really belted him hard. Later on, he also got cancer of the lung, which went to his brain, and he passed away.

Before his funeral my dog Boomer and I went down to Seawall for a walk. I was sitting there just at dawn—the sun hasn't come up over the horizon—and flying in from Long Ledge, by the Western Way bell buoy, right up the channel, was a flock of gulls in squadron formation, the way the Air Force flies. I said aloud, "Arthur, it's you. I know it's a sign from you. I am watching now because I have never seen gulls flock like this."

It was a big flock and they sure were flying not like gulls but like Air Force planes. I observed them closely because I knew it was a clue. They were heading right up the Western Way, and I thought to myself, "They will go up and, when they get to where there is a settlement on Cranberry Island, they will shear off and fly as a salute over the island." This was my thinking because that's where he was raised, but it didn't happen that way. They went straight up to the north instead, so I says, "Arthur, I don't understand it."

Boomer and I got in the truck and went to Ship Harbor to continue our outing. We walked down the path all the way to the intertidal zone. We sat on the beach, just quiet; the sun had come up and I looked towards Wonderland. Coming from the Cranberry Islands, right over Wonderland, towards Ship Harbor were seven cormorants flying in a perfect "V" formation.

Now, when I was younger, there were not near as many cormorants as there are today. They are a lone bird and always fly low over the ocean with their wing tips barely clearing the water. They very seldom elevate and never in a "V"; that is not the cormorant's way. Furthermore, about the only time you would ever see two of them together was in the spring at mating time and then you might see, at most, a pair of companions flying, but other than that they are a solitary creature. Because no one bothers the cormorants around here, in the last fifty years cormorants have multiplied and become numerous enough to fly in "V" formation. It seems like it might be an evolutionary thing with them because they haven't got it in perfect pattern yet. When they do formations, they wibble, wobble, wibble, wobble all over. It is a riot watching them try to accomplish this. They lose elevation, and the flock falls apart.

Yet here come seven cormorants with the lead bird and three on each wingtip as if they had been trained by the Air Force. They were jet black against a cobalt blue sky and headed west-southwest. It looked like they were going to proceed until they get to Bass Harbor Bar and then, I predicted to myself, they would head west.

Just like I thought, when they got to Bass Harbor Bar, they pulled sharply to the westward, took up elevation, and went up, up into that cobalt blue, until they were completely out of sight in the sky.

I knew why they were going west. Dana Mitchell, my Penobscot friend, told me that, in his culture, when the human spirit goes back home after death, regardless of where it is, it heads west. I was still sitting there thinking about this when I looked up in the sky to the north of Ship Harbor and saw a plane in that cobalt with the sun gleaming right off her, illuminating her, making her bigger than life. She was a tremendous plane—no Cessna but a major, heavy-duty government plane. She headed south. I said to myself, "I wonder at what point she is going to head west." Well, when she got to Ship Harbor, that plane just flew west out of sight. That was Arthur. It had to be a phantom jet. Arthur was at its controls, going home.

I was still sitting there looking towards Bass Harbor Head when this incredible array of auspicious omens like a scheduled parade continued. Here comes an eagle flying east-southeast, level and on a steady course. When he gets right where I am, he shifts and shoots directly for the sun. I thought, "Arthur, I am getting it. A new day is dawning for you, isn't it?"

Yet I still couldn't figure out why those gulls didn't go over Cranberry Island, though. That one baffled me. I was thinking about this as Boomer and I slowly headed up from the intertidal zone and, just as soon as I stepped up onto the main shore and began on the path that leads into the woods, I said to myself, "Arthur, I've got it! I now know why the gulls done what they done. You were raised in Cranberry Island, but you were born in Manset! So those gulls split the difference; they flew right up the Western Way, between the two shores of Manset and Cranberry Island. I got it at last."

Frank Withee

Not everyone believes in spirits and signs, and I'm not going to try to convince you. I can only tell you my own experiences and let you interpret them as you will. I wonder myself sometimes if I'm not susceptible to overdramatizing the ordinary to make a good story, finding magic where there are only birds and clouds and coincidences. Let me tell you something else that happened recently, and you be the judge.

Frank Withee was a man I met in the Army, December of 1961. He came up and introduced himself to me when we were working in the 14th infantry motor pool. He stuck out his hand

and said, "I am Specialist E-4 Frank Withee of Headquarters Company. I drive that little baby over there." He pointed towards his truck. Of course, it was the biggest truck in the motor pool.

I says, "I am Private E-Zero Wendell Seavey. I'm in B Company. I drive for the second squad of the 81 Mortars, and that's my little gem right over there."

He says, "How do you like Army life?" He was a lifer. He reminded me of the cartoon character, this old gruff Sergeant Orville Snorkel in Beetle Bailey.

I says, "I hate the Army life and I cry for my mother quite often."

"Oh, that's just because you're new here. After you get used to it, you'll love Army life."

"Really?"

He says, "What are you doing this Sunday?"

I says, "Oh, probably swimming down to Waikiki Beach and looking at the beautiful women."

He says, "Forget that foolishness. I work at a pony farm. I'll pick you up in front of Quad E at 8 o'clock on Sunday morning. You come and work on the farm with me, and at the end of the day I'll take you to my place and introduce you to my wife Shirley and my kids, and you can have supper with us."

The relationship lasted over forty years.

When Frank died on the 3rd of November, 2004, I had just left his bedside at Maine Medical Center in Portland twenty minutes before. I was driving home, and my mind was on my friend and his family. After a couple of hours I saw a sign that said "Bangor, 26 miles," and I thought I was near home, but the next thing I knew I was on a strange road sixty miles north of Bangor. I found out where I was by asking a woman at a rest stop.

When I finally returned home two and a half hours later,

Ann told me, "Mark my word; you are going to get a sign from Frank."

On the 6th of November I went for a walk with my two dogs to a very isolated spot three miles from my house, Old Point on west side of Bass Harbor. There is a cottage there owned by Julia Child's brother-in-law. While resting on a bench, I saw a small chain laying next to me on the porch, and I wondered what it was. I went over and picked it up, and two dog tags that were down in the crack of the porch came out. I said, "Dog tags! Who could have lost dog tags here?" I took them over and set down on the bench to look at them; they read, "Wendell S. Seavey, U.S. 51469107." I exclaimed, "My God, they're mine."

I looked up in the southwestern sky, and I said, "Frank, how *did* you do that?"

At the funeral I asked his family if I could place one of the dog tags in his coffin as a small gift from me.

They all nodded yes.

My Sons

My sons, Wayne and Frank, are both good boys. They're giants compared to me, both more than a little over six feet and over two hundred pounds; they like to joke about how I must have been turned into a midget when no one was observing. During childhood we had lots of great adventures together, and both boys went fishing with me often. They also got exposed to more of the world than most Maine kids growing up during their time.

After Frank completed his basic training at the Great Lakes Naval Station, he did three months of special training at the same base. That was the time I told you about meeting up with him. After that he got transferred to the *U.S.S. El Paso,* which was an amphibious ship that carried the Marines and their equipment wherever need be. He did his full tour of duty on the *El Paso* in the Atlantic, Mediterranean, and Red Sea. Just about two days before he was scheduled to be discharged in Norfolk, there were some hijinks among the men—what we used to call "playing grab-ass" in the Army—and a mattress was set afire aboard ship, not exactly what you want in a confined space at sea. The fire was put out before anything came of it, but one of the men, a cheese-eater, singled out Frank and ratted on him, just plain wanted to get him in trouble. Matters escalated and, before you knew it, there was going to be a full court-martial in the spring of 1992. That was when I told Frank that I wanted to come to Norfolk and talk to the captain of the ship. He did not want me to do that; he said, "Stay where you are." He continued to work on the base in Virginia, and the proceedings against him continued.

The trial was coming up in September, and his lawyer wanted me to be there because he considered calling me on the stand as a character witness. Frank had no say in the matter, but I think, by then, he was glad enough to have his dad come down.

Ann and I drove to Norfolk for the trial. We got a motel room; Frank even stayed with us. The afternoon of the trial the judge said that he wanted more examinations done. As we were driving across the base afterwards, I told Frank that I wanted to go to the *El Paso* and talk with Captain Pernini, the one who initiated the court-martial.

Frank said, "I have no desire ever to set foot on the *El Paso* again."

I said, "Look, Ann and I traveled these one thousand miles for you; you're going to go this last mile for me."

Reluctantly he guided us to where the *El Paso* was at pier. He complained, "It won't do you any good because Captain

Pernini leaves two-thirty every afternoon." It was already half past three.

I said, "You don't know he's not there. That may be the way it always has been, but you don't know where he is today."

When we got to the gate, it was locked and under guard. I said, "Frank, talk to the guard and get me through that gate."

He explained that he was stationed on that ship and I was his father. The guard let us through. As we were approaching the gangplank, Frank, much surprised, noticed that Captain Pernini's car was on the pier. He said, "What is he doing here? He's never here at this time of day."

I responded, "He doesn't know it, Frank, but he's waiting to see your father."

He was thunderstruck; he couldn't believe Pernini was still there, although he well knew about the psychic activity in his family.

When we got up to the deck of the ship, I spoke to the officer. I said, "I want to speak to Chief Petty Officer Whiller." That was Frank's immediate superior.

When Petty Officer Whiller appeared at the gangplank, I said, "Can you get me an audience with Captain Pernini this afternoon and, if not, I am willing to come back tomorrow."

"Wait here, and I'll go speak to the captain."

When Whiller came back, he said, "Follow me. The captain said he will talk to you."

I was led by myself to a large officers' conference room. The captain greeted me at the doorway and dismissed the others. He was a little bit larger man than I, very stoic and serious-looking; he had powerful, penetrating eyes. We were two men about the same age. He said, "I will meet with Mr. Seavey in private."

Once we took our seats in the conference room I said how sad I was about all the shit that had happened, and I explained to him how patriotic Frank had always been, even since a young boy; that he always had the American flag in his bedroom; he would wear no clothes except those that were made in the U.S.A.; and he always wanted to join the Navy when he got older. "I think what went wrong was that Frank went in as an enlisted man," I said, "and I don't think it challenged him enough. He should have joined for six years and become a commissioned officer."

Captain Pernini said, "I think Frank has the ability to become anything he wants to become." He told me that it was in the hands of the court and he had no power over it now.

After some Army and Navy talk, I changed the conversation. "Captain Pernini, I noticed you have two daughters. I no longer want to talk to you as a military man but father to father." I was looking right in his eyes and, as soon as I said that, they softened.

Pernini said that the man who reported Frank was troublesome and had since gone AWOL. Then he added, "Well, maybe I do have a little say in this matter." He provided me with three or four things that he wanted Frank to complete. He said, "If Frank will do those, I will see what I can do for Frank." I am sure readers of this book will understand why I leave those matters between Captain Pernini and Frank Seavey.

That is when we ended our meeting. Immediately thereafter an officer came into the conference room and announced, "I will see Mr. Seavey to the gangplank."

Captain Pernini addressed the officer, "You are excused. I will take Mr. Seavey to the gangplank myself."

I'm embarrassed to say this, but I'm going to because it is the authentic end of the story. Captain Pernini added, "Frank is lucky to have you for a father."

Then the Captain and I shook hands at the gangplank, and I went down and met Frank on the pier.

I told him what Captain Pernini wanted him to do, and I said, "You make sure you do it because he's going to check up." I also told him, "It's my opinion that the judge is just waiting for a sign from Pernini. If Pernini puts his thumb up, the judge will spare your head. And, like in the days of ancient Rome, if he puts his thumb down, that judge will take your head off, symbolically, of course. " The judge was strict; the day before he had sentenced a man to forty-two years in a federal prison. I don't know what he done.

Frank followed through; two or three weeks later they had the trial. He had to do three months in the stockade, and he received an honorable discharge.

It's been said: all's well that ends well, and I figure this ended about as well as it could have under the circumstances.

Today Frank is married with three children and working for a dairy company in Bangor.

Wayne was different from Frank. He went right off into fishing. That's all he ever really wanted to do, follow in his grandfather's footsteps. My father was a local legend in this area, a man of great integrity, and Wayne heard all about him on the wharf. You could say he followed in my footsteps too, as far as fishing went, but we'll leave it at Gramp.

For better or worse, Wayne was more than a fisherman. I'm afraid he was every bit the hell-raiser that his old man was, and then some, and that's saying something, given the reputation of the No Good Boyo. Yet I couldn't hold a candle to my son in this respect. He burned it at both ends the first seven years out of high school—wine, women, and song, nothing left to the imagination; sowing his wild oats; he done it all.

Then he had an auto accident that almost took out his life. One afternoon in 1994 he crashed his car at high speed somewhere on Route 102 between Southwest Harbor and Ellsworth;

he smacked his head against the front windshield. The impact threw him into the back seat, so it banged his head into the rear windshield too. He ruptured his spleen and was bleeding internally, and the surgeon who had to remove it said that, if he was a half hour later getting to the hospital, they couldn't have saved him; he would have been dead.

Sue, Ann, and I were all called to the hospital. Wayne was conscious. First thing he said to me was, "I could have died from this one, couldn't I, Dad?"

I said, "You come about as close as you could come without doing it." I added, "You're twenty-five now. You've had seven years out of high school to sow your wild oats. Now it's time to call it quits. If you don't, you'll be hooked on this for the rest of your life. There comes a time you have to say, 'I've done enough of it.' Wayne, only you can stop this. If you continue to live in the fast lane, you're going to end up dead. If you do, I'm going to come to your funeral, and I'm going to cry, and it's really gonna hurt me, and I'm really gonna miss you. And then, no matter how painful, life goes on."

Soon after that he met Julie, and he changed his way of living altogether. He dropped his wild ways, the partying and fast driving. He got married, had a daughter Jordan, became a great dad, and was Mr. Responsible for five years. I went fishing with him some of that time, but I'm afraid I was a little slow for his operation, and he wanted a younger, stronger man to go with him than what I had become.

Wayne is still a responsible fisherman and father, and a great son, but he and Julie are no longer living together. In fact, she's now married to my friend Billy Soukup's son Bill, and Wayne is living with Tricia, a Native American from northern Maine.

Let me put it this way. Wayne almost died once, and he knows as well or better than most that he's got just this one life, and he's going to try his hardest to live it as Wayne Seavey and figure out who Wayne Seavey is. If that means a little more creativity and adventure than most can handle, well 'twere it ever so.

Overboard

M arch 19, 2002, was a day that I went lobstering with Wayne. There was an eighteen- or twenty-mile-an-hour easterly wind when we set out, nothing to write home about, just disagreeable. It was fine for fishing.

We were hauling our traps at about one o'clock in the afternoon and were on the next-to-last pair. The wind was hitting the boat on the port side, as Wayne pointed her southward. The tide was flood, to the east, so the wind and tide were going against each other. It was kicking up some good whitecaps.

I usually stood right behind Wayne's bait box, facing the bow of the boat, but this particular time, I had gone around so that the starboard side of the boat was to my back. We were both working on traps when the boat went down into a very deep roll like falling into a valley in the sea. It threw me towards the starboard side almost as if an aikido master had pushed me. The combing took me right in back of the knees and flipped me up over the side, just like that. It sent me over the boat, and I landed in the ocean. I tried to grab the side as I was going over but couldn't get a hold of it.

I struck the ocean right on my shoulders, fully dressed. I had on my oil coat with the hood up, and I was wearing a barvel and my boots. It took me by total surprise. I said to myself, "My God, I am in the ocean!" Well, I thought all I had to do was tread water for a minute or so and my son would come haul me up.

What Wayne had seen was my boots going over the side. When my feet hit the water, the wind pushed the boat forward and the tide pulled me under it. I went in under the bilge and got trapped there. The next thing I said to myself was, "My God, I am under the boat!"

I could look out from under and see daylight. When the boat hit the water, she was making a lot of bubbles, and the water itself was kind of murky. Everything looked as if I taken Saran wrap and put it over my eyes—hazy and blurry. I could see the light of day out by the turn of the bilge, so I got onto my left side and tried to swim out from under her. It didn't work. There was so much force between the tide pushing me under and the wind blowing the boat down over me, I couldn't get free of her, not that way. I was thinking that maybe I ought to try and dive under the boat and come up on the other side.

Wayne could not move the boat because he did not know where I was. Had I been around the propeller and he made the wrong choice, it would have cut me to nothings, so it was a risk he couldn't take. He thought I was under the boat but wasn't sure if I had sunk completely. He was thinking of putting a gaff handle down, hoping that I could see it and get a hold of it so he could haul me out. But the visibility was so poor he would have had to get it right in front of me for me to recognize it for what it was.

I cancelled out the idea of trying to dive under the boat. All I had was the air in my lungs and, being no pearl diver, I didn't know if I even had enough of it to get out alive, let alone complete a dive. So I decided that my best bet was to keep on my side and hopefully swim out from under her. I kept my head down because the boat was whacking me and I was afraid if she hit me square in the head that would have been it. I just swam a sidestroke and kept at it.

About thirty seconds later I came out from under, facing away from the starboard side.

It takes far longer to tell this story than it took in real time. I heard Wayne holler, and he grabbed me by both shoulders and said, "I have got you, Dad!" He is strong as a bull. He gave me a hell of a pull and hauled me out of the water. I stood right there on the platform and just looked at him.

"Well, Wayne," I said, "you have just saved your father's life."

"Are you hurt, Dad?"

"No, I am just fine."

"I have got a pair of sweatpants, dry winter socks, and a T shirt down in the cabin. You go down and get changed. and I'll get the boat closed in and the gas heater lit. Go ahead."

I hesitated. "Do you want to haul that last pair of traps?"

"To hell with the last pair of traps! Go down get changed. We are going home."

I had saved my own father's life once, many years before, and it extended it for nine years. How long Wayne has extended my life remains to be seen.

At the time, the anxiety of the adventure didn't bother Wayne too much, but the next day it kind of settled in on him what could have happened. I said, "Wayne, if I ever drowned, I would never want you to give up fishing because of it. Never blame the ocean. It is very impersonal; it would have been an accident. Don't get angry at the ocean. These are the chances we take."

"No, Dad," Wayne replied, "I wouldn't have been mad with the ocean, but I would have had to sell that boat. I never could have gone in her anymore."

Farewell to the Reader

Since I graduated from high school on the last day of May in 1956, I have spent two years in the Army, five years in the boatyard, almost two years in a health-care facility—nine years on the land—and the rest of it has been on the water fishing: lobstering, hand-lining, gill-netting, shrimping, or scalloping. Forty-one years on the water so far at the time of my book's publication.

We never know how long we're here for. It could only be one day, or it could be a hundred years. That's not up to us. I was born with a caul, so maybe that's kept me from drowning more than once. I stepped away from a car when I was a child. I could have died then, and there would be no story beyond that to tell and no one to tell it.

Chris Kaiser went on a vision quest in the spring of 2004, seeking the vortex to the other world. He had been fasting for three weeks at the bidding of the spirits. His body was found six days after he went missing, floating and decomposed in Hamilton Pond, where he thought the vortex was located. I believe he died four days earlier. That night I was sleeping soundly when my dog Boomer began whining. Boomer always guarded his master's bed, and his response indicated an intruder. But not quite. It was as though something was there that was bigger than he could understand or defend against. He went running out of the bedroom into the living room, knocked over a lamp, and tried to fit himself under a chair that was much too small. He was shaking and terrified for a good hour. No doubt about it, Chris had come to say his final good-byes to me.

Some people might say I have followed in my father's foot-steps, but he had his path to walk and I had mine. We done it differently. His life was as straight as an arrow: fishing-oriented from the word go. My life has taken some curves here and there.

Anyone has regrets, but I have none that are overwhelming. No matter where I went or who I met, it has always been reward-ing. I think I was supposed to meet all those people. You never know from one year to the next when there might be another curve. So like the tides, go with the flow and, if we meet, it could be beautiful and, if we don't, that can't be helped.

Excerpts from
Wendell Seavey's Letters,
Journals, and Stories

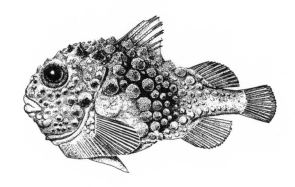

March 11, 1961, to Mom and Dad

I have not been able to write letters because we have been in the field for the last nine days. We were driving up Mt. Kahaka and those roads are steep and slippery with mud. I had food for the men in the truck and shells in the trailer. One of the water cans fell off the truck and I ran over it with the trailer. It stove itself to hell. Then I broke the fan belt and boiled the engine. So I was broke down on a hill. Then another truck hauled the food. I was left with truck and trailer that night.

Tell Darrell he does not want to get in the Army. It is no good. The Navy or Air Force would be much better for everyone. I'll probably be home next summer and will talk to him. If he does not go to school, he might as well go in the service and get it over with because, if you don't join, the Army will get you sooner or later on, just as they did me. If you're in good health, you just can't keep out. If he does go to school, they will get him as soon as he gets out. There is no missing it. So one might as well join the branch he wants to and try to like it. They will get him one way or the other. The Marines and Army are no good. You can let him read this, but it probably won't do any good because one learns the hard way.

December 30, 1961, to Mom and Dad

Tell everyone to write. I am very lonely now. I am training to load, aim, and fire the 106 mm. gun. She is a big gun; it takes three men to shoot her. Just the back blast from her could kill you if you stood within 85 feet directly behind her when you fire her. And she could hurt you at 135 feet from behind her. So if she can do that from the behind, you can think what the shell that comes out of the barrel can do.

I am also training to aim and load the 81 mm. mortar gun.

It takes three to work that gun. She is used for killing a big bunch of men.

Also I am taking advanced infantry training and training with the M1 gun and soon the M14 gun. I am training in truck driving and in computing. That is aiming the big guns at targets we can't see when shooting at them, plus how to kill men with your hands. It is hand-to-hand combat and they teach you only enough to make sure you would get killed if you tried to use it. All the other men have one job to do, and that's it. I would make a good convict after I get out of this outfit.

We were training at crossing a river where the bridge has been blown out. We made rafts out of our raincoats and put our rifles and clothes on them and swam with the stuff across the river. I was swimming with one of the sergeants and he got all wore out when we were only halfway across. I kept him up until they got him on a raft. Then I swam his equipment and mine across. When we came back I swam two rifles, two helmets and two helmet liners, and his clothes and my clothes, plus him, and he was nothing but dead weight. They were alongside of us with a raft, but I got him across without their help. He said he would come back and haunt me if I drowned him! Two days later Headquarters sent a sergeant to find out if I knew how to swim. I wonder how much proof it will take to convince them.

A lot of the people are dying back home. I've got three letters and six people are dead. Before I get back, at that rate nobody will be left.

I am glad to get letters and will write everyone in time. But when you're training to be a combat man, it is not easy and you don't have much time. So I'll write mostly one letter home and you can let the others read them. I'll close now.

March 12, 1963, to Mom and Dad

That weather you're having back there is sure a lot different than what we're having here in Hawaii. You folks must be some tired of nothing but storms by now. Maybe March will go out like a lamb. But it may also go out like a tiger if it keeps up.

I told you in my last letter I got the fudge okay. It is some good. This morning when I thought the coast was clear I got into my locker and was filling my pockets with fudge, only to look over my shoulder to see the platoon sergeant behind me holding his hand out. So in order to keep his mouth shut, I kind of had to give him a couple of pieces of it. Last I see of him he was walking off, smacking his lips.

Was I surprised when you said you heard Crosby and his wife were getting divorced. And Ruth and Austin. I guess marriage don't mean anything. It is mostly a show. Really it don't mean anything at all. People seem to live together until they get tired of each other, then swap around. Marriage nowadays is nothing but a joke.

The only thing holding me up from getting promoted to E4 now is that damn platoon sergeant. My squad leader is trying his best to get me my E4 stripes. He says there is no reason why I should not have more rank when I get out in August, but this platoon sergeant won't put me in for it. That's the trouble with the Army. You can deserve something, but one man can hold you up. He is also the man that stopped my leave. That is the trouble when your life is in the hands of others. They can hold you up for any reason they want to and there isn't much you can do about it. If Captain Schofield had stayed, I'll bet I would have been E4 a long time ago and, before I got out, I would have been ready to have gone up for sergeant. Any of the men that are here now that were here when Schofield was here will tell you if he had stayed I would have been a sergeant before my time was up. That's the way it goes. If a man in the higher ranks likes you, you can go ahead fast. But if they don't pull for you, then you can't make shit—leastways in the Army. The squad leader has put me in for E4 today. Once again, whether that platoon sergeant will blackball it again only time will tell. In another five months I won't need the approval of any of them, but it would help right now.

March 17, 1963, to Mom and Dad

The weather has been overcast and we've had showers for the past couple of days. Today is the same. Yesterday I took my camera with me and stopped off at Honolulu's International Airport and took eleven pictures there. They have just rebuilt it all new. The old airport was too small to handle all the business. Air transportation is sure growing big nowadays. Planes carry a lot more people now than ships do. It takes a week to go from Hawaii to California by ship, only five hours by plane. Passenger planes now fly about 600 miles per hour. They say in ten years these planes will be outdated and passenger planes then will be flying about 2000 miles per hour. One will be able to fly around the Earth faster than the sun goes around it.

I took the last picture of the Aloha Tower. That is the tower down on the waterfront where a lot of the big passenger ships come in to dock.

I just saw Charles Bartlett this morning. I was writing this letter at the YMCA and looked across the street and there goes Charlie with a lady on his arm. They went down one street and I went down another where they could not see me. Then I crossed over to their side and we just happened to meet each other on the street. They were going to church, so we didn't have time to talk very long, but long enough so the next time I see him he will have no choice but to tell me about his girl. That was the first time I had see him in a long time. He has been hiding too long, so this morning I thought I'd ambush the old buzzard and see what he has been up to. HA! HA! Now I know he has got him a girlfriend. I don't know all the details at this time.

May 21, 1963, to Mom and Dad

Yesterday we were on the range firing the B.A.R. rifles. They shoot a 20-round clip of ammo in seconds just by pulling the trigger back once. If one has a good loader by his side to put a clip in the gun as fast as you shoot it, you can really put out some lead. The M-14 is supposed to replace the B.A.R.

Glad to hear Irving and Dad are getting a few fish. Too bad they can't get ahold of some herring. That was nice a couple of years back when we could get them up to the Hub in a truck. That was just great that year. Where are they fishing to now? And what's the price of fish? Is anyone going trawling this year?

Tomorrow I was supposed to go into the field for a couple of days, but they are giving a man an undesirable discharge and are sending him back to the States. So I got the job of driving him to the airport to load him on. We have to be there two hours before the plane takes off and I have to stay there until the plane is halfway back to the States before I leave. They do that in case the plane has trouble and has to come back. After the halfway mark the plane might as well go on as come back if it has trouble, so after that we go back to the post. That is better duty than going out in the field anyway.

So Ellis came back and Edgar is going, huh? Did he take his wife back after she ran off with Lawrence? What's Ellis doing for work now? Has Russ had anyone looking at his boat? He ought not to have any trouble selling her.

I plan to go to the beach tomorrow if it doesn't rain. Am glad the snow is gone back there. Is the lobstering picking up much? I just wrote to Tucker Spurling over to Manset.

98 more days and I leave Rock Hawaii.

May 23, 1963, to Mom and Dad

I don't consider my time as wasted at all, even though I didn't learn any trade. Although there are times when I am mad and might run the Army down to the lowest notch, I've learned a lot just the same from the Army. That's the way it goes.

The weather is some hot. At the end of each day you can wring the sweat right out of your clothes.

How is Clarence's arm now and how did he hurt it?

I'll bet those smelts and lobsters tasted good. It would be nice to have some seafood once again. Last Friday I tried some scallops we had for dinner, but a golf ball would have been just as good. For some reason they can't keep fish as good as they can meat and make it taste much at all.

I hope to get on a ship that is leaving the first part of August. If not, I'll be on the one that's leaving the last part of the month.

June 16, 1963, to Mom and Dad

Those halibut that Dad and Irving are getting must be helping out. Are many of the other boats fishing this spring? Do they plan on still going for pollock and selling them next winter? Glad to hear Darrell is shaping up some and is going to help himself when he can.

Well, we had an inspection by the General out on Dragon Field on Saturday. As usual my truck came out the highest. They said that truck and trailer was outstanding. You would think that they would realize that the truck did not get in an outstanding condition by itself and that it took an outstanding man to get it that way and that man should have more out-standing rank than the others. But it doesn't seem to work that way. Oh well, I am so short now that rank makes no difference.

I went to the beach yesterday afternoon and today you couldn't tell much difference 'tween me and a lobster.

December 11, 1970, to Richard and Lindy Grossinger

November was a very busy month for me, lobstering most all the time. The month was windy but not so bad but what we could make fishing days out of them. When I got a day off all I wanted to do was rest. The lobsters came in good that month but, since the snow came, the lobsters are headed for deeper water or, as the boys in Augusta would say, "No such thing; they have just stopped crawling in shallow water and are now crawling in deep water."

Richard, I was reading your book *The Provinces,* and Mr. Reginald Uzman sure has us Maine fishermen out to be numbskulls. First he says the lobsterman is stubborn, thick. Then he says: "This is a famous fisherman's myth, that lobsters migrate, that lobsters move great distances. That's because they think they're following lobsters. What they're following is an optimum thermocline, an isotherm of 12° C. The lobsters in colder water are numbed into lesser activity. They don't come out to feed, so they don't get caught in the traps. In the winter the water is colder closer to shore; the reverse is true in the summer. The lobster's availability is purely a function of the temperature of the waters. The lobster has no higher motives, like migration; he wants to survive and reproduce, and it is my thesis that, although lobsters can survive at less than 12° C., this is the temperature regime required for their eggs, which they carry a whole year. The lobsterman, as I said, achieves a certain degree of empirical success, and then he stagnates; they set their pots in the same places; they emulate each other; it's really a case of the blind leading the blind."

Well, whichever idear one believes, the way you catch them is no difference. You got to have your traps in the right place at the right time. So whether the eye seeing dog follows his blind master or whether the blind master follows his dog I know not, but they both seem to end up at the same place at the same time.

In about another month Mert Rich and I are going shrimping in his boat. That will be a new line in the field for the both of us. In another four months or so I can let you know how that turns out.

April 28, 1971, to Richard and Lindy Grossinger

It has been some time ago since I've last written to you. Even though I don't write much I think of you often.

We came through the winter no worse for the wear. The kids had a couple of bouts with the flu and I was laid up for a week with a cold. That was the last part of January, so that's all history.

Merton Rich and I went after shrimp but didn't do much at it along with many others. For about a week and a half we done good, but it didn't last very long. If it hadn't been for one spot we found, we wouldn't have done much at all. Many did not even find that one spot.

That was my first try at dragging. Although we were dragging for shrimp, I know that fish dragging is done basically the same way. I can tell you I don't like it. As far as I am concerned, it destroys too many other forms of life for what you catch. I like fishing that doesn't hurt the ocean bottom and doesn't hurt other forms of life or, if it does, it is as little as possible. There is something about dragging that to me seems very crude. I doubt if I ever go again.

I think it is high time we began to start taking care of this old Earth. We are going to have to reconsider our ways of doing things and our outlook at it. I think man's selfish outlook and ways of doing things are now starting to back him into a corner.

I am checking the notes you made when you were interviewing me for your study. You made copies for me to correct, and I can't believe I said those things. Perhaps you mistook me for another lobsterman. I am joking, of course. I think I was just speaking wharf language for you, telling you what people here think. I have changed so much since then that I don't believe my own words: "God created man, not the lobster, in His image. Anyone can see from how ugly he is that the lobster was created in the devil's image. It's man's job to subdue the wild beasts and tame the Earth. You can read it in Genesis; he was given this territory by God. He was set over the beasts in the field and the birds in the air and the fish in the sea. The way some people talk you'd think man was making things worse and it was the lobsters and the other animals that were doing God's work. Well, man wasn't made to be idle or starve like some people believe. He was made to go out in the elements, to go against storms, to learn what the devil is like and defeat him. You can't stand up to the devil in life unless you've gone out on a cold winter day and seen him face to face. Then you meet him and learn his ways. It teaches you how to live, which the minister can't, nor the school teacher with all his books."

On page 288 of *Book of the Cranberry Islands,* you also use my words, and I remember this discussion. I had just read your writing about me in the *Oecology* issue, and I was going to give as good as I got. I said: "Richard, you sit down by a typewriter in a nice warm room and type, and sure it's easy to write about how nature is so good and man is the evil one who's destroying all this beauty. But things don't look quite the same once you get right down there with her. Nature's not quite so good and friendly. It's cold and storms and winds, and a man has to do everything in his power to keep from getting destroyed by nature. If man didn't subdue nature, nature'd subdue man. I know, you and all your friends think that nature is good, and we're the evil lobstermen just killing and taking selfishly for our own interests. You come very easy to say that it's nature as the work of God and the Devil working in Man to destroy it. Well, I'm not so sure it's nature and God against man and the Devil. It's man who was made in God's image, and how do you know that nature's not the work of the Devil trying to destroy man?"

I no longer think it is man and God on sides against the devil and nature. I am beginning to think man is too selfish to give a damn what either nature or God thinks about his actions as long as he can git what he thinks he wants.

It's funny how a man can get an idear in his head and go along with it so long and be blind to any other thought. Well, I guess you have listened to me bitch and rave long enough in one letter, so I'll go on to something else.

I know you remember old Harve Moore, the man who sat in the chair so much at Thurston's wharf. Maybe I should say Lester's stepfather. He died April 18 at about 9 A.M. He was bringing his boat into the wharf and just before he got to the wharf he dropped dead. The men tried to bring him around, but nothing could be done. He was seventy.

My sister's boy, Chandler Kelley, Jr., has bought a boat and he will soon be going lobstering. Maybe he has seen the light and is going to straighten out now. Here's hoping anyways.

May 16, 1971, to Richard and Lindy Grossinger

Since I last wrote to you, another old-timer died from the wharf. He was Henry Sawyer. My sister had one of the ESP flashes and predicted his death two weeks before it happened. It happened when Henry's daughter came up to my sister and took her by the arm and greeted her. After she left, my sister told of the funny feeling that came over her and told Olive, my other sister, that Henry's death would be soon.

The price of lobsters has been up this spring, but the catch has been way down. The weather seems to me much more like fall than spring. It's hard to get good eating fish these days and, when I do, eating the catch is expensive. I had some ocean perch that wasn't bad. It may be bait, but it's better than haddock at $1.50 per pound.

I got caught up with a tub of gear the other day southward of Spurling Shoal for the second time in a year. No buoy, so someone must have parted with it.

October 27, 1971, to Richard and Lindy Grossinger

This has been a very busy time of year for me and I get very little time for reading. Like Thoreau said in *Walden,* "When my hands were busy I done very little reading." But I do read a little every day. Right now I am halfway through *The Greening of America* by Charles A. Reich. I read seven or ten pages a night according to how long I can stay awake, and a couple of pages before I go haul my traps in the morning.

I was also reading *The Provinces* and was pleased to see that the Canadian biologist you interviewed was not quite so hard on us fishermen. I like what he said. Most of it speaks to my experience with lobstering: "Fisherman always find more movement among lobsters than we've been able to demonstrate. Of course, in some areas if the lobsters didn't move they'd be covered with ice and it would grind them up. They're pretty negative with regard to light. Shine anything and, all else being equal, they'll shun it."

I never did know a lobster who liked light; there's not much of it where they live.

The fishing was not too good this summer. The pollock never came in at all and the codfish were hard to find also. There's not enough fish for a chowder. But it did hold us over until I set my traps out in August. The lobsters are slow this fall also, but in the past two weeks they have improved, and so has the price, from 80 cents to a dollar, and that's a big help.

Sue and I have been reading Scott Nearing and decided to try a garden ourselves next year. The book of his we just read was called *Living the Good Life*. I liked the book very much and hope to meet him and his wife someday. If the ocean keeps on drying up, maybe a garden would be a new answer.

October 15, 1972, to Richard and Lindy Grossinger

We sold our house at Southwest and moved back to Bernard. Those were three weeks I care not to repeat. Our house in Bernard is across to the left from the post office. We have a big field in front and a very good view of the mountains and harbor from here. We have the same amount of rooms here as we had at Southwest plus a good-size barn. I walk less than two minutes down over the hill and I am at the wharf. Sue and I love it here and the kids do also. The house needs lots of work done, but it will be good once it is over with.

I went trawling for hake this summer, and the haking was tops.

We are going to have a garden plowed this fall. Then we will lime it. Right now I am lobstering. There don't seem to be very many lobsters this fall, but now the price is a dollar a pound.

Father Jim is in Rome for three months.

June 24, 1973, to Richard and Lindy Grossinger

I read your story about the name of Seavey today from *The Provinces*. I want to thank you very much for it. Here's what I like about it: you found the roots of "sea" and "war" in "Seavey"; I am a peaceful man by nature, but my ancestors battled the sea. These are my favorite parts:

"November 1, 1466: Richard Sewy with William Martyn Senior and William Browne, in breach of assize for brewing ale."

A Seavey after my own heart!

"1489: William Sewy amerced nine pence for having wounded William Browne with a poniard."

That particular weapon did not come down through the family!

"1510: William Sewy fined 1 pence for being among common players of football."

I imagine Wayne takes after him!

"September 11, 1583: The ship *John* returns from Newfoundland with a cargo of oil (Owner: Elizeus Zevye). Exeter port-book."

I'll save that tidbit for the next time someone says his ancestors were fishing the banks before mine.

"June 25, 1640: Saco; charged by Philip Swadden of Piscataqua that 'William Sevey about ten days past, did pull down all the rafters of the stage that Mr. John Beaple fisht in this place,' charged by Nicholas that 'Steven Crafford pertener with the said William Sevey, did ruinate the flakes, short and long layers, with other things belonging to the fishing craft.'"

We Seavey pirates were cutting traps back when lobsters were hog food!

"July 31, 1641: Purchased by John Winter at Richmond Island

five hogsheads of mackerel from William Seavey at the Ile of Shoulds."

That's a lot of mackerel by today's standards!

"1722: Captain Stephen Seavey has purchased an island in Portsmouth Harbor, Isles of Shoals, henceforth known as Seavey's Island."

This fits with my own understanding that my people came most recently from New Hampshire on my father's side.

"March 21, 1728: Newcastle; being of sound and perfect memory but crazy and infirm in the body, William Seavey leaves to Hannah and his son William all his household goods, two acres of salt marsh, one-half his cattle and sheep, and the negro woman Ammi; fifteen pounds each to daughters Hannah and Hephsibah and sons Thomas and Ebenezer; three pounds each to his son-in-law, Captain Samuel Bamfield and grand-daughter Mary (Banfield) Langdon; twenty shillings to his son Stephen."

I'm glad we held some salt marsh but not so glad to hear we were slavers!

"May 18, 1723, Lt. Gov. William Dummer's War (or the Three Years' Indian War): ordered Corporall Seavy to send Ebenezer Seavey and Benjamin Larraby to Roger Dearings Garrison thear to Remain till Further Orders."

I hope none of them was killed. I wouldn't want any Larraby ghosts coming after us!

The winter lobstering held up much better and much later than it has in past winters. I think one reason is because more men went shrimping and not so many went lobstering—so that took some of the load off the lobsters. The spring lobstering has also been much better than it has for the past few springs. Answers to that I dare not guess.

I've had my traps up for about two weeks and have been

hand-lining for codfish since then. Been getting between six and nine hundred pounds per trip. The price is ten cents a pound.

I plan to haul my boat and paint her before I start trawling.

Sue and I had the front lawn plowed up and planted a garden there for this summer. It measures forty-five feet wide and sixty feet long. We have a fence all ways around it. Our potatoes are growing in seaweed and hay. Their spot is about twenty feet by twenty feet square. They appear to be coming along okay. We think it will take about three compost piles to do the job from here on out—a lot of work and fun plus we have a lot of good food.

We've started three apple trees, but it will be another four or five years before we expect much from them.

October 14, 1973, to Richard and Lindy Grossinger

This summer Sue and I took separate vacations. She went to Boston for a week and done her thing; then I went for a week and done mine. It worked out great for both of us.

This fall I am taking a course at College of the Atlantic on Thoreau. The class meets once a week for two hours. It has been seventeen years since I've been to school, and I enjoy this far better than I did seventeen years ago. They are trying to blend the college and the local people together, working and studying together. This is the second year they have been doing that.

Not all the fishermen approve of my new interests. A few Sundays ago while I was fishing I got a call on my radio-telephone and someone who didn't identify himself—but I knew who it was—said, "Don't you know it's Sunday? You oughta be in church with all the good boys. The Lord don't want you out fishing."

Sue is taking a spiritual class once every two weeks and is

very involved in church work now. Today she was voted in as the president of the parish council.

We have studied astrology for the last year or more. Sue has got into it far deeper than I have. Some of our interests are the same and some differ.

As for fishing and lobstering, I went hand-lining for cod in July and had a good month. In August I painted my boat and went on vacation and done a little haking up into September. That was not so good. I am now lobstering and so far that hasn't been so good. Maybe later on it will improve and maybe not.

As Harve Moore liked to say, "Even if I'm not making money, I'm not getting lazy."

May 1, 1974, to Richard and Lindy Grossinger

The first half of the fall was very poor lobstering, but about the middle of October the price went to $1.50 a pound and the lobsters started to crawl, so we made a good fall's work. The winter fishing was good until the first of March, and there has been poor fishing ever since. This is the poorest spring that I've seen since I've been lobstering. We're all hoping that things will improve.

I took a class at COA last fall. Then when that was over, I took a class for about three months on spiritualism in Brewer. That proved very interesting, but it wasn't for me.

Many changes are taking place in the church, and Sue enjoys working for some of these changes. She is also on the warrant committee for the town of Tremont, so she is involved in town work.

There is a man on Big Duck Island who is a Gestalt therapist. He is working at the Jefferson Manor at Bangor and at COA Bar Harbor and has weekend workshops out at the island. He is proving to be very interesting, and sometimes I work as an errand boy, hauling people and things back and forth. That has got people talking, I'll tell you.

September 19, 1974, to Richard and Lindy Grossinger

I want to say at this time I have warm feelings of the days when we used to have our talks and the meals and good times the two families had together. Time sure flies or maybe time stands still and we fly, but either way it has been many weeks since you and your family were last here, and now fall is upon us.

Life has had its ups and downs with us this summer. Our car died and we now have a 1969 station wagon. My boat engine died and I replaced it with another just like her. Our garden done good; summer fishing was bad; and so far lobstering has been good.

Sue is busy in church work and town work. I am busy at bread labor and am reading all I can get my hands on about the Gestalt philosophy. In spite of it all I seem to be just as impossible and crazy as ever.

February 1, 1975, to Richard and Lindy Grossinger

As for a record of how I fish from 1969 to present for your anthropology committee, you will find it lacking because I just record what is earned and what is spent. I don't record number of pounds per day or price per pound. Some fisherman may do that. But this is my way of keeping records for the Government for income tax. There are receipts with number of pounds and price of lobster for the day in which the Government can check on if they want to see if I keep good records or not. I have been checked for years '71 and '72, and the Government was happy with my book-keeping.

I am not willing to go through all the years, but what I have done is to take September '69, December '69, February '70, and

May '70 to just give you a sample of how I do my book-keeping. It doesn't matter what the year, month or price is of what I sell, I use the same system. But I am not willing to put my books up for anyone to go through except for the Government. So I hope this sample will be enough to please those grading you.

January 16, 1976, to Richard and Lindy Grossinger

I've seen some people get a lot of help from George Cloutier who does Gestalt and one-to-one therapy out of Duck Island. For some, Gestalt does a lot, but it is not for everyone; that is for sure. The island is a place where they can live and work as long as they want to under real-life conditions. George feels that many have been in mental hospitals so long they have lost their will to help themselves, and this is what Duck Island does. He doesn't use pills and pain-killers. He feels people with bad problems have hid from their pain long enough and, until they are willing to work on themselves and go through the pain and hell to get this out of them, then there is not much one can do.

My fishing was down this year, so when it comes to silver and gold, these things I have not got. Sue and I are still living what some feel is a radical lifestyle. Some feel it is right on and others shake their heads. We feel it is right for us. She is still involved in town and church work. We both have our different wants and needs but give each other the freedom and space we need to do it in.

I would say mostly things are much the same here. The weather has been wild this winter, very cold, snowy, rainy, icy, and heavy winds. It has been four or five years since we had such a solid winter. Mary is now nine. Wayne will soon be seven. And Frank will soon be six. So the little family grows.

May 30, 1976, to Richard and Lindy Grossinger

I've been sick in bed for the last two days with a cold, and tomorrow will be another day inside for me also. This is the worst cold I've had in twelve years.

About two weeks ago George and Lee from Duck Island were on vacation when their main house on the island got on fire and burned down. Everything in it was lost. There was a person sleeping in it at the time and two others sleeping elsewhere. The woman in the house woke up and was able to get out and get the dog and cat out. The dog was afraid and got in under the house and got burned up, but none of the people got hurt. We were unable to get to George and Lee, so they never found out until they landed the plane on the island a couple of days later. That wasn't much of a welcome home. They are going to build another house this summer starting in a week or so. He is still holding workshops there.

August 11, 1976, to Richard and Lindy Grossinger

We have had a busy summer this year. I have been working at the Oceanarium on Mondays, Wednesdays, Fridays, and Saturdays. Also making the Duck Island runs, sometimes two runs a day. Working at the Oceanarium has not been as enjoyable as what I feel it could have been. I think that the fishing room doesn't flow the way it should but, with some changes, I believe it would. The room flows counterclockwise but, in order to get the full meaning, it should flow clockwise, and that's the way I want to lead visitors, but it's going against the natural flow, the way it's organized. I've talked to David Mills three different times about it, but he doesn't want to change it, so that is that. This is my last week here. Then I'll paint up my boat and start lobstering.

Hurricane Belle has been coming up from Florida this week, packing winds up to 115 mph but, when she got to Connecticut, winds dropped to 55 mph and it went inland through Vermont. We had winds about 35 mph gusting to 50 last night, but today is sunshiny and just great.

The weather has been quite foggy and rainy this summer. Weatherwise this summer has left things to be desired.

Out at Duck Island they are building a log cabin twenty by forty feet from the logs right on the island, so they have their work cut out for them. This will replace the one that burned down last spring.

October 21, 1976, to Richard and Lindy Grossinger

I've done good lobstering this fall. At the first of it my catch wasn't that big, but the price was never below $1.30 a pound, and the weather was the best I've ever seen it for this time of year. The price has gone to $1.50 now, and my catch is around 200 pounds per haul, so I've been able to get some well-needed money.

Mary is taking ballet two times a week. Frank will soon be taking guitar lessons. Sue got him a small guitar yesterday in Bangor. She is still on her year's sabbatical from church work and seems to be doing good. We got us a 1975 Subaru station wagon this fall; our other old car had just had it.

January 10, 1977, to Richard and Lindy Grossinger

The lobstering is still good for winter and the price is $2.80 per pound. I've all my fall gear up and just doing winter fishing. I quit hauling people to Duck Island in early October because it was just too much to fish all day and run to the island nights. I think I'll take up with them in the spring, but so far I haven't missed doing it. I have met some people I really enjoy, and they enjoy me also. But the most of them are like the waves that are made from tossing a rock into the water. A big splash for a moment and then they fade into nothing. Often one sets back and learns that if you want something rich that lasts, one has to find it in one's own self. This is the big lesson I've got from Duck Island. And it is well worth the effort that went into it.

February 15, 1977, to Richard and Lindy Grossinger

Today as I sit at the table writing to you the snow is falling lightly outside. Thank God it's not falling inside. Sue is getting ready to take Mary to the doctor. We have all been sick with the flu back here in the lovely state of Maine. Yuk!

Sue was first to fall to the germ warfare, then Frank, Mary, me, and Wayne. I just got almost over the flu when added attractions came. I got an ear infection and had to go to the doctor and have a spear lanced through my ear. It was such fun I nearly passed out laughing two or three times.

We have got the flu U.T.A. (up the ass). Kids under sixteen should not read this letter without a grown-up with them.

So here I set for another week, enjoying my rest, books, and TV. Wonderful. Wonderful. Wonderful. If they had lobsters in Hawaii, I would sail my boat, kids, wife, and all on the morning tide.

It has been three weeks since I've hauled my traps. Today I did get to the boat and shovel the snow and ice out of her and warmed up the engine. The boys are back to school, and Sue is better too. That means she is able to set up in bed and blink her eyes without help. Mary is showing signs of improvement over yesterday, which means she is not going to have to go to the hospital like we thought. Things are looking up. I can see the silver lining.

Richard, I really enjoyed your last letter. About that one note you wrote on me in the *Oecology* book seven years ago, I want you to really know that I have no bad feelings about that whatsoever. It was a real good learning experience for me, and I am now really glad it happened. I've learned a lot from it and now that is in the past and the past is gone. So please do not have any bad feeling about that, Richard, because it doesn't bother me at all. We both had a lot to learn and I am sure that is why it happened. So in the long run it did happen for the best, I feel.

April 3, 1979, to Richard and Lindy Grossinger

It sounds like you are having a full and interesting life in California. As for us, life has changed somewhat also. I have given up hand-lining and trawling altogether and last summer went gill-netting with Merton Rich and his son Bruce, who is twenty-three now. I was going to go with them summer before last but fell and hurt my hand and couldn't work hard that summer. I really enjoy gill-netting much more than trawling and hand-lining and have no desire to return to the old way of life. I still go lobstering during the spring, fall, and winter.

Duck Island closed down last September. George and Lee wanted to do other things after running the island for five years. So that has gone with the wind.

A year ago a friend of the family that we got to know from Duck Island and who moved back to New Mexico sent me a check and a letter saying for me to come to NM for a free vacation on her. The next day I got a call from her asking if I was coming. Which I said, "I sure am." So on the 19th of January I left and got back on the 6th of February. After telling the family how well I liked it out there, Sue said, "When are we going?" Which I said, "How about next winter?"

So on the 18th of December we headed out and got here on

the 26th. We will be here until the 30th of April, then will be headed back to Maine. Kids are doing well in school after a couple of rough days. Sue has read more books on the Indians of the Southwest than any five people I know of. I am working five days a week at a seafood store and show slides on lobster-fishing, bird life, and scallop fishing on the Maine coast in the schools, clubs, and Indian pueblos. Then on weekends we travel and see 101 things to visit and do in NM. We find this a very beautiful state and have no regrets of coming, although at times it has been painful. Not all fun and games.

Will go gill-netting again this summer and the kids will finish school.

April 24, 1979, to Richard and Lindy Grossinger

Frustrating to be so close and yet so far from you people. We do wish we could get to visit you in California, but time and money will not permit us to come your way.

California must be a very interesting place to live. Maybe, like you say, it couldn't be home, but so what? It must be well worthwhile to live there.

Sue has no calling to live in California at all, but I sure as hell would like to. Maybe someday I will, but it would be so far off that there isn't much sense for me to even think about it because my wants and needs may have changed so, that when it comes so I can, the calling will no longer be there.

I will return to Maine next month with a far different outlook on life and Maine than what I left with. This trip has been a real eye-opener.

I am shocked at what little culture the White people have in this country, and what little love there is for anyone different than what we ourselves are—be it the color of our skin or the way we talk or believe or what have you.

The Indians seem to have culture and know what and where home is to them, but as for us Whites, do we know? I wonder for the first time. The Indians feel we have lost our roots so long ago we don't know where we come from or what our culture was or where our home was. Or wherever it was, where it is today. And our style of life is to rob the land because we have no love for it because it is not home to us. Like we are outsiders.

This will have a big effect on my outlook from here on out. I never thought much about the wisdom of the Indians before, but they seem to know things which we lost a long, long time ago.

My ancestors were living in what we call New England today years before the *Mayflower* came over. Once I thought that was quite something in itself. Now I feel like, so what? They had lost their roots long before that.

What does and what will this mean to me? How will this affect my life and outlook? I just don't know.

I think my mother's mother was a full-blooded Indian. I am not sure because I know very little about her. But maybe I can find out more about my roots by checking her side of the family out than I have from my dad's.

Well, these are some of the bones this trip has given me to chew on.

A week ago Sunday on Easter Sunday we went to see the corn dances at Santa Domingo and Santa Anna. We have been treated very well by the Pueblos while visiting their towns.

The kids have said they hated Albuquerque but loved the beauty of New Mexico. They enjoyed meeting the Indians. Sue asked them if they would ever want to come back here again; they said maybe, but after they had grown up. As for me, this has been a full trip and I feel finished with this place and don't think I'll ever return.

We'll leave here on the 30th of April and will see the Grand Canyon, Utah, Wyoming, and then head for Maine.

April 30, 1980, to Richard Grossinger

Hello once again. We got your latest book, *Planet Medicine*, less than a week ago. I just started reading it and am on page 38 right at the moment. I am finding it very interesting. Since our trip to New Mexico and trying to learn from the Indians their ways of life, I have become more holistic. I guess that means arriving at a point where our body, mind, and spirit will function in harmony. So your book is right in line of where my interest is at. I want to thank you very much for having your book sent to me, and I will read it from cover to cover.

Other books I've been reading lately are *Zen in the Martial Arts* by Joe Hyams and *Centering: Your Guide to Inner Growth* by Sanders G. Laurie and Melvin J. Tucker. I also got a book on aikido by Yoshimitsu Yamada. I do wish there was a dojo nearby so me and the kids could study aikido. Not that I have visions of becoming a martial artist but as a way to keep on learning.

Carl Jung went through a crisis from thirty-eight to forty-three where he knew he had to change his philosophy of life. The philosophy he lived by the first half of life was not the same as what he needed for the last half of his life. Now I am at that place in my life, a kind of hard place to be at, an unsettled place to be at, but one should deal with it, I am told.

We have done all right at fishing and lobstering since returning to Maine. I went gill-netting with Merton and Bruce Rich last summer, then went lobsterfishing ever since in my own boat starting in September. The weather was just great—warm, mild, and calm all summer and fall. Around the ninth of January it started to get windy, and we have had plenty of wind ever since. The winter was windy and cold, but not much snow or rain until mid February to the middle of March. That was when we got our real winter weather. We are getting normal spring weather now. I took the winter traps up in early March and am now setting traps out for spring lobstering. Getting about a quarter of a pound per trap, and the price is $3.75 a pound, highest I ever sold them for. Gas is about $1.20 a gallon. Bait is $9.00 a bushel. When or where will this all stop I have no idear. My guess is things are out of control. Whether all the King's horses and all the King's men can get it back together again remains to be seen.

Understanding and control of ki may help those who believe in it, at least for their personal life. One thing that does help is to have a lot of flexibility because of the great speed with which everything changes. I think a lot of people are starting to wonder as to what has taken place and what is going to take place.

As a family, we are all fine and doing well. Frank is ten, Wayne is eleven, and Mary is thirteen—fourth, fifth, and seventh grades. Sue is still reading tons of books. She has been reading a lot about the Jewish religion and history lately. Like tracing one's roots in religion.

December 2, 1981, to Richard Grossinger

Thank you for the t'ai chi ch'uan book which you sent me. Like I told you over the phone, I am taking t'ai chi classes this fall at the high school once a week. They run for ten weeks; then I will see if I want to keep taking them or not.

The teacher, Mary Green, a woman of Chinese descent, is excellent in how she demonstrates the movements. I've seen other teachers who had the movements down, but she is the living soul of them. She is as graceful as a mountain lion. She starts each class off by making us imagine a golden light coming out of the bottom of the earth, coming through our feet, and radiating throughout our bodies. As she puts you into that meditative state, she wants you to be as fluid as water. She herself is as fluid as a cat.

I am afraid I am too stiff to relax into it. I am too rigid a man to get into the shapes. I just can't do it. One time out of frustration she struck me gently to try to get me to give up control, but she has a student as thick as a brick. I wish I could do what she can do, but I can't. Maybe next lifetime things will be different.

As for us as a family, life goes on with all the change, pain, delight, and problems that come with raising a family. Nothing stays the same for long.

Mary will be fifteen in January and is 5 feet 10 inches tall, a beautiful girl or maybe I should say a woman. She got on the honor roll and is taking up cheerleading and enjoys high school. Wayne will be thirteen in February and is in the seventh grade. He is into basketball, baseball, and sports. He owns his own skiff and set traps in the harbor this summer and baited bait pockets for the lobstermen this fall. He hates school but is doing good. Frank will be twelve in February. He is on the honor roll and is into basketball. He gathers bottles and has a paper route for his "cash crop," as we say on the farm.

Sue is a wife and mother, still reading tons of books. She turned forty this fall and is very proud of it. She is on a committee to get a library for Tremont School.

As for myself, I turned forty-three this summer. I worked in the lobster room at the Oceanarium part-time this summer and am now full-time lobstering. I got my weight down to 150 pounds, which was what I weighed twenty years ago when in the Army.

So life goes on about the same in Bernard as when you were here, just different actors to play the same roles as the old actors die off. Such is the drama of Bernard.

October 30, 1986, to Ann Murphy
(formerly Ann De Cleene, now Ann Seavey)

Wayne has worked as a cook in the second-best restaurant in town. When the first cook had a night off, Wayne was first cook, and he has fed up to 150 diners himself. He bought a motorcycle in June unbeknown to us. We found out about it in late August when the State inspector came to check out something that wasn't right. Wayne had forged his mother's signature and put his friend's number plates on it. He was fined, and the record will be cleared in three years I think. He no longer drives our car. The restaurant burned down about three weeks before closing time. They don't know how the fire got started. No one was hurt.

Mary started dating a local fisherman, age 27, this spring. They are going to be married on November 2nd. She is three months pregnant. He has drinking and drug problems. I told her, you don't have to marry him, but that made no difference.

Life is a bitch at times, Ann, as you well know. Sue and I are housemates only now, and we had a fight this month, and I let her know that we were more friends than husband and wife and, if we could stick it out until the kids were raised, that would be fine, but if it got unbearable we could part ways even sooner. Since then things have so far been much better between us.

Sometime, I think everything be damned. I would like to walk out and head for California and not even look back. I have become an angry man who wished he had stayed single. Maybe someday I'll cool down, but I need a change badly. Well, Ann, I am going to hang in here as long as I can stand it and I hope I can last it out. Time will tell what is next.

December 17, 1986, to Ann Murphy

The whole family went to Lynn, but Sue and Mary stayed there until December 7th while the boys and I headed back home. She sold her father's flea market business and helped her mother get things straightened out. The boys and I lived here by ourselves and got along fine. No trouble at all. They stayed to home, though they could have gone out a lot more. They invited their friends here to meet me and I them. They did their schoolwork and never skipped school. We went out to eat once. There was none of the tension there is when Sue is around. They cleaned their bedrooms without even being asked.

I think I will go back to Bass Harbor Marine for a year and a half or until Frank is out of high school. When I go back to work at the yard, I think I'll move out at that time and get a rent on the other side of the island. Sue and I won't finish our divorce until the house is sold and everything is divided up. She and I don't hate each other, but we just can't be ourselves around each other. Time to toss in the towel. The kids can live with me or her; it is up to them.

There is a friend, Dina. She and I had nothing to do with each other until we went on a hike together around Jordan Pond last June. We have grown to love each other. We think we are soulmates. We are having a relationship with each other since July. She has been married twice and has a daughter in college. She is going to divorce her husband and move back to Maine in early January. She wants to get her M.S.W. degree. Where she will study, I don't know for sure. Maybe Bangor. Maybe God only knows. Where our relationship will go or develop into I do not know, but I feel I must let you know of her. She will be 44 years old in January.

Ann, you are a special person in my life and I hope you

choose to remain so. I love you and have always loved you and don't see that changing. My eyes don't miss much, although I let a lot pass by. I know you know that. You are nobody's fool in any sense of the word.

Know I am not the man that you used to go fishing with ten years ago. I am going to get in touch with a Wendell I've never let happen or got to know before. It is high time, I feel. My lord, what an ass I've been for so many years. I want to be free of all this shit our society says we must do to be happy. Can you still love the new me or would you rather say fuck you Wendell or tell me to go to hell.

I am changing, and I'll keep on changing until I die. After that? Well, one life at a time.

December 27, 1986, to Ann Murphy

I do want you to know that Dina and I have no plans to live together or get married. We both enjoy each other and both want our freedom.

If you come to Maine next summer, try to come alone so you and I can have some time to be together and talk things over between us. There is a lot of unfinished business between us and there always will be if we don't get together and really talk. I was no more done with you that day in your kitchen ten years ago than anything, but it was the only way I knew to keep our families together. Ten long years have passed, Ann, and other than us seeing each other for an hour or two every three years or so, that has been it. I care about you, but I have no desire to remarry anyone at this time. I want to taste freedom and be free to meet whoever I want whenever I want wherever I want and not be hog-tied to anyone. Most of all, I want to become myself. Free! Free! Free! World, Beware!!! Ann, if you return to MDI, we will see a lot of each other. Or in time I will come to Canada and see you. You can count on it.

My plans for now are to work at the Summit House until late winter or early spring and then get my old job back at Bass Harbor Marine. When that happens, I'll move out of the house here and get a rent somewhere on the west side of the island. Mary is going to live with her mother. Whether the boys live with me or Sue, I don't know. I think Frank would be better off living with me because he and his mother fight so, but he says he will move back and forth. Wayne will be done with school in June, so he is a short-timer. I plan to stay around MDI until Frank is done school; then I'll be free to travel if I am into it. I hope Sue and I can go our own ways as friends. If not, it can't be helped.

I know now after working in the Summit House for 1½ years that there is something about me that can't be tamed. My parents tried it and failed. The Army tried it and failed. And the Church tried it and failed. And last time up to bat was the Institution of the Nursing Home, so proudly it stands. It tried it and failed. Now, long at last, I am ready to admit to myself I am untamable. So I've asked myself what is my real job on Earth and, as near as I can tell, it is to become myself.

I do want you to be a part of my life and I a part of yours. Now some of my old friends may not be able to stand the new me and, if they can't, then they and I shall come to the fork in the road with each other. I expect some will be like you and shout Ya-Hooo oo oo, and others will say go fuck off, Wendell; we liked the old bottled-up Mr. Nice Guy best. Sorry, folks but, long at last, he died along the trail. Couldn't stand himself any longer.

I have no answers, but I sure want to live the question. Quite a switch for the guy who thought he used to have the answers, right Ann?

Where will I be on my dying day? Who will I be with? Will I be alone? What will I be doing? I know not.

December 30, 1986, to Ann Murphy

I wish the wind would start blowing again. Both the summers of '82 and '83 that I have spent at Bass Harbor Marine I've never seen so few sou'westers. Believe me, I am not complaining, but from what experience I've had living in Maine over the past 46 years one could almost set their watch by the time the sou'westers would start. Each afternoon we would expect a 15–25 mph smoky sou'wester. During those summers we would work at the docks day in and day out and rarely have to move all those boats off to the moorings.

Back in the days of Noah, there was a spring where it rained for 40 days and 40 nights. Well, the spring of '83 topped them all because it rained for 90 days and 90 nights that spring. Noah only thought he had seen rain! On one of those rainy days Marcia Madeira said she was thinking of building an ark and asked if I'd be willing to help. I replied, "You bet your sweet buns I will. You won't hear me knocking it."

The summer of '83 was so dry that the only other summer to come close to so little rainfall was the summer of '47. That was the year of the great Bar Harbor fire.

February of '84 was the mildest February that I can recall, and March of '84 was the worst weather I can remember of. We had temperatures down to zero. From November 1981, to the spring of 1982 I had never seen so many windy days straight in a row. And when it did stop blowing, it was only to take a 2-second breather before it started up again. About a million years ago, or around the time I was in the fourth grade, I read a rhyme in my English book that went like this: "Whether the weather is good or whether the weather is not, whether the weather is cold or whether the weather is hot, we weather the weather, whatever the weather, whether we like it or not."

Mark Twain has been quoted as saying, "If you don't like Maine's weather, just wait a minute and it will change."

About ten years ago I was visiting retired fishermen at the Fishermen's Institute in Gloucester, Mass. I was talking to an 89-year-old man named Mr. Seymour who had spent a total of 63 years gathering the harvest of the sea, doing both offshore and inshore fishing. I asked him if he could see any difference in the weather pattern of today from what it was when he was a young man. After a reflective pause he said, "I answer you this way: you can't predict the weather nowadays like you used to be able to years ago."

January 26, 1987, to Ann Murphy

I used to hate high school. It was like some kind of prison to me and, as a kid, I couldn't wait to get out of there. Then after I was out of school, even before I went into the Army, I used to have this recurring dream that I was a freshman in high school and it would be a while before I was out, and it was such a heavy dream to me. I've had this dream all through the years until I felt it was like a prophecy of something about my real life. Last year I dreamt I was in my senior year. Still heavy, still not free. Last night I dreamt I was at my graduation. I was dressed in slacks, a white shirt, and a red sweater with a tie, wearing a golfer's hat, and I was young and free. What a dream, and it was in color! Maybe I have gone through school, whatever it is, the one I needed to go through, and am free at last!

March 10, 1987, to Ann Murphy

Things are busy and greatly changing for me. I turned in my resignation on Thursday, February 20th, to the Summit House

Nursing Home. The following Tuesday I told my assistants, and on the 27th I told the residents. Nothing has been the same since. There has been tears and hugs, anger and guilt trips. But now I am back to being my foolish and impossible self on the job, and the staff are responding. As for my new job, I am going back to Bass Harbor Marine. I begin working there on April 13. My last day of work here will be April 11.

Sue and I are going to separate in April if I can find a rent. I want a two-bedroom close to my work. I've taken over the payments on Frank's 1977 Dodge pickup truck, so I should have a set of wheels.

Sue and I seem to have reached an acceptance of this. I think she is even excited about it.

I am taking two courses under Adult Education. One is Celtic and Arthurian Myths, and the other is Handwriting Analysis.

As for Dina, she and I have our ups and downs. As far as soulmates goes, soulmates fight as badly as anyone else with each other, maybe more so. I think whenever you put two people together, there will be plenty to fight about. We are back to being friends and no longer lovers. I expect this will be a cat-and-dog relationship much of the time. Oh well.

March 22, 1987, to Ann Murphy

Last weekend I went apartment hunting and the first apartment I looked at I took. It is a yellow house, and it has a spiral stairway that goes up to a bedroom like you would find in a lighthouse tower. The walls in the bedroom are paneled in wood, and there is a built-in bed with a skylight over it. It is in Southwest Harbor.

Sue and I called her mother on March 6th and told her the news. She is the most understanding person one could ask for. She said, "You both are well thought out and I never agreed with the church stand on divorce." She still loves me, she said, and I am still welcome in her home. How about that? Sue is in line now about my leaving and we both know we are not husband and wife. Friends we are, but husband and wife we are not.

As for Dina and me, we separate more each week. Now she doesn't want me to call her anymore. I think I always loved her more than she did me, so it serves me right.

Oh well, as I am about to leave home, I leave a free man, free as a bird. It is the halfway mark of your and my lives, and there is still a lot of time to do whatever it is we are meant to do. I am sure happy to have met you and hope that what we have done with each other so far is nothing compared to what is left for us to do with one another.

May 24, 1987, to Ann Murphy

It was 22 years ago on the 6th of May that my boat was launched. It took a few days after she was launched to put the finishing touches on her. Then Dad and I went lobstering in her, and on May 23rd I made my first trip hand-lining in her with two other men and we came in with 4000 pounds of pollock and codfish, and on May 24th, Dad, another feller, and I got 12,745 pounds of pollock that day. Dad and I had a full great year fishing and lobstering in her, and on May 4th, 21 years ago, my Dad died, and on the 7th he was buried. So ended a way of life and a man I loved deeply. I hung on the best I could for another 17 years until I saw it was hopeless to hang on any longer. Then 3 years, 5 months in a boatyard, 21 months in a nursing home, now back at the boatyard.

Mary is due to have her baby any time now. The baby's head has already moved into place, and she is a time bomb ready to deliver at any moment now. Frank may live with me this summer. Nothing for sure.

Frank and Wayne both have cars which their mother bought them. In turn, they are supposed to pay her back. Her decision—I have no more money to give. I have my paycheck and $600.00 in the bank.

I hope you and John will be able to make it with one another and will be able to live and share a happy life together. For better or worse, I am a single man again. Dina and I are still good friends but no longer lovers. She has her lovers and I have mine. She thinks I am just a clown that gets in his own way and she gave me up as a lost cause. Either she is insane or I am insane or we are both insane or neither of us is insane, but we didn't make it together either way one looks at it.

I climbed Sargent Mountain yesterday, and today it is back to work. The weather has turned beautiful again. I wish you luck with your stained glass and in finding a job you will like. I hear through the grapevine that Betty Spurling is mad at me for leaving Sue. I don't know at times if I can even keep up with all that is happening. Guess I'll have to. I've been avoiding my shit for so long that now I am covered with it all. I will either move on ahead or get killed by it all. There is no turning back now even if I wanted to, which I don't. This will make or break me.

June 27, 1987, to Ann Murphy

On May 27th at 11:49 A.M. Mary had a baby boy named Brian Alexander. He is a healthy boy and all seems well about him. Wayne is cooking at a restaurant in Bar Harbor and plans to go to Florida late in the fall. He graduated on June 12th and is doing well. His car is broke down. Frank is now working for a mason. He wanted hard work and out of doors and so he has it. He also has a girlfriend.

As for me, I am working hard at the boatyard and am glad I made the move. I needed to get outdoors working once again.

I have no regrets in living by myself. It is a great learning experience. My guess is I'll work at the boatyard for about another year and a half. I think that what I am doing is slowly saying goodbye to this place. But only God knows these things. I've never felt like such a stranger in this world since I can remember. It is like being in no man's land. I used to feel like I knew what I was doing and where I was going, but now it is like I don't know shit. Maybe someday I can make some sense out of it all. I feel I must go through this dark space and someday I'll find home again.

A couple of men stopped me on the street the other day to invite me to go hand-lining and trawling with them. That will feel good, whether there are any fish or not—just to be able to go through the motions one more time. Fishing was always such a part of my life. I know the bible says, "We should not ask why the former days were better than these, for we ask not wisely concerning these things." Sometimes I wonder about that. There once were roots and stability to this life of mine and to the sea. Now it is all shifting and changing.

August 20, 1987, to Ann Murphy

Thank you for the letter you wrote me on July 8th. It was a very wise letter filled with insight which I am very thankful for. Yes, I am feeling like I want to go back out on the water once more. I don't want to own my own boat but I would like to go with someone else, even if it was just for a change. I may do a little weekend lobstering this fall, but I do need a steady job until the kids are self-supporting. Frank has one more year of school.

Thanks for your feedback on delightful Dina. I agree with every word you have said about her. My opinion of her is she is pretty, moody, seductive, and not to trust one damn bit. It is quite a fucking game she plays and is she ever good at it (no pun intended). But I am starting to get my bellyful of her and, if I marry her and have ten kids, for Christ's sakes, Ann, cut my balls off or my head, whichever you can get to first. She is a cock-teasing bitch or maybe witch. I am not sure. Well, fuck her and the broomstick she flew in on. Enough on her.

I have been having quite a summer after I got over my blahs. Been wining and dining and swimming, hiking, folk-dancing, movies, fucking, and have regressed back to about 33 years old, although it really adds up to 49 years.

My grandson is a fine baby and I love him. He and I went to the nursing home yesterday, and they loved him more than me. See if I take him again!

Working hard at the yard. Got my weight down to 155, fighting trim. I am as black as a black and am calling everyone brother. No regrets in leaving the nursing home, although everyone misses me. Let's you and I take that job. Maybe you be the director and I'll be your assistant. Write to Betty and ask her whether she'd let us do that. But, of course, you would have to quit your job where you are and leave John, your house, and Canada, so I guess that would be more than you could stand. HA! HA! Too bad!

When are you coming to Maine for a visit? Soon I hope. The water in the lake is perfect. My son Frank lived with me for about a month this summer while he was working here in Southwest as a mason. Last Sunday he moved to Bar Harbor where he is now working three nights a week at the Central House, a restaurant. School is about to start, and he is going to do his last year.

Well, Ann, do write again and let me know all the great things that are happening in your life. Any idea when you will be getting to the USA again? Will close for now and hope to hear from you soon.

September 15, 1987, to Ann Murphy

Hello from the upper town dock at Southwest Harbor at 9:15 Tuesday morning with the sun shining brightly and a refreshing north wind blowing on my back. Just a few houses down from where old Ralph used to live. It is now the middle of September, but by the time you get this letter through the pony-express system in Canada it will be more than likely the middle of October.

Wayne has got done cooking at the Brick Oven and night before last he moved in with me, bag and baggage. He is now going lobstering with Tommy Lawson out of Southwest. Tommy is doing well, so Wayne should make some money this fall. Mary couldn't get baby sitters, so she is now on welfare. Sue has put in her resignation at the Summit House because she refuses to work any more nights and the head nurse will not give her any days. She plans to sell the house and rent an apartment.

I fell last Saturday between a boat and the dock and sprained my lower back. Am now healing up from that. I may work for Dave and Audrey this week, as I can't lift for a while and this will keep money coming in while my back heals.

I do hope to get on the water some weekends later on this fall. I agree with you I need to be on the water some, even if it's just a little bit. How come you're so smart in knowing what is good for me? Even like letting go of Delightful Dina? How come I don't know these things myself? I thought I was supposed to know all there was to know. Even fooled myself for a while. Maybe I was the only one who got fooled. Oh well, maybe the starting of wisdom is when you finally realize you know nothing.

October 31, 1987, to Ann Murphy

Wayne is doing great lobstering, making a lot of $$$. He and his girl have broken up, so all the young women of MDI are calling asking is Wayne home? I say no, but what's your mother or grandmother doing tonight? CLICK *buzz* is all I hear.

My back has all recovered from my fall, so I am healthy once again. Am going out with women, but so far I have not met anybody that I am really excited about.

I get a lot of housesitting jobs and within a year I should have slept in every house on Mount Desert Island. Maybe in time I'll be known as the George Washington of MDI.

February 24, 1988, to Ann Murphy

Hello woman. Sounds like things are happening for you. Good to hear you and John are getting it together. Who is there on this earth that we could live with and not want to kill every now and then?

Wayne moved out of my apartment in early January and is sharing a place with two other guys. He is still lobstering but not making much money this winter. But he is going shark-fishing come May. Frank is doing well and after school is planning to join the Navy. Good luck to the Navy! He turned 18 on the 5th of February; Wayne turned 19 on February 22nd.

Mary and her baby are doing well. She is seeing a young man about 25 years of age. He is a smart guy and full of fun. It is only friendship for now. I am glad to see her get out once again.

I am now reading *Road Less Traveled* by Scott Peck, also taking a workshop on Monday nights in Bar Harbor about the book. I love it. Read another good book called *Coming Apart*. All about love relationships and their breakups. The relationship between me and Dina is all over. We just didn't jell. So much for all that soulmate shit. It boiled down to the fact I fell in love with her and she dumped me. I'll bet I will be a lot wiser the next time around if there is another woman out there in the universe fool enough to try it with me. I've had a few affairs but nothing emotional or no primary relationship with anyone. If one comes along that I like and who likes me, then look out world because here we go again.

I am still happy at work but am thinking of maybe going gill-netting next summer and lobstering in the fall. So I may get out on the ocean one more time yet before I leave the good state of Maine. Plan to spend the rest of the year here, but I think then it will be time to see other places and do other things. I guess what I am doing is getting things in order to leave. Just watch. I'll marry some woman with a slew of young kids, then see what an unwise thing I did and blow my brains out. Then you can write my story that I never got to.

Good luck at your work, old friend of mine, and don't behave yourself. Be sure to write again when time permits within the next two or three years. Just joking.

August 15, 1988, to Ann Murphy

Work at the boatyard is going great. We are as busy as bees at the hive or ants at the hill.

The divorce hearing comes up on September 7th in Bar Harbor. Sue does not have to go to the hearing. She and I sat down and made out papers together. It takes ten days after the hearing for the divorce to become final if the judge approves of it.

I am not going to go lobstering this fall because I would feel like I should stick with the guy until Christmas if I did. I am staying at the boatyard and, after the divorce is final, all I have to do is give the boatyard two weeks' notice and I am free to be on my way to the West Coast.

Sounds like you are coming to Maine just as I am leaving. If I am still here, surely I want to go on that bike ride with you. If I am not here, we will have to do it another time, either here or on the West Coast.

Been trying to figure out who I am and why at times I feel like I've missed the boat so often. Life is rich, exciting, and full for me. I've already turned 50 going on 23 except I am getting stiff in the wrong places to quote Ralph Phippen, at the wrong times damnit, to quote me. How many lives must I live before I finally get it right. In the meantime, I'll try to enjoy what's left of this one.

By the way, Frank went into the Navy on July 29th, Great Lakes Boot Camp.

September 14, 1988, to Ann Murphy

I'll be heading along Route 90, which will take me quite a bit south of you folks. If I had a newer truck, I'd come to Toronto, but I am starting 138,000 in the hole. I hope I am doing what the Holy Spirit wants or I am in deep trouble. Take care, old friend.

October 30, 1988, truck stop, Eureka, California

I am traveling alone—so it appears because no one else is with me—but I am anything but alone. The Holy Spirit is with me. I am sharing in a love greater than any I have ever known, a love without fear, a love that will never abandon me, a love that doesn't let you down and lunge for your jugular. When a man and woman fall in love, it is as though they give each other a beautiful gift. It looks good, it feels good, it tastes good, it smells good, but then you each open your gifts and what do you find under the wrapper? Frustration, compromise, anger, and guilt. Separation and exclusion, not togetherness and unity.

We must realize that we have everything within ourselves. The only thing we need to do for one another is to forgive.

I guess that's about all the sage wisdom you'd care to hear from Lama Seavey at this point.

November 13, 1988, Tulsa, Oklahoma, at sunset

A strange feeling comes over me; it hits me like a ton of bricks. I don't feel lacking in anything. I don't feel as if another person has what I haven't. I don't feel I am looking for another woman. I guess I feel like a trucker who is about to drive on a route he has never driven before. I have been given glimpses of this route in my dreams, and I know it is going to be beautiful. In fact, a power much greater than me is driving my truck.

I am watching the traffic and buildings and expressways, and I look off to my left side and see not what the song promises, "a full moon over Tulsa," but a car lot crammed with motor vehicles, a mile of them. Then I look to my right and see the same thing, stretching for at least a mile—and all at once I feel saturated with this illusion or hallucination called "Life on Earth."

Can this country produce! I am not sure it is a good thing.

Where do I go and what do I do now? Surely this must be a transition I am going through, and I know the past routes have been dead-end streets, and there is nothing back there for me. While I am at this point still in a human body, alive and well and dwelling on the Spaceship Earth, what will it be from here on? I've never felt like such a stranger to this life before. This must be my trip through the desert.

It looks like I'm coming full circle and headed to Maine, but what a different outlook on life! What will I do there? Who will I meet? What am I to say? If I fall back to my old ways, then I will have to return to the desert again to renew myself?

I am now fifty years old and I've never known a Seavey or a Carter to reach a hundred, so I'm more than half over. I better get more in touch with this world or in tune with it, before I wake up from this life at some point and God asks me, "Well, Wendell," or whatever I am known as then, "what did you think about life on Earth as a person?" and I look and God and say, "I don't know. Was I ever there?"—and then I get sent back to do it all over again, God forbid!!! Once will be plenty for me, thank you ... but then again maybe not if I can get to be an aikido master or tea pourer the next time.

What a liberating feeling to have made this choice on my own and gotten to know my desire for myself. I can go back to Maine with a peaceful mind, believing that this is truly where I belong.

January 9, 1989, to Ann Murphy

I was shocked and deeply saddened to hear of the loss of your home and all your things. What a bummer of a piece of luck! I am at a loss as to what to say or write. We are far apart in miles and I really don't have much more than a pot to piss in or a window to toss it out of—but should I be able to get you something you need or do something for you that you need, then let me know what that is and I'll surely try to.

Yes, I had quite a trip for myself and I am an Atlantic not a Pacific person, but that is a long story. Hang in there, and do look me up when you get to Maine.

March 28, 1994, to Roger F. Duncan

Hello, I am writing to you about your book *Coastal Maine: A Maritime History*. In my opinion, this is a great book and I feel it should be taught in all of Maine schools. This would give Maine students a very good knowledge of where we came from, the events that have led us to where we are, and the problems that we face.

I was born in 1938, my mother was born in 1895, and my father in 1896. Dad was of the last generation of what I call the last of the early American fishermen that went fishing under sail, that you write about in Chapter 26. He was introduced to the sea by men who were born in the 1860s and '70s. He fished out of Portland most of his younger life; he fished from Canada to Boston over the years.

My favorite memories of childhood are of going down to the dock and listening to those old men tell their tales of years gone by. My ancestors were English and I can trace my roots back to Devon, England. They were the stock of men you write about in the chapter "The Fishing Settlements." They had settled here by the early 1600s.

I can well identify with you in the chapter "The Decline of the Fisheries" in which you talk about your summer back in the 1930s when you went fishing with Captain Riley McFarland. For me it would have been the late 1940s and early 1950s. Since finishing high school in 1956 I have gone lobstering, tub trawling, hand-lining, and scalloping.

In the 1970s I read many of Scott and Helen Nearing's books and then got to know them personally and attended some lectures they gave at College of the Atlantic. The College, founded by Ed Kaelber and Father Jim Gower, had its beginnings in discussions in my kitchen. The present President, Steve Katona, was a marine biologist involved previously with Allied Whales. I took him on many trips to study the ocean.

I have lectured to various groups, including hospices, schools, and organizations on Mount Desert Island. For several years I worked in the Oceanarium in Southwest Harbor for David and Audrey Mills. Here, the public from all over the world learn about the environment of the North Atlantic. I went to New Mexico for four months and presented a slide show on lobstering and bird life to both children and adult audiences, to the Native Americans and public-school systems and the New Mexico Park Service.

Dear Mr. Duncan, I am sure you are well aware of how we have plundered, pillaged, and raped our ocean to get her bountiful harvest this past century. But we, as fishermen, through our so-called rugged individualism, ignorance, and greed and our effort to make a living have betrayed our ocean and have turned it from a Garden of Eden into a watery graveyard.

We must change our outlook and our old ways that no longer work for our best interest, or the interest of the ocean or the generations to follow. If we continue on our present path, we will betray them all.

Your book is a marvelous piece of work and I feel it can become a cornerstone to start building to reeducate people about gathering the harvest of the sea. I can envision the coming together of fishermen, U.S. and Canadian, marine biologists, environmentalists, universities and colleges such as COA, aquariums, science museums, Greenpeace, Native Americans with their wisdom and knowledge, all these movements working together to put Humpty-Dumpty back together again.

We must create a new dawn, a new beginning. Our present ways are failing. There must be a peaceful reeducational rebellion because fishing is in a real crisis. We must see that we can become strong and do something about this crisis rather than be fearful, angry, and frustrated, and do nothing.

April 6, 1994, to Steve Katona

I am writing to you about my concern about the ocean and its ecology and the decline of the fisheries. I know that you are aware of the great problems that we are facing today. Steve, we have known each other for many years and we both know of our common interest in the ocean and its preservation.

I would like to get people together to produce a documentary film to alert and educate the public as to what has happened to the North Atlantic because of fishing practices. Historians can lay down the foundations of time; scientists can give the cold, hard statistics; biologists and environmentalists can present their findings; fishermen of the past and present can contribute their thoughts and insights.

The film could be used as an educational tool for young fishermen who have no sense of the history of their industry as well as a guide to legislators of Canada and the United States who do not have an in-depth understanding of the breeding cycles or healthy home habitat of different species of marine life.

April 23, 1994, to Richard Grossinger

I have been thinking much about you this year and rereading many of your books you have sent me over the years for which I am truly grateful.

I am recalling back to the late 1960s when you, Lindy, and Robin were here and you were doing your ethnographic fieldwork for your Ph.D. in anthropology and we had our discussions with each other. It is hard to believe how much I have changed since then. I was reading your thesis on page 309 where I told you: "All this ecology stuff is written by men who have never been out in the ocean." Well, give Wendell a rap on the knuckles for that one; I don't know what I was drinking that day, but I'm not the same Wendell Seavey any more.

On page 315 of your thesis, well, I think you better knock me on the skull or just throw me overboard for that one. I told you: "Man can't expect to figure things out for himself. He's meant to sin. He's meant to make mistakes. That's why God sent His only Son down to earth, to atone for man's sins. So that man wouldn't be damned to hell for mistakes he couldn't help. That's the reason for confession; man doesn't know the way to avoid sin, so he has to confess. It's foolish for man to try and know everything. God works in mysterious ways. Ecologists can't make the world right either. Only God can. And it's foolish of them to try."

That makes a certain sense, but it's sure a snarled line. I think I was just getting to know what I believed. I had an old belief in place and a new one not yet fitted.

I was after all the one that gave the prognosis of the doom and gloom the fisheries would face one day if we didn't change our ways and outlook of harvesting the sea. I remember that, as you interviewed others, you said to me, "Wendell, you are the only one who is talking this way."

Well, Richard, that day has come, I am sorry to say. It has not only come to the North Atlantic fisheries but the planet. The newspapers and TV are full of news of this disaster. Look at the April 17th, 18th, and 19th issues of the *Boston Globe*. This will help you understand the magnitude of this problem.

During March, after much prodding from my wife Ann and our dear friends Betty and Tucker Spurling, I have decided to do my best to wake people up as to what has happened and why this has happened.

Richard, if you pick up your book *The Slag of Creation* those were good words you wrote about me on pages 134, 209, and 210. They show my whole journey. On page 210 you wrote, "Wendell is a new age ferryman, for an ecological college, for scientists mapping bird migration and whale populations, for collectors of solar data and Gestalt therapists. His affinity is Hermes, Mercury is the metal; he is the go-between for remote but approaching connections. He has a steady income for the first time in his life (except for the 36 hours he lasted at the sardine factory after his marriage, handing out fish to the cursing women, battered like the doughboy, until he took his ship out into the water and fished the offshore shoals). It is not only money; he is learning things he finds he cannot any longer do without. With the I Ching, Dane Rudhyar, a garden, and a mulch heap, he is keeping late late hours for an easterner, but the discipline remains, subtly removed, and some of his fishing partners, after abandoning him as loony, are looking again. Wendell is getting very smart very fast in a dangerous and holy text. It may not be fish, but it does recall the fisherman's lineage, when Marduk was king and Tiamat the abyss. He'll be a true Phoenician handliner, if he survives, not just the aroused sea and fragmented rocky garden, but the later rebellion of the family and the mind."

How about that!!!?

Other people we have contacted so far are Bob Bear, a marine biologist; Susan White, a documentary film-maker at the University of Maine, Orono; a man in Canada who has worked as an international lawyer for farmers and unions; two women in Canada, one who works for the University of Toronto, the other for the Government of Canada; Commissioner of Marine Resources William Brennan; and Dana Mitchell, a native American of the Penobscot Nation, who is now the elder tribal leader and travels many different places speaking on Indian affairs— he is involved in a Native American children's after-school and educational club his daughter started on Indian Island by Old Town here in Maine and with saving parks and wetlands in the Baltic Sea in West Germany. Our next letter will be to Colin Nickerson of the *Boston Globe*, writer of the fishing articles.

Hopefully our trails will cross again when the time is right.

May 31, 1994, to Richard Grossinger

I am most interested in the work of conservation and consciousness change. My new friend Chris Kaiser has a philosophy that what you think is the physical world is really "the dance of spirits constantly communicating with you symbolically," which I think ties in with what you wrote about "the crisis of the ocean," which is, as we both know, part of the crisis of the Earth, which is a crisis of the human spirit and its identity.

I send my best regards to you and your family. Maybe someday we will all meet again.

December 20, 2000, story told to a group of friends

I went to the airport last week to meet Ann's plane and had some fun with an airport cop while I was there. Her plane was due in somewhere around 7 o'clock in Bangor and, well, I have never gone to pick her up when the plane isn't two hours late and this holds true this time as well. It is two hours late as usual so I think to myself, "What am I going to do with myself for these two hours?" I hate to go window-shopping, just walking through the malls or looking at WalMart's junk, so I think, "There has got to be something to do."

Here I am sitting in the airport and I'm watching the airport police guy. I notice that every twenty minutes—he is just as punctual as the sunrise in the morning—he gets up, walks out of his office and goes right to the door. The doors automatically slide open and he goes right to the left and looks at all the vehicles. He is doing a good job. I can see he has got four or five ticketed already when I first get there. What he does, I notice, is he makes a little chalk mark at the high noon on the wheel and then goes on checking the tires one after another to see if they have got the chalk mark. If they do, he writes a ticket and places it under the windshield wiper and on he goes. If they don't, he makes his little chalk mark and goes out again twenty minutes later. He has got a system that works so well and I am sure that no one had ever interfered with this system before. He has no reason to do anything except act like a robot. He is on automatic pilot. There he goes: doors open, turns left down the row, got 'em, and then back in the office every twenty minutes.

I watch this and think, "Ah ha!" You see, I had this Nissan van that has "Hot Flash Anny's Stained Glass" printed on it. It is really bright and you can see it from ten miles away. So anyway here is this cop who goes and makes his little mark on my van and then he's back in his office. I go out, take my shoe and rub all around the whole tire so it looks even. I just brush his chalk mark off, but I make sure I make it looks the same around the whole rim of the tire. Then I move the van fifty feet or so. Twenty minutes later, out he goes again. He makes his chalk mark and I rub it off and move the van. Out he goes again and I alternate, sometimes moving the van this way and sometimes that way. Well, this goes on three or four times, and my goodness he's getting suspicious. He makes a mark there, he makes a mark here, he makes a mark on the fender itself. He suspects something has happened to the tire but can't figure what. Anyway, out I go and brush them all off and just put the vehicle down here a little farther each time. Well, out he comes again, but this time I see we are going to break tradition. He is coming out the door and he is ready for bear. He ain't going out there to the other cars until he just stands there and looks at that van. He goes over and looks at it. He gets right down on his hands and knees but what he doesn't realize is that I have been walking right along behind him and I said, "Oh, excuse me sir, I am just pulling out of here." I startled him and he leaped like a jack in the box, gave me the filthiest look, and away he went back into his office. Of course I couldn't do it again, so I go way down to the end of the airfield and I see Ann's plane finally come in. I waited until I saw all the luggage and passengers come off the plane and then I go back over to the door and go in, find Ann and say, "Grab your luggage out of here quick; I'll explain it to you later." That was the night I harassed the airport cop.

Wendell Seavey:
Land Marks

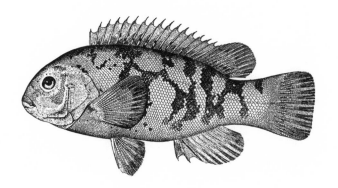

Land Marks

(Western Shoal)
Little Duck just starting out by Long Island, and Black Ledge on end of Marshall Island.

(Pencil Shoal)
Schooner Head hid behind Richard Head, and Western Sister ½, ⅔ out by SW Point.

(Meeting House Ground)
About five or six feet of Long Island out by NE end of Big Duck, and Baker's Island on Schooner Head.

(Lad's Shoal)
Baker's Island lighthouse on western crotch of Western Mountain, and high part of Long Island by Mer Point. To set down, hold the mountain mark still over the stern.

(The Middle Ground)
Schoodic Mountain out by Little Duck Island, and Gooseberry Island on Placentia Head.

(The Reefs)
The two Duck Islands together, and Gooseberry Island on Placentia Head. [hard bottom]

(The Cottle)
Blue Hill Mountain over Placentia Head, and Mer Point on Pemetic Mountain just to the westward of Cadillac Mountain. [hard bottom]

(Gorge Hen's Reef)
Baker's Island light on middle of Pemetic Mountain so you can
see water between Mer Point and Long Island.

(Bull Ground)
Have the house on Gott's Island head out by the little island,
and Green Island so you can see it on the NE part of Big Duck.

(Aberner Ground)
Placentia Head on big Green Island, and the beach on the little
island out by Mer Point. [hard bottom]

(Shell Ground)
Big Camden Mountain on Southern Cove, and Mer Point light
is on Pemetic Mountain just to the east of the Bubbles. It is
about SSW two tubs of trawls [six or seven minutes' running
time] from the Aberner Ground. [There is not much bottom.]

(Robinson)
Blue Hill Mountain on Placentia Head, and Mer Point light is
on the flat place on Schooner Head Mountain.

(Bank's Ground)
Baker's Island light is on the western part of Schooner Head
Mountain, and the quarry at Black Island is on Mer Point.

(Clousen)
Blue Hill Mountain on Placentia Head, and Baker's Island light
out by Mer Point.

(Handline Place)
Baker's Island light on Pemetic Mountain, and Black Island just coming out by Mer Point.

(Eastern Muddy Ridge)
Baker's Island light on the Middle Dog Mountain and so you can see water between Long Island and Isle Au Haut.

(13)
Have Baker's Island light on the Bubby Mountain, and Mer Point light on the quarry of Black Island. You can run in five minutes for the Bubby, then set off two tubs of trawls and bring Baker's Island light onto Green Mountain.

(Tucker's Rock)
Baker's Island light on eastern crotch of Western Mountain, and the high part of Long Island on Boat House Cove.

(Picked Hummock)
Trask Point out by Long Island and Baker's Island starting out by Mer Point.

(Gilbert Hummock)
Sargent Mountain in the "V" on back of Long Island, and Johns Island run down with Swans Island.

(Marks for the Outer Peak)
    A. Ock Hill over Mer Point, and one leg of the bell-tower hid behind the light.
    C. On an ebb tide set, set for the light. Good for two or three tubs of trawls.
    D. The Inner Peak is about a mile or more inside.

(Marks for the Outer Pratt)
    A. Blue Hill Mountain over Mer Point, and Baker's Island light in the middle of Green Mountain.
    C. The Inner Pratt is the same except Baker's Island light is in the sag of Green Mountain.
    D. For a flood tide set, set in for Green Mountain.

(Marks for the Western Muddy Ridge)
    A. Have the point of Black Island down by the quarry just out by Mer Point, and Baker's Island light almost on top of Pemetic, the third mountain from the eastward, but just so it is a little to the eastward of the top of the mountain.
    C. Ebb tide set, set just westward of the Rock.

(Spurling Shoal)
Green Island out by NE point of Big Duck, and Blue Hill Mountain on western end of Little Duck.

(Wall Shoal)
Just so you can see water between Little Duck and maybe Baker Light. I have lost this one.

(Grumpy)
Camden Mountain in western crotch of Isle Au Haut, and Carver's Harbor out by Western Ear. [Good bottom with Blue Hill out by western end of Long Island and Burnt and Spoon Island run on.]

(Good Places for Halibut)
    A. Just south of the Rock with the three chimneys lined up. Set one tub of fine gear.

C. Go SSE of the Rock for about seven minutes. When you're in about 45 fathoms of water, set up towards the Lodge. Good for two tubs of halibut gear.

D. (The Millician) Green Island out by Rich's Head, and with Schoodic Point just starting to come out by Little Duck Island. Eastern end with Gott's Island Head on the eastern end of the fourth mountain.

E. Have Schoodic between the Little and Big Duck Islands, and Green Island in the notch of Black Island and Placentia western end. Eastern end, the lone tree on Long Island so you can see it.

F. Eastern end, have Bass Harbor Head onto the sandy beach on Placentia Island, and Mer Point light out by Green Island set for Long Island Harbor.

F. With Johns Island touching on Crow Island and the field out by Green Island, the south end. [two tubs]

Wendell Seavey

Regional Mount Desert Island

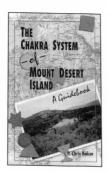

The Chakra System of Mount Desert Island

P. Chris Kaiser

Wendell Seavey's hiking buddy presents the sacred geography of Mount Desert Island and guides the reader to power spots.

$14.95 paper, 1-55643-271-2, 140 pp.

Acadia
The Soul of a National Park

Steve Perrin

This book provides illustrated walks throughout the landscape in which most of Wendell Seavey's story takes place.

$19.95 paper, 1-55643-468-5, 360 pp.

On the Integration of Nature
Post 9-11 Biopolitical Notes

Richard Grossinger

The author paints Mount Desert vistas and tells the story of Wendell Seavey, Chris Kaiser, and the countercultural community on the island.

$12.95 paper, 1-55643-603-3, 150 pp.